HOW TO
MARXIST ...
PHILOSOPHY

ALSO AVAILABLE FROM BLOOMSBURY

HOW TO BE A MARXIST IN PHILOSOPHY

By Louis Althusser

Translated and edited by G.M. Goshgarian

Bloomsbury Academic
An imprint of Bloomsbury Publishing Plc

B L O O M S B U R Y
LONDON · OXFORD · NEW YORK · NEW DELHI · SYDNEY

Bloomsbury Academic

An imprint of Bloomsbury Publishing Plc

50 Bedford Square	1385 Broadway
London	New York
WC1B 3DP	NY 10018
UK	USA

www.bloomsbury.com

BLOOMSBURY and the Diana logo are trademarks of Bloomsbury Publishing Plc

Originally published as *Être marxiste en philosophie*, Presses Universitaires de France, 2015

First published in English 2017

British Library Cataloguing-in-Publication Data
A catalogue record for this book is available from the British Library.

ISBN:	HB:	978-1-4742-8053-2
	PB:	978-1-4742-8054-9
	ePDF:	978-1-4742-8052-5
	ePub:	978-1-4742-8055-6

Library of Congress Cataloging-in-Publication Data
A catalog record for this book is available from the Library of Congress.

Typeset by RefineCatch Limited, Bungay, Suffolk
Printed and bound in Great Britain

CONTENTS

INTRODUCTION

G.M. Goshgarian

I

On 11 June 1984, Althusser called one of his many unreleased manuscripts to the attention of the Mexican philosopher Fernanda Navarro, who was to publish an introduction to his late philosophy in the guise of an interview in 1988. 'I've reread a manuscript that comes under "philosophy", a manuscript that, though it's unfinished, seems pretty good to me. At any rate, I read the whole thing. It takes up the question of philosophy's absolute beginning and Descartes' feint in his "order of reasons". Did you read it while you were here? I don't disown it.'[1] Coming from a past master in the art of self-deprecation, this counts as high praise. Navarro was fascinated by the manuscript: 'Althusser showed me a philosophy manual for "non-philosophers" . . . that I could use as a reference work for my project. Delighted, I began to discover it, to devour it.'[2] It was in the light of this guided discovery that the Mexican philosopher patched together *Filosofía y marxismo*, the only philosophical text that Althusser was to release in the decade left him after he strangled his wife Hélène Rytmann in a fit of madness in 1980.

A French version of *Filosofía y marxismo* was published in April 1994. It became the prolegomena to the reference text for Althusser's late philosophy with the appearance of 'Le courant souterrain du matérialisme de la rencontre' in fall of the same year.[3] Extracted from a chaotic mass of manuscripts dating from 1982–83 and almost certainly revised thereafter, this fragment had soon sparked a fascination for the late Althusser that shows no signs of diminishing.

The posthumous celebrity of the Althusser of the 1980s has no doubt been bolstered – calculation or contingency? – by the occultation of the Althusser of the immediately preceding period, whose most important texts were not published for decades to come or, in some cases, have still not been. For the untimely thought of the Althusser of the 1970s continues to provoke a fierce hostility that mellows into disdain and yawning indifference only when his detractors succeed in assuring themselves of its utter irrelevance to their present. That is all the easier to do in that, with rare exceptions, even his well-disposed commentators have helped maintain the buffer zone around the philosopher of the encounter by confining their engagement with his 'dogmatic predecessor' to his proclamations of the crisis of Marxism, widely celebrated, on Antonio Negri's warrant, as the first harbingers of an Althusserian '*Kehre*'.[4] As for the solutions to the crisis proffered in the texts supposed to have heralded this turn, they belong, by common consent, to another age.

Yet an informed reading of *Filosofía y marxismo* blurs the line of demarcation thus drawn between the late and the superannuated Althusser, a staunch defender of the dictatorship of the proletariat, among other currently unthinkable ideas. For the 'interview' of the '1980s' is, in essence, a patchwork of extracts from, or résumés of, texts that Althusser produced in the 1960s and 1970s – as if the interviewee wished to flag the fact that the founding concept of his late philosophy, the encounter, appears throughout his work, if under various aliases: 'accident', 'accidental node', 'accumulation', 'combination', 'combination of circumstances' [*concours*], 'conjunction', 'conjuncture', 'entanglement' [*enchevêtrement*], and even 'encounter'. This is one index among many that 'Althusser's turn', if turn there was, came about by way of a re-turn.

To be sure, the mere presence of such terms in his earlier work proves nothing. Is not the basic principle of the materialism of the encounter (or 'aleatory materialism') the idea that a new structure can irrupt as the unpredictable result of a concatenation of a whole series of elements 'whose internal dispositions and meaning var[y] as a function of the changing place and role of these terms'? A mode of production, for example, can surge up as the result of a 'meeting' [*rencontre*] of 'elements' with 'different and independent origins', and yet the capacity, ascertainable after the fact, to 'join together and constitute that structure (the structure of a mode of production) … by coming under its jurisdiction, *becoming its effects*'. To settle the question of the 'Althusserian turn', accordingly, we might try to determine, in the light of this principle (the formulations of which just cited come, respectively, from Althusser's and Étienne Balibar's contributions to the 1965 collective work *Reading Capital*),[5] the precise moment in which the various elements of aleatory materialism came together and 'took' (in the sense in which one says, in French, that mayonnaise 'takes', as Althusser put it in 1966)[6] in such a way as to constitute the effects of this conceptual structure through the retroaction of the result upon its becoming.

One of these elements, Epicurean atomism, is all but absent in Althusser down to the mid-1970s. Was the *Kehre* brought on by an aleatory swerve precipitated by his (re)discovery, in the work of the Epicureans, of the aleatory swerve? There is reason to think so. In the preceding decade, Althusser had several 'brief encounters', '*relatively* accidental', with Epicurus and Lucretius.[7] Yet none of these flirts 'led to a fusion', to continue to cite the March 1969 letter that was published six months after he sent it to a comrade whom he felt constrained to ask, in another, private letter, to 'bring . . . her passion for him and her behaviour toward him under control' in the wake of a 1968 encounter that had, precisely, failed to 'take'.[8] Only with the June 1975 'Is it Simple to Be a Marxist in Philosophy?' in which Althusser locates 'the premises of Marx's materialism' in Epicurus, Spinoza, and Hegel, and the March 1976 'The Transformation of Philosophy', in which Machiavelli and Epicurus are the two philosophers expressly singled out for having practised an anti-philosophy anticipating Marx's, do we catch a glimpse of the dizzying promotion awaiting the Philosopher of the Garden at the École normale supérieure.[9] What was the result of this encounter and the ensuing fusion between the early Althusserian theory of the encounter and the later Althusserian reading of Epicurus, assigned the role of aleatory materialism's founding father once the encounter 'took'?

The result was at least, and perhaps at most, a translation of Althusser's theory of the encounter or 'accident'[10] into Epicurean terms, accompanied by a translation of certain key concepts of Althusser's earlier work into the terms of the theory of the encounter. Thus we are told that 'the developed concept of contingency' is called 'the encounter', and that conjuncture is 'a word that repeats "encounter", but in the form of a junction'.[11] These reformulations are at the heart of an exposition of an aleatory materialism about which the reader will decide, after comparing it with previous avatars of Althusserian materialism, whether it stems from a *Kehre*, a continuing break, a linear evolution, or a simple reprise.

She can make the comparison without immersing herself in 'The Underground Current'. For the first presentation of the materialism of the encounter to propose these redefinitions makes up Chapter 16 of the book she has in her hands, the 1976 manuscript that Althusser recommended to his Mexican Eckermann in 1984. The Althusser of the *Kehre*, if his conversion is to be dated to his declaration of allegiance to Epicurus and Lucretius, is, at least chronologically, the Althusser of another age. As if to flaunt a paradox, the Marxist philosopher finished the first draft of *How to Be a Marxist in Philosophy* in July 1976, a few weeks before putting the final touches on a 400-page book centred on his defence of the dictatorship of the proletariat.[12]

II

If the date at which Althusser espoused aleatory materialism is open to debate, few will deny that, by 1957 at the latest, his flirt with anti-philosophy was beginning to resemble an affair likely to last. It was in October of that year that there took place, in Paris, under the auspices of the 'Cercle ouvert' (Open circle), a lecture-debate entitled 'Chacun peut-il philosopher?' (Can everyone be a philosopher?). The discussion quickly escalated into a verbal joust around the recently published *Pourquoi des philosophes?* (*Why philosophers?*), in which Jean-François Revel affirms that modernity can safely forget philosophy, long since replaced and relegated to the rank of second-rate literature by the sciences. As proof of his claim, Revel cited the gobbledygook that impostors such as Heidegger, Lacan, Sartre and Merleau-Ponty were then busy palming off as profundity. Intervening from the floor in the discussion after the speakers' debate,[13] Althusser took up the cudgels for his friend's book, the main thesis of which he professed to share.

In fact, he defended a much broader thesis: that nearly every major philosopher shared Revel's. It was of course true that philosophy's 'basic pretension' is to possess knowledge beyond ordinary mortals' ken, knowledge that, in its own estimation, entitles it to exist: 'the philosopher always knows, more or less, what the radical origin of things is . . . what the true meaning of what others know is . . . [and] the meaning of the acts in which they are engaged.' Nevertheless, in 'a more historical perspective', it becomes clear that the philosopher seeks his titles to existence, not in philosophy as such, but in an antagonistic encounter with it: the great philosophers define themselves 'as a function of the philosophies that they reject'. Philosophy is a 'combat' in which every combatant 'feels the need to get rid of existing philosophies'.

The attempt to do away with philosophy is thus philosophy's founding act. Every philosopher (except perhaps the first) is an anti-philosopher.

But how can one be an anti-philosopher without being a philosopher? How can one 'take a sort of originary distance from the world' of philosophy that would not be philosophical? How can one 'reject philosophy without founding a philosophy?'

The young Marx shows us the answer by example, according to the young Althusser (he would turn thirty-nine a week later). Hardly had the science of history been founded than its founder mobilized it in an assault on the rear base of the philosophy of his time, its dominant ideology, with a view to neutralizing all philosophy, past and present. He thus demonstrated how to be a Marxist in philosophy without becoming a Marxist philosopher, how to overcome philosophy non-philosophically: by practising the science of it.[14]

It was by practising it as a science that the Althusser of the early 1960s sought to do away with all hitherto existing philosophy. His Marx, after being seduced in his youth by the sirens of an empiricist anti-philosophy, had rejected philosophy by founding a philosophy, the scientific philosophy of dialectical materialism, the pendant to the Marxist science of history. More exactly, Marx founded this scientific philosophy *in principle*, above all in *Capital*, without ever quite managing to work it out in *theory*. Whence the historical task of Marxist philosophy: reading *Capital* for Marx, in order to bring out the philosophy it contained 'in the practical state'. This was the mission that conferred his titles on the Marxist philosopher, who knew better than men themselves, if not the sense, then the essence of everything they knew and did. Althusser says so literally in *For Marx*, which makes dialectical materialism the general Theory of the essence of theoretical practice in general, and thus also, by way of a silent appeal to Spinoza, the general Theory of the essence of practice in general, hence the 'Theory . . . of the development of things in general'.[15]

One would be hard put to characterize better, in so few words, the idealistic philosophy of the essence of everything and its opposite that Althusser is at pains to deconstruct in *How to Be a Marxist in Philosophy*, from Plato through Kant to Lévi-Strauss, without forgetting Althusser. Whence another Althusserian re-turn, a self-critical one this time, made explicit in a passage of the book about the 'mistaken idea' that Marx founded a philosophy in founding a science of history. Involved here is, more precisely, a re-turn to a re-turn, for this self-criticism is a reprise of one written in 1972,[16] itself a revised version of the detailed 1966–67 self-criticism of which Althusser was to release only a few fragments in prefaces to re-editions and translations of *Reading Capital*.

The mid-1960s self-criticism crystallized after a lost battle during which he had defended a science of history threatened, in his view, by pseudo-Marxist reformists intent on recasting Marx's revolutionary theory as the highest stage of bourgeois humanist ideology. This philosophical defence of Marx's singularity had political stakes: the basic orientation of the French Communist Party and the international communist movement, which Althusser was trying to bend, as he avowed in an unpublished 1967 jotting, in the direction of 'left-wing anti-Stalinism'.[17] It was in the wake of his failure to do so that he became aware of the idealist Trojan horse within the confines of his own materialism, and went on to reject as 'theoreticist' the notion of a scientific philosophy just briefly evoked.

The indubitable *Kehre* precipitated by this self-criticism put his thought back on the strait and narrow path, as it were, of anti-philosophical deviation. By way of a continuing self-critique, it led to the anti-philosophy ratified ten years later in *How to Be a Marxist in Philosophy*. At the same time, it led to the encounter-fusion of this deviant philosophy (communism is above all 'disorienting' (*déroutant*), Althusser says in 1972, 'it diverts you from the road you were on')[18] with the materialism of the encounter, at the heart of which one finds what he would call, in 1976, the 'deviation-deviance' of the clinamen. In retrospect, it made the 1961–65 'brief encounter' or, perhaps better, paradoxical coexistence between the elements of a nascent aleatory materialism and the pronounced idealism of the theoreticist deviation 'relatively accidental'. But this deviation was evidently no such thing: it was the royal road leading straight to the philosophical orthodoxy of what Althusser had called, in 1957, the 'great tradition'.

His later, heterodox philosophy began to emerge, or re-emerge, in public in a 1967–68 team-taught 'course of initiation into philosophy' aimed at non-philosophers, scientists above all,[19] the first five lectures of which Althusser himself delivered in November-December 1967.[20] In the February 1968 'Lenin and Philosophy', a lecture purporting to initiate professional philosophers into Lenin's philosophy, these elements crystallized in the idea, already briefly set out in the May 1967 conclusion to 'The Historical Task of Marxist Philosophy',[21] that philosophy is a continuation of politics by other means, the privileged means being the exploitation of the methods and results of the sciences.[22]

In one sense, this was nothing new: theoreticist philosophy in its Althusserian variant had also engaged in politics by way of the exploitation of a science, the science of history, producing eminently political effects despite all: thanks to Althusser and the Althusserians, a left-wing anti-Stalinism had succeeded in making itself heard in the PCF. The *theory* of philosophy proposed by this philosophy, however, prevented it from accounting for its own practical operations. Claiming to be a science – even a science of the sciences – a defining characteristic of which, according to Althusser, was to work on an object of knowledge distinct from its real object, it effectively confessed that it was incapable of being transformed by the world it theorized, or of transforming it: it could aspire only to knowing it.

Althusser extricated himself from this impasse by doing an about-face. He acknowledged that Marxist philosophy, far from being a science, is dependent on a (proletarian) ideology, and thus has an 'organic link' with politics. He observed that the 'vast majority' of philosophies also have an organic link with politics, albeit one they 'stubbornly deny'. And he affirmed that Marxist philosophy is distinguished by the fact that it has 'renounced denial'.[23]

What purpose does such denial serve?

Althusser's response is twofold. 'The dominant classes deny that they dominate.' 'Philosophy *represents* the class struggle, that is, politics.'[24] The dominant philosophy accordingly represents this denial, a crucial component of the dominant classes' politics; it does so before (*auprès des*) the sciences, which harbour the potential to expose it for what it is. Philosophy represents this denial by conjuring away its own domination by politics and determination by the sciences, while reducing them, one denial leading to another, to 'a state of submission and ... apologetic exploitation that serves extra-scientific values'. The relationship of foreclosure that philosophy maintains with its '*real* relation to the sciences' is thus at once the condition and the effect of its complicity with the dominant classes' politics.[25] The unacknowledged place of this real relation is what is filled in and blacked out by philosophy's pretension to knowing 'the radical origin of things'.

As defined in and through Althusser's anti-theoreticist *Kehre* of 1967–68, accordingly, the historical task before the Marxist in philosophy is basically negative: it is to expose philosophy's complicity with the politics of the dominant by uncovering the 'philosophical' relation it maintains with its real conditions of existence. This is not a task for Marxist philosophy as such, says Althusser at the end of 'Lenin and Philosophy', but for a science of philosophy exterior to philosophy and capable of producing 'objective (and therefore scientific) knowledge' of it: a '*theory of philosophy*'.[26] He had come to the same conclusion ten years earlier, endorsing, at the end of his defence of Revel, the anti-philosophical programme adopted by the author of *The German Ideology*: 'the slogan "put an end to philosophy" had a very precise, very concrete goal: its sole meaning was to coincide with a historical discipline that allowed [Marx] to forge a theory of philosophy'.[27]

Yet even an extra-philosophical theory of philosophy is philosophical, for a reason stated, as we have briefly seen, in Althusser's 1957 intervention: 'to get rid of [philosophy] (that is, in order to remain true to the goal preoccupying us)', 'the great philosopher' has to 'found a philosophy'.[28] It is unclear whether Althusser thought, in 1957, that constructing a Marxian theory of philosophy offered a way out of this circle. His 1967 initiation into philosophy is, however, unambiguous: one 'must guard against the illusion of being able to provide a definition – that is, a knowledge – of philosophy that would be able *radically* to escape from philosophy ... one cannot radically escape the *circle* of philosophy. All *objective* knowledge of philosophy is in effect at the same time a *position within* philosophy.'[29] The consequence is nevertheless emphatically not that there can be no objective, scientific knowledge of philosophy. It is, rather, that Marxism must pursue a double strategy, developing a scientific theory of philosophy's double relationship with politics and the sciences while consciously representing the extra-philosophical science premised on that relationship in an intra-philosophical struggle that is necessarily political and ideological, as that science itself claims. In that sense, to acknowledge that there is no 'radically' escaping what *How to Be a Marxist in Philosophy*, silently circling back to the 'Cercle ouvert', will call the 'infernal circle' of philosophy is to acknowledge that the Marxist theory of philosophy, albeit aphilosophical and apolitical, cannot *not* have philosophical and therefore political effects. The business of the Marxist in philosophy is to produce them by representing the science that takes philosophy for its object before the political practice that philosophy ultimately is. It is not to found a new philosophy. 'Less than ever', Althusser proclaims near the end of 'Lenin and Philosophy', unabashedly ignoring positions he took in the first half of the 1960s and even in the first half of this lecture, 'can we say that Marxism is a new philosophy'. It is a 'new practice of philosophy' that 'can transform philosophy'.[30]

He sets out to realize this program in *A Marxist in Philosophy*, following a path traced by way of metaphor in 'Lenin and Philosophy', which proposes to deconstruct the high tradition of idealist philosophy by taking its distance from the distance that the philosophical tradition claims to take from the world. Thus the concrete task of the Marxist in philosophy is said to consist in transforming the idealist philosopher's mythical 'originary distance' into '*the emptiness of a distance taken*'[31] – the emptiness that will become, in 1976 and beyond, the void that surges up in the wake of an 'originary deviation', where there was, prior to its sudden emergence, only the 'void' of an excessive fullness. To be a Marxist in philosophy is to make a void from a false void that has been preventively filled with the 'originary meaning of things', in order to clear a space for a non-exploitative, (anti-) philosophical representation of scientific knowledge.

How, exactly, is the Marxist in philosophy to go about things? Althusser answers by way of another celebrated metaphor: by drawing a 'line of demarcation' through the deceptive fullness of the philosophical field.[32] Well drawn at the right time, it transforms the philosophical field into a *battle*field, precipitating an encounter whose stake is the fate of the scientific practices, with the stake of this stake being, as we saw, class domination and the struggle to overcome it. Thus what takes place in philosophy is ultimately only the endless repetition of the production/evacuation of one void through the creation of another, by means of a distantiation/differentiation of which the whole panoply of philosophical battle is the evanescent trace: a 'philosophical nothing'[33] consisting of theses, antitheses, categories, and other 'philosophical objects'[34] which, albeit non-objective, nevertheless incarnate a crucial objective: an ongoing defence of the sciences against the constant threat of their exploitation by ideology and its main 'theoretical detachment', idealist philosophy.

In that specific sense, philosophy has no history. More exactly, its history is, in the last instance, the history of the endless drawing and redrawing of the same line of demarcation between the two principal factions in philosophy, of which one, materialist and dominated, openly takes sides by denouncing the unacknowledged assumption of a partisan position by the other, whose refusal to acknowledge its partisanship is the main mechanism of its domination.

In its concrete effects, the 'new practice of philosophy' that Althusser champions in 1967–68 is oddly reminiscent of the old practice of anti-philosophy that he mocks in his first self-criticism. Written from his high theoreticist positions of 1965, that self-criticism takes the form of a self-portrait of the would-be Marxist philosopher as naive anti-philosopher, bent on confining philosophy to the role of science's *'evanescent* critical consciousness', with, as his sole aim, 'the continual critical reduction of the threa[t] of ideological illusion' – a naiveté said to have reduced the history of this (anti-)philosophical 'external conscience' of science to that of its 'continuing death' (*mort continuée*).[35] Yet it would be a mistake to treat the 'new practice of philosophy' heralded in 'Lenin and Philosophy' as a mere negation of the anti-anti-philosophy of *For Marx*. For that would be to forget that every science progresses by way of a 'continuing break' (*coupure continuée*), to recall another anti-theoreticist idea that Althusser introduced or reintroduced in 1967–68.[36] Althusserian Marxism would have to sustain several further breaks before the new practice of philosophy could encounter that toward which its analogue, Derridean deconstruction, is driven by its internal logic, according to a draft of *How to Be a Marxist in Philosophy*: the dictatorship of the proletariat.

III

One of the textual lineages to which *A Marxist in Philosophy* belongs runs from the 'transformation of philosophy' programmed at the end of 'Lenin and Philosophy' to 'The Transformation of Philosophy', a lecture that Althusser delivered in Granada in March 1976 and substantially incorporated into the book a few months later. *A Marxist in Philosophy* also includes a version of the fifth lecture of his 1967 initiation into philosophy, an analysis of theories of knowledge since Descartes that was not published with the preceding four lectures in 1974. If we add that *A Marxist in Philosophy* presents itself as 'that which cannot *not* be the sketch of a scientific theory of philosophy', whose 'hesitant beginning' 'Lenin and Philosophy' declared itself to be,[37] and also, explicitly, as an instantiation of the 'new practice of philosophy' called for in that 1968 lecture, the 1976 book would seem to be the direct if belated sequel to the texts marking Althusser's 1967–68 turn.

But it is also the reprise of an unwritten 1969 book.

After plunging into a severe depression in April 1968 – the beginning of a 'major, virtually uninterrupted illness' that dragged on for four years, 'apart from a sunny interval in spring 1969'[38] – Althusser wrote, precisely in spring 1969, a text titled 'Qu'est-ce que la philosophie marxiste-léniniste?' (What is Marxist-Leninist philosophy?). Hardly was it finished than it was transformed into a considerably longer manuscript renamed 'On the Reproduction of the Relations of Production'. It was from this text that Althusser extracted the fragments patched together, after some rewriting, in his renowned 1970 paper, 'Ideology and Ideological State Apparatuses'. The rest of the manuscript was put aside. It was not published in its entirety until after Althusser's death, in French in 1995 and in English some twenty years later, under the title *On the Reproduction of Capitalism*.[39]

In the first chapter of this book, Althusser sets out to write a very short history of philosophy, taking as his point of departure a question that he will ask again in the first chapter of *A Marxist in Philosophy* and elsewhere: Was Gramsci right to declare that 'everyone is a philosopher'? The 1957 'Cercle ouvert' debate had started out from the same question: 'Can everyone be a philosopher?' In 1957, Althusser dismissed it with a one-liner.[40] Twenty years later, he seems to acknowledge that his Italian precursor was right: 'philosophy', declares *A Marxist in Philosophy*, in sum, 'is not the preserve of professional philosophers'. In fact, he puts an Althusserian thesis in Gramsci's mouth: everyone is a philosopher to the extent that he lives 'within an ideological framework impregnated with the fall-out from philosophy'.[41] In other words, the 'spontaneous' philosophy that nearly everyone professes has in fact been inculcated in him or her by an ideology that the philosophy of the philosophers helps fashion.[42]

True to the program outlined in 'Lenin and Philosophy', the first chapter of *On the Reproduction of Capitalism* closes with a promise 'to produce a scientific definition of Philosophy' in its double relation with 'class relations and the state' on the one hand and 'the history of the sciences' on the other.[43] An introductory note entitled 'To My Readers' even identifies this definition as the 'goal' of the whole work. The rest of volume 1, Althusser informs us at the end of the first chapter, is basically a 'long detour' leading to it. Why start with these ten pages on philosophy, only to leave the questions they raise 'in abeyance'? 'For reasons that are very important both theoretically and politically', he says in 'To My Readers', that 'will appear at the end of volume 2'.[44]

How to Be a Marxist in Philosophy takes the place of this unwritten second volume. Since it is a place roughly charted in volume 1, we can try, speculatively, to fill it in for Althusser, if only as a way of indicating the direction his thinking on philosophy took after 1967–68. Let us begin by bringing a familiar passage of the 1969–70 paper on ideology together with the fifth lecture in the 1967 initiation. According to the latter, philosophy maintains a 'philosophical' relationship with its real conditions of existence. According to 'Ideology and Ideological State Apparatuses', 'ideology is a "representation" of the imaginary relationship of individuals to their real conditions of existence'.[45]

The passage that points to a relationship between these two relationships, imaginary and 'philosophical', occurs in the original version of the prologue to the well-known scene illustrating the interpellation of the subject by the Subject: in this case, somewhat surprisingly, of Moses by God. It contains a phrase absent from the ISAs paper: 'we shall, moreover, expressly return to this demonstration once we are in a position to speak of philosophy again'.[46] In His relationship with the subject, this hint seems to suggest, the Interpellator and Law-Giver God of volume 1 was due, in volume 2, for demotion to the rank of philosophy's lieutenant or place-holder.

If so, Althusser may well have gone on to discuss, in volume 2, the interpellation of Everyman by a Philosophy that 'duplicates itself' in its subjects as God duplicates Himself in His, 'even in the frightful inversion of His image in them'. What philosophical interpellation might involve is suggested, in turn, by the fifth lecture, which notes that philosophy represents 'the dominant rationality in the sciences' in a guise that changes from age to age: dianoia, observing reason, thinking substance, experimental reason, and so on.[47] On science's behalf, philosophy thus interpellates a subject that, incarnating the law of right reason (duplicated even its frightful inversions), is Everyman. That is, philosophy creates man in science's image by creating an imaginary subject of science in philosophy's. It is perhaps in that Althusserian sense that volume 2 would have confirmed Gramsci's claim that everyone is a philosopher.

Let us take one more speculative step. In *On the Reproduction of Capitalism*, Althusser writes that the 'concert' of the Ideological State Apparatuses is 'dominated', not without 'false notes', 'by a single score', 'the score of the *State Ideology*': that is, the ideology of the dominant class, which it is each ISA's task to play in an arrangement adapted to its own audience. More precisely, 'the overall unity of the system formed by all the state apparatuses is ensured by the unity of the class politics of the class holding state power and by the State Ideology corresponding to the fundamental interests of the class (or classes) in power'.[48] Would Althusser not have gone on to say, at this stage in his reflection, that philosophy justifies the subjection of the dominated to this unity by forging the imaginary unity of a universal subject of science or right reason? And, further, that it denies its own exploitation of the sciences at the behest of the State Ideology by demonstrating the harmony of both Science and State Ideology with its imaginary representation of the dominant rationality? Is the interpellation of Everyman as reasonable subject and law-abiding citizen of the reasonable state not the main practical task before a philosophy that assigns itself the role of guarantor of the whole and of the originary meaning of things, thus duplicating its own imaginary-philosophical relation to its real conditions of existence in that of its subjects to theirs?

Be that as it may, this speculation brings us back to the question of philosophy's conditions of existence. Would Althusser have limited them, at the end of volume 2 of *On the Reproduction of Capitalism*, to 'class relations and the state' on the one hand and 'major events in the history of the sciences' on the other, as the first chapter of volume 1 seems to suggest?[49]

The fate of the fifth lecture offers an answer in the practical state. Althusser intended to publish a version of it in the *Revue de l'enseignement philosophique* in 1968, but changed his mind after correcting the page proofs.[50] We do not know why. It is, however, easy to see that this December 1967 text is markedly out of phase with a thesis central to the February 1968 'Lenin and Philosophy'. Although Engels rightly affirms, Althusser says in 1968, both that philosophy is, ultimately, an endless struggle between an idealist and a materialist tendency, and also that the shifts marking its repetitive history are determined by the great scientific revolutions, his conception of that history is '*missing* something *essential*'. Missing is the Leninist thesis that philosophy, via its relation to the sciences, '*represents* the class struggle'.[51]

The same thing is missing in Althusser's 1967 lecture, which broaches the history of philosophy from the standpoint of its relations to the history of the sciences alone.[52] It seems likely that that is why the lecture was ultimately not published. It is certain that, as soon as his health allowed, its author made good the lack that 'Lenin and Philosophy' pinpoints not only in Engels, but also, tacitly, in Althusser. That is, the first chapters of both 'Qu'est-ce que la philosophie marxiste-léniniste?' and *On the Reproduction of Capitalism* propose a schematic overview of the history of philosophy that devotes equal attention to its determination by 'scientific' *and* 'political' events.

Althusser nevertheless concluded, shortly after finishing the 1969 manuscript, that he had once again overemphasized the determinant role of the sciences. In mid-1970, restating ideas advanced in an unpublished 3 May 1969 'Afterword to "Lenin and Philosophy"', itself akin, astoundingly enough, to reflections aired in an unpublished November 1967 note to his collaborators,[53] he wrote that Marx's radicalization, and thus politics, had played the determinant role in the emergence of the science of history, which would nevertheless not have come about without philosophical 'translation' of that radicalization.[54] In 1972, he went on to affirm, in a self-critical passage of 'Reply to John Lewis', that Marx's philosophical revolution had 'commanded' the founding of historical materialism. 'Philosophy', he added, ostensibly conceding a point to Lewis, 'is 'concerned' not only with politics and the sciences, but with *all* social practices'.[55] It is a major concession that, despite appearances, accentuates the determinant role of politics in the broad sense; for it is the fact that the social practices are, by virtue of the ideology they 'secrete', a potential source of resistance to the State Ideology that motivates their promotion here. This concession goes hand-in-hand with the stipulation, perhaps not accidentally found on the same page, that philosophy, 'politics in theory' since 1967, can be more precisely characterized as, 'in the last instance, class struggle in theory'.[56]

There is of course no answering our question of a moment ago as to whether Althusser would have restricted philosophy's conditions of existence to 'major events in the history of the sciences' and 'class relations and the state' if, as planned, he had written volume 2 of *On the Reproduction of Capitalism* in 1969. But the dizzying shifts just evoked show that, if he had written it a few years later, those conditions would almost certainly have been identified as 'all the social practices', with the privilege once granted scientific revolutions restricted to the first of them, the one that gave birth to mathematics and also philosophy by providing the first 'real philosopher', Plato, with a geometrical model of rigour and a – literally – reactionary, that is, reactive, political reason for proposing it. Readers of *How to Be a Marxist in Philosophy* will decide whether we have bent the stick too far in the direction suggested by a rarely remarked and probably disingenuous two-line concession to John Lewis. Let us, in the hope of influencing their verdict, highlight one of the major consequences of this 'Lewisian' rectification.

It is that the philosophy that helps wage the class struggle of the dominant strives to reduce *all* social practices to a state of submission. The denial characteristic of idealist philosophy accordingly takes the form of an affirmation of the primacy of theory over practice *as such*, and of Theory or philosophy over all other forms of theoretical practice. It takes the form, in other words, of philosophy's totalizing, totalitarian assimilation of the non-philosophical, and of its claim to being a general Theory of the development of things in general. It is with reference to the subaltern status to which philosophy assigns the *whole* of its putative outside that Althusser, from this point in his thinking on, draws the fundamental line of demarcation between idealism and materialism – or, perhaps better, between Philosophy and anti-Philosophy.

This mandates another redefinition, which draws a line of demarcation between two different ways of drawing a line of demarcation.

The presentation of the two basic philosophical tendencies in 'Lenin and Philosophy' exemplifies the theoreticism that it takes for its target, for it comes down to affirming that each of these two tendencies 'exists in its own camp . . . according to its proper conditions of existence', until, 'one day', the two camps 'come up against one another (*se rencontrent*) and come into conflict'.[57] It may, however, be ventured that this idea is found in 'Lenin and Philosophy' only because it is found in Lenin, who thought that 'basically, there are only idealists and materialists'.[58] Althusser himself had long practised a conception of the philosophical encounter that, thinking the combatants as an effect of their combat, precludes any such neat distinctions. He had even stated, if indirectly, the principle informing his practice in a 1966 comment on the state of war in Rousseau: 'Particular interest is constituted by the universal opposition which is the essence of the state of war. There are not first individuals each with his own particular interest. . . . Opposition is primary'.[59] 'Reply to John Lewis' reformulates this principle negatively in the passage quoted at the beginning of the present paragraph, a passage encapsulating the theory of the encounter that 'Reply' in fact denounces. The passage bears, it is true, on class struggle in the broad sense, not on philosophical class struggle per se. Class struggle in theory, however, obeys the laws of (class) struggle tout court: in philosophy as well, it is the combat that makes the combatants.

But, in philosophy as elsewhere, the dominant classes deny they dominate: they do not go looking for a fight, while waging one with exemplary ferocity, in line with a strategy that consists in *containing* the adversary, in both senses of the word. Simply to emerge, materialism must therefore first look for idealism's outside, which is to say for itself, *inside idealism*. Did Althusser's Marx not wrest the fundamental materialist category of the 'process without a subject' from the heart of Hegelian speculation?[60] Moreover, although idealism alone has a vital interest in penning a domesticated version of its adversary up in its own domain (how can it exploit it if it expels it?), the rigours of philosophical battle are such that materialism, too, must wage an unending struggle against an internal foe. Witness Althusser's thirty years' war against Marxian idealism, including his own 'rationalist-speculative', 'theoreticist' opposition of science and ideology. It is thus also with himself in mind that he describes the idealist-materialist knot that must at least provisionally be cut if an encounter is to take place:

> A 'philosophy'... is not a Whole, made up of homogeneous propositions submitted to the verdict: truth or error. It is a system of *positions* (theses), and, through these positions, itself occupies positions in the theoretical class struggle.... It is not a question of, on the one hand, a homogeneous good side, and on the other a bad side. The positions of the two sides are usually mixed up together.... The idealist and materialist tendencies which confront one another in all philosophical struggles, on the field of battle, *are never realized in a pure form in any 'philosophy'.*[61]

It is in this tempered form that Lenin's theory of the two camps reappears in Althusser's (post-)Leninist philosophy. Yet anyone who has read the late Althusser or, for that matter, the Althusser of late 1957, will have noticed that something essential is still missing from this evocation of the entangled encounter between idealism and materialism: the idea that the latter has to wage battle, not only against its adversary on the philosophical field of battle, but also against that *Kampfplatz* itself. That thesis leads straight to the concept of the dictatorship of the proletariat. If we have lost sight of it, it is because it forms the ground on which we have been advancing for some time now.

IV

Althusser finished writing *How to Be a Marxist in Philosophy* in the midst of his 1976 campaign against the French Communist Party's imminent abandonment of the concept of the dictatorship of the proletariat, of which the party leadership had served notice at the beginning of the year (on TV). But that may be chalked up to contingency. 'The dictatorship of the proletariat is the critical point in the whole theoretical and political history of Marxism', he wrote in 1966.[62] He could have made the same declaration ten years earlier or twenty years later: from beginning to end, Althusserian

Marxism turns on the concept that bears the unfortunate name of class 'dictatorship' in the Marxist tradition.

Its stakes are summed up in the thesis that social classes are the effect of exploitation, the reproduction and thus the existence of which ('to exist is to be reproduced')[63] are ensured by a structure of ideological, political, legal, and other relations of domination, crowned by a state in the dominant class's hands. From his first, 1959 book, *Montesquieu: Politics and History*, Althusser thought the always revocable perennity of such a structure, based on the exercise of a force ultimately determined by exploitation, as the effect of a combination of contingent circumstances made necessary by their encounter and fusion; he thought the state as a crystallization of the excess force possessed by an exploiting class over that of the classes it exploits, an excess generally obtaining on all levels of a society subjected to the exploiters' domination or 'dictatorship'. The terminology of *void*, *encounter*, and *take* that he elaborated from the mid-1960s on translates so effortlessly into that of the irruption of a class society conceived along these lines that it is hard not to conclude that the former terminology is a generalization of the latter.

Yet that terminology must be modified before it can be applied to the dictatorship of the proletariat. Althusser's hypothesis, like Marx's, is that this dominated class, if it were to become dominant, would have, like every other dominant class in history, to wage a struggle to establish and maintain its ascendancy at all levels of the social structure. (This seemed all the more obvious to Althusser once he came to the conclusion, in 1972, that a socialist mode of production was a 'yellow logarithm': post-capitalist society would, he contended from then on, long be characterized by the antagonistic coexistence of two basic modes of production, capitalist and communist.) The new dominant class must therefore, like every other, create a state of its own as an instrument of its domination – without, unlike other ruling classes, disguising that domination.

The proletariat, however, is not an exploiting class, whereas the historical function of the state and the whole structure of domination over which it presides is, according to Marx, to guarantee the reproduction of a relation of exploitation. It follows that the proletariat has an interest in precipitating, through its parties and through mass organizations, the demise of its own state. Althusser goes so far as to declare, in a 1976 'Note' to his study of the dictatorship of the bourgeoisie, *On the Reproduction of Capitalism*, not just that 'a communist party has no business entering the government of a bourgeois state ... in order to "administer" the affairs of a bourgeois state', but that it 'has no business entering a government of the dictatorship of the proletariat', either, inasmuch as its task is not to manage 'its' state, but to struggle for its decline and disappearance.[64]

The class dictatorship that, on the communist hypothesis, will put an end to classes must accordingly erect a 'semi-state' or 'non-state' (Lenin's creative 'translation' of Engels).[65]

The last stage in the continuing break effected between the texts of Althusser's 1967–68 turn and *How to Be a Marxist* depends on this paradoxical concept. We can take the measure of its fundamental importance in the evolution of Althusserian aleatory materialism by comparing the peroration of 'Lenin and Philosophy', which announces the 'new practice of philosophy', and a passage earlier in the same lecture that might seem to pave the way for it by explaining the lack, a century after *Capital*, of a great work of Marxist philosophy. Why this lack and this lag? 'Philosophy exists only by virtue of the distance it lags behind its scientific inducement', the great scientific event capable of sparking a great philosophical transformation. 'Marxist philosophy should therefore lag behind the Marxist science of history.' That is why Marx – the Marxist Marx – kept silent on philosophy. Fortunately, in 1968, the long deferred Hegelian dusk was about to fall. 'Marxist philosophy's' owl of Minerva would soon 'take wing'.[66]

Sometime between 1973 and 1976, class struggle in theory got the better of the owl of Minerva.

As Althusser saw the matter both before and after the 1973–76 turn within his turn, idealist philosophy gains ascendancy, philosophically speaking, over all the social practices and the ideologies they engender by deforming them in order to subject them, philosophico-imaginarily, to the unified, hierarchical order over which it thinks it presides – a theoretical system whose rationality and forms of demonstration it borrows from the sciences. This philosophical reduction to order turns out to be comparable to, if not, indeed, calqued upon, the order that the ideological class struggle of the dominant seeks to impose on all practices and the corresponding ideologies by means of its ideological apparatuses. It is thus the dominant classes' dictatorship, orchestrated by their state, which the dominant philosophy serves: it resolves, at the level of abstraction specific to it, the contradictions that a class dictatorship encounters in its interminable, usually preventive war to meet the resistance that exploitation necessarily engenders. In this sense, idealist philosophy is, in the last instance, state philosophy.

The Marxist philosopher's task was, accordingly – according to the author of one strand of 'Lenin and Philosophy' – to devise a counter-philosophy to combat the call to order issued by philosophy on behalf of the exploiters' state. That is, his task was to unify the ideological elements capable of fusing in a conceptual system that would serve the political struggle of the dominated. In so doing, Marxist philosophy would make good the lag analyzed in 'Lenin and Philosophy', in the wake of many other Althusserian texts of the first half of the 1960s.

It is this idea of the creation of a comprehensive philosophical counter-order or counter-system that disappears with the extinction of the Marxist owl of Minerva, because it turns out to be incompatible with Althusser's conception of proletarian dictatorship and, consequently, with his contribution to the underground current of the materialism of the encounter. Whence yet another Althusserian self-criticism, cast as a positive revaluation of the mature Marx's silence on philosophy. The Althusser of the 1960s had failed to understand, or had perhaps only forgotten or wilfully suppressed,[67] what this silence signified: that it is hard to reject a philosophical order *philosophically* without simultaneously founding one. But a philosophical order, in its systematicity and its hierarchical modalities, is by its nature complicit with the order policed by the classical state, the state of an exploiting class. A proletarian philosophical order, like a proletarian state, is, on this view, a contradiction in terms.

It follows that what Althusser had to say in 'Lenin and Philosophy' about the inevitable lag between a scientific revolution and the corresponding radical philosophical 'reorganization' was itself the effect of a lag, inscribed in what appears, from the standpoint of his later anti-philosophy – and perhaps also from that of his anti-philosophy of the 1950s – as the strict incompatibility of two strands in 'Lenin and Philosophy'.[68] What would soon, if it had not already, become Althusserian aleatory materialism could not be forced into the mould into which Althusser had been trying to fit it from the beginning of his theoreticist deviation. The philosophy that serves the dominated classes' struggle to establish their own state while simultaneously ridding themselves of it requires (on Althusser's 'late' hypothesis) a deviant form, even – since a deviant philosophy, too, remains 'philosophical' – a form that constantly deviates from itself. The name that best suits such (self-)deconstructive (anti-)philosophy is the one imposed by its origins. Just as the paradoxical historical task of the revolutionary proletariat was to establish a non-state, a state that (as Engels put it), '[is] no longer a state in the proper sense of the word', the task of Marxist philosophy was to invent a non-philosophy.[69]

Where were the models for it to be found? 'For my part, I would closely investigate the cases of Epicurus and Machiavelli', Althusser remarks in his spring 1976 lecture, 'The Transformation of Philosophy', adding, in the nearly contemporaneous 'The Facts', that an 'unusual and illuminating link' existed between these 'true precursors of Marx': 'above all, Epicurus, Machiavelli, Spinoza, Rousseau, and Hegel'.[70]

As for the positive task before this aleatory philosophy-non-philosophy, Althusser confines himself to noting that it is called upon, not to impose on the elements of a nascent communist ideology 'a constraining ideological unity', but 'to promote the liberation and free exercise of social practices and human ideas' and therefore, necessarily, to help 'invent *new forms* of community that would make the state superfluous'.[71] The same applies to what is called, in a Marxist terminology currently out of fashion, the dictatorship of the proletariat. The Althusser of the materialism of the encounter was, decidedly, the Althusser of another age – past or to come, the question remains open.

With that, we have reached the threshold of *How to Be a Marxist in Philosophy*.

V

In the letter that he wrote to Pierre Macherey at the end of summer 1976, Althusser announced that he had just finished 'an introduction which was meant to be an introduction to philosophy for non-philosophers, but, in the writing, turned out to be . . . for philosophers. I believe, and no mistake, that the other kind of introduction is all but impossible to conceive. I, at any event, have come a cropper.' The text he was referring to then bore the title 'Introduction à la philosophie'. He sent Macherey a photocopy of the typescript, which he lightly revised that fall before deciding to overhaul it in 1977–78, doubtless in hopes of making it more accessible to non-specialists. The new version in fact evolved into a different book, which Althusser entitled 'Initiation à la philosophie pour les non-philosophes'. In an allusion to the title of his presentation at his 1975 habilitation, 'Is it Simple to Be a Marxist in Philosophy?' he eventually gave 'Introduction à la philosophie' the title 'Être marxiste en philosophie'.

Neither of these two books was released in his lifetime. *Initiation à la philosophie* first appeared in 2014; in 2017, Bloomsbury released it in an English translation titled *Philosophy for Non-Philosophers*. *Être marxiste en philosophie* was not issued in its entirety until 2015, some twenty years after its burlesque 'Prelude' appeared posthumously in the journal *Digraphe*.[72] The book is here published in English translation for the first time

HOW TO BE A MARXIST IN PHILOSOPY

BY LOUIS ALTHUSSER

PRELUDE: GRUSHA'S DONKEY

The whole thing came together spontaneously. We have to let you in on it, after all. We had a sprawling, cool house and a big yard for when night fell. Wind went rustling through the treetops and the water lisped in the fountains. It was summer. The company of philosophers, that is, everyone, the famous ones and the others, came with the moon, drawn by the scent of men and a desire for conversation, and the coolness came wafting in from the foliage. There was fruit on the abandoned tables, with crunchy chocolate-covered cornflakes. They arrived one after the other, one with the other, or one by one, those still alive together with the dead, though we never did find out who was dead and who wasn't. No way of telling, from the boom of Socrates' laugh, whether he'd already quaffed the hemlock; no way of telling whether little Meno, shivering in the water of the truth, had already hit on his two right angles; whether Descartes had already discovered his pineal gland, or Kant, Copernicus; whether Marx had already stood Hegel on his head, or had yet to (a mass of that size!); whether Bergson had already thought of the thingamajig with the cones, or Wittgenstein had already concluded that when there's nothing left to say, the thing to do is shut up. They were there without age or time, and without history, and there was no way of telling whether or not their future was behind them or their past ahead of them – whether they were carrying it like a bag of figs hanging from the back of their necks or in front of them on a platter to prop up their breasts and their consciences. How to put it? They were there *qua* good philosophers who dwell in the eternity of the concept – philosophy, which is 'eternal' – and are so thoroughly haunted by it that they lose all sense of past and future, that is, as (Saint) Augustine has explained so well, of the present. Hence this fraternity and this mix of different epochs, which made each of them everyone else's contemporary. The great disorder of time amid the disorder of ideas! It often happened that one of them found himself talking or holding his tongue in place of another, so familiar were they with each other's thoughts. They even knew each other's surprises like the backs of their hands. Everything had already been said and done, everything was so, and was forever to be said and done again, since nothing is ever as fresh as an old idea, or as old as a fresh one. Eternity. Women were in short supply, of course. Aristotle, who always had 'nature' at his fingertips, explained that it hadn't really made women for philosophy. Yet, despite Kant's grumbling, some of them too, of all stations in life, had been invited, without waiting for the women's liberation movement. Things were moving along nicely. In the heavens, the stars said not a word.

Little by little, carried along by the flow of the remarks they'd been trading back and forth, they had said to each other, 'After all, why not compose, for ourselves, something like a gigantic, impromptu exchange of the ideas of the living and the dead about philosophy? Everyone can say what's on his mind and, despite all the well-known positions and oppositions, we'll at least have considered everything from all angles; and who knows but that, in hashing over all this rhetoric of truth, we won't find something unprecedented to shake it up with?' This idea too materialized spontaneously and, since each of them expected to have the best of it, all of them agreed, even Kant, who told the others that philosophy is a battlefield while keeping his plan for perpetual peace to himself, thus winning all the way down the line.

That's how things got started: at top speed, the first night, when, right off the bat, a Stranger brought everyone up short by saying in a loud voice: 'I demand the floor!' Everyone looked at his neighbour in silence. Apparently, no one had been counting on this. And since the Stranger insisted, vehemently, and since everyone was dumbfounded, except for Kant, who said to his neighbour, 'But this isn't the Jacobin Club, after all!', and since the Stranger kept insisting, getting louder all the time, Socrates' voice emerged from his beard to answer, calmly: 'But you don't have to demand the floor, my friend, because you've just taken it'. (Silence.) 'Consider, rather, how strange this "floor" is, so different from all the wild game and all the powers in the world, since, to take it, you need only ask for it. Moreover, which of us owns it, so that we might give it to you?' And Socrates was off on the subject of the floor, asking one little question after the next, as was his wont: whether one has it, or gives it, or takes it, or holds it, or yields it; whether the floor is of the same general stock as the voice, the voice of the same general stock as language, and on and on. Caught in the trap, the Stranger answered, his question concealed in his responses. Naturally, everything came surging back again: truth and error, truth and lies, promise and betrayal, at which point Kant naturally found a way of getting in a word about 'the right to lie'.

Socrates was the sort to lay insignificant reflections like that on you: all he had to do was to open his mouth, and his interlocutor would shut his and start thinking, or pipe up and blurt out a truth. That is known as *dialogue*. A way of talking that amounts to talking for others, as if *they* had the floor. The upshot was that the Stranger fell silent. But they'd been teetering on the brink of disaster, reflecting that way without a chairman to run the session.

We also had a big session on the One, during which Parmenides shone (everyone knew his line, of course, but since he was very old and a bit gaga, they let him run through his spiel). But you could tell that Spinoza, Hegel, Marx and Freud weren't going for it, to say nothing of that sly little devil Hume. There had been too much respect in the air, however, and too much of that old parricide business that Plato had been mixed up in (to become a philosopher, you have to kill your father in philosophy; but does one ever bring that off, mother mine?), so that the session had ended up taking a commemorative turn. Even in philosophy, you sometimes have to know how to shut up.

On the other hand, Aristotle and Plato laid into each other but good on slaves. The question was whether slaves could reason or, being nothing but animals endowed with the power of speech, had been deprived of reason 'by nature'. Aristotle, who thought that, in certain cases, 'my word, the matter is open to debate', had cornered Plato, for whom it wasn't, on the *Meno*. 'Let's see now: you conceded quite a bit of reason to that young, handsome slave of yours, didn't you? You'd think he'd been Euclid!' And, pushing his advantage, Aristotle had naturally wound up with a speech about the day in the future when there would be no more need for slaves, because 'the shuttles would weave all by themselves'. He tried to catch Marx's eye, sure that that one had hit home. But Marx wasn't there. Yet another meeting: that blinking International! And a long way off at that: in London!

There was also an extraordinary session of the kind to set your head spinning, when Reverend Father Malebranche, who thought that he'd never in his life discussed anything other than the existence of God, and his glory, and his grace – in other words, everything – had to put up with Mercier de la Rivière and his Physiocrat friends telling him he wasn't a theologian by a long shot, but, rather, their mentor in political economy, for having had the gumption to say that the world was governed by laws, the most general and the simplest – in short, the most 'economical', the most 'profitable' – since he'd pushed economic thinking to the point of demonstrating that God, like any other landowner, had arranged to have the best overseer, the best steward, run the world: Saint Michael. The Reverend Father didn't know what to make of this tribute, which proves, as Jaurès would more or less put it, that 'a little religion estranges you from the secular world, whereas a lot can reconcile you with it'.

The Reverend Father seemed distraught. A man who'd called tails and tossed heads! He came away from the session shaking with doubt about the nature of his philosophy, especially after Marx and Weber stepped in to ask just what philosophy was, after all, to be able to contaminate everything this way, even religion, behind the backs of those who fabricate it 'for the greater glory of God'.

This session sent a strange wind rippling through their minds: it was as if all of them were discovering that there can be inverted relations between philosophy and religion and, underlying them, realities which, albeit indispensable to philosophy, are *non-philosophical* – political economy, say. It was as if all of them were discovering, and all at the same time, that there can be events in philosophy, although it is 'eternal'. Silence. In the heavens, the stars said not a word.

I believe it was a little later that we started using strong language, the night Wolff lit into Kant. 'You've showered me with compliments', he told him, 'me and everyone else besides, but only the better to squash us under the weight of your pretensions.' 'Who, me?' said Kant. 'The most peaceful fellow who ever trod the earth? The man who, of all men, has had the greatest good to say of man?' 'What's that?' said Wolff. 'Didn't you write that we were all metaphysicians? And that, since we were philosophers, we were like wolves among men, perpetually at war with each other? You treat us as if we were dogs tearing each other to pieces in a courtyard; and what takes the cake is that you mix philosophy up in these contingent quarrels, by writing, black on white, that it is a battlefield and nothing else.'

'But that's absolutely right', said Lenin. 'All philosophers are at war. And underlying the philosophical struggle is the class struggle.'

'Class struggle or not', said Wolff, 'this gentleman' – and he pointed at Kant – 'who treats us like rabid dogs, has simply taken it into his head that he's in possession, in sole possession, of the secret of perpetual peace, and not just in politics, but in philosophy too! You'll see when they publish his shorter works. The gentleman helps himself to rather more than his due: war is for the others, peace is for him, and once he's had his say – silence in the ranks! As if he himself, with his disguised Spinozism, weren't in the process of declaring the worst war there is: the war for atheism! Besides, it didn't take Fichte, Schelling, and Hegel long to show us just what his philosophical peace was worth!'

Wolff was beside himself, and a murmur ran through the assembly. Since Lenin had come to Kant's defence, it was Lenin, in the end, who came in for a thrashing. 'You wrote that philosophers were flunkies of the bourgeoisie!'

This was a good deal more serious; for, between Wolff and Kant, it was, ultimately, still just a moral question; it was a political question with Lenin. And when social classes loom up on the horizon of memory or forgetting, passions are unleashed. Contrary to what they supposed, however, Lenin wasn't the only one in his camp. The mighty Machiavelli, whom history had showered with insults for telling the truth, came to the little man's defence, defying anyone to prove that power is based on anything other than class struggle. Hobbes explained how everyone had hated him for trying to forge, in *Leviathan*, a theory of the dictatorship of the bourgeoisie. Spinoza explained how fish eat other fish, from the biggest on down, and how people, those fish with sad passions, aren't any less fish than anybody else. And Spinoza, who knew a little something about the matter after Machiavelli and Hobbes, said simply: 'But have you never noticed that it's always the same people who hate the same people, even in philosophy; that it's always the same people who start things; and that it's politics that speaks through this hatred, the politics of the rich and powerful?' Rousseau too, another unpopular sort, evoked the origins of society and the bogus contract that the rich make the poor sign to extort submission from them, 'and what do the philosophers do? They're the priests of power.' Hegel himself broke his silence to remind them – and he of course supplied the reference, in *Principles of the Philosophy of Right*, a remarkable text, do you know it? – of the immense accumulation of wealth on the one hand and poverty on the other.

The match may not yet have been won, but they had to retreat into their silence. Then, to everyone's surprise, Lenin spoke up.

'Let me tell you a story', said Lenin, 'a story for the hell of it, a story about Russian peasants. You have to imagine it happening out on the black steppes, in a small village like all the rest: poverty-stricken wretches in log huts. It was one of those long winter nights, and everybody was asleep – everybody but Anton, the old man, who'd woken up with a start to the sound of someone pounding harder and harder on the door of his hut. Dawn was only just beginning to creep from the mists of night. Anton swore every oath in the book to get himself out of bed. Finally, he opened the door. Standing in front of it was that young half-wit Grusha. He seemed to be in a dither. 'Come look! Just come and take a look!' He refused to say at what. Anton ended up following him to his field down paths buried in snow. The loveliest tree in the region, an immense oak from which they hanged thieves, stood in the middle of the field. 'Look what they've done to me!' said Grusha, groaning. Anton looked. He saw the oak, a long tether and, at the end of the tether, a placid donkey, waiting in the cold for whatever freezing donkeys wait for. 'The bastards! They've tied my oak to a donkey! And I can't untie my oak!' Calmly, Anton approached the tree and untied the donkey. 'There's nothing to it, you moron! It's not your oak you have to unfasten, it's the donkey.'

They couldn't figure out what Lenin was trying to get at.

'I like this story', the Stranger said. He thought for a moment. 'It seems to me that, sometimes, to solve a problem, you have to know how to change its terms. Isn't that the point? Isn't that what Lenin and all those who've spoken in his name do? I'm the Stranger, so I can tell you without beating around the bush that you have strange conventions in your Western philosophy. They rattle me, whereas *you* take them in your stride. But Lenin and the others change the terms of the problem. . . .'

'Imbecile!' said Socrates.

All in all, it went pretty well. We never knew where we were headed, but we were always headed somewhere, or nowhere, which inspired Dietzgen to say that philosophy is the 'path of the paths that lead nowhere'. That one didn't miss the mark. Everyone looked at Heidegger, who claimed to be a peasant, but wasn't happy. 'You haven't understood me well', he said, and set off on explanations that were very hard to follow, which he kept going back over, interminably, until we got the feeling that he had something important to say about philosophy as the destiny of 'Western' reason. It went pretty well.

The only problem was those who bolted before the discussion was over, at those moments that seemed to hang suspended, when we had the feeling that THE question hadn't been settled yet, but that we were 'hot'. That was the moment, if ever, to remain at one's post. But, Lord help us, at those moments, most of the religious philosophers found an excuse to slip off to pray; the political philosophers scooted for rallies; Kant found a pretext to steal away to satisfy some mysterious need of reason; and Hegel's chin started twitching, meaning, obviously, that he had very important things to say – but in his case too, it was only so he could leave, since 'Frau Hegel was waiting for him at home'.

What was to be done with all of them gone? We would have to proceed differently.

We had, at the outset, agreed to draw up reports on each session, immediately afterwards, and had hired a good secretary to take notes. We were going to turn the whole thing over to Maspero, who would do whatever he had to to publish it. But no go. What with all those who were stealing off (I've cited only the examples that can be decently mentioned, for don't forget that philosophers are also human beings), another procedure was called for; it would be assuredly less analytic, but what can you do? We would pay a price in terms of disorder, but we'd have a text in hand.

Thus we unfortunately ended up leaving out everything that had made the discussions so lively – all the personal remarks, the colloquialisms, the provocations, the surprises, all the personalities of the Garden (since access was unrestricted, they were past counting, the famous and the unknown alike) – and charged the Secretary with the task of turning out something like a resume of what had been said, even if that meant unifying scattered remarks and restoring an implicit unity – a resume that wouldn't go too far towards betraying the initial project of a haphazard exchange.

You'll see for yourselves: something of it survives, perhaps, in the untimely turn of a discourse that often treats philosophy as its own myth. Which is a way of taking it as seriously as can be: its necessity.

1

Our experience confronts us, at the outset, with a preliminary question: How should we present philosophy? Does it call for specific forms of presentation?[1]

Everyone knows that philosophers have expounded their thought in very different forms, running from dialogue (Plato, Berkeley, and others) to the tale (Voltaire) and even the novel (Thomas More's *Utopia*), thus covering what we might call the whole gamut of literary genres. But everyone also knows that most philosophers, and almost all the greatest among them, have chosen other forms of presentation, very different from these, ranging from demonstrations in the geometrical mode (Spinoza in the *Ethics*) through the deduction of theses (Saint Thomas in the *Summa theologica*, Kant in the *Critique of Pure Reason*) to meditations that rigorously respect 'the order of reasons'[2] and so on. Here it is no longer a question of literary genres, but of forms of presentation that are as formal and scientific as possible.

This hesitation is not philosophically insignificant. For one of the stakes of this choice is what Kant called the possibility of presenting philosophy in a popular form. Kant himself, after rigorously expounding his theses in his great *Critiques*, tried his hand at the genre of popular philosophy, but without much success. This led him to the conclusion that philosophy offers a very special kind of resistance to being presented in popular form.[3]

This conclusion is rather paradoxical, since all philosophers, genuinely aristocratic thinkers aside (and even then), more or less believe that 'every man is a philosopher' (Gramsci),[4] hence that even the most abstract of philosophies can and should be made accessible to all ordinary people capable of reading and writing. Every attempt to popularize philosophy[5] thus finds itself in a quandary: on the one hand, it should be possible to expound philosophy to anyone capable of thinking; on the other, it is hard to make it accessible to everyone without betraying it.

We may say straight away that this difficulty is no illusion, but well and truly constitutes a philosophical question. We will have to take it seriously and answer it correctly when the time comes.

Better, we should anticipate this answer now, so that we can put our presentation of philosophy in a form that does in fact make it accessible to ordinary readers, as long as they are willing to lend us a minimum of attention and really think about what we say. Hence we should anticipate, in our practice, the theoretical answer we shall give in due course. We can already say that such anticipation is characteristic of philosophy, for philosophy always precedes itself. That too is something we shall have to explain when the time comes.

Everything just said presupposes, obviously, a certain conception of philosophical language. Philosophers are well known for inventing and using abstract terms employed nowhere but in philosophy. To mention just one (there are many), Kant and Husserl talk about a 'transcendental subject'. They mean by this not subjects such as you and me, psychological, legal, moral, political, and empirical subjects, that is, finite and mortal subjects, but a sort of reality that takes the form of a subject, yet is free of all empirical determination – better, that constitutes the a priori condition of possibility (another term specific to philosophy!) of every empirical entity (perceptual, known, or of some other kind). We shall also have to ask why philosophers feel the need to forge such terms, which belong only to them.

The same philosophers, however, also use philosophical terms that coincide, at the verbal level, with words used in ordinary language (they are written the same way): for example, God, the subject, morality, science, the soul, the body and so on. We should not be taken in by this verbal identity. For, most of the time, when these words are used by philosophers in their own discourses, they do not have exactly the same semantic content that they do when used in ordinary language; they have a different meaning. This gives us a glimpse of a crucial feature of philosophers' terminology. The words they use (whether they are peculiar to them, or also occur in ordinary language) take their meaning less from common usage than from their *specifically philosophical usage*. More exactly, they take their properly philosophical meaning from the context of the philosophical discourse in which they 'function'. Still better, they take that meaning from the necessary relations existing, in a body of philosophical thought, between the different terms. Thus there is, in every philosophy, something like a rigorous system that necessarily relates the meaning of each term to the whole set of the other terms.

Of course, we are not talking here about just any term, just any auxiliary word, but about the words essential to the constitution of a given system of philosophical thought. For the clarity of our exposition, we shall call these terms or words *categories*, an expression deriving from a Greek word meaning to judge/condemn. Among the terms that can be considered categories are God, soul, body, substance, time, place, space, matter, spirit, subject, ego, world, universe, perception, knowledge, beautiful, good, moral, practice, respect, power, political, economic, consciousness, self-consciousness, unconscious, etc. – on condition, to repeat, that we agree to take these terms in their properly philosophical sense, that is, *in the sense imposed on them by the relations which they necessarily maintain with the system of the other terms in a body of philosophical thought.*

It is on this condition, which is not unproblematic, that the vocabulary of philosophical categories can become accessible to non-professional philosophers, and that a popular initiation into philosophy can become possible. We shall do our best to facilitate the 'transition' from the ordinary meaning of words to the philosophical meaning of categories by stating, on every occasion, the ultimate reasons for this 'transition', this difference, and this resemblance within difference. We cannot, however, hide from our readers the fact that this undertaking calls for an effort of collaboration and reflection on their part. Without it, even our most painstaking explanations will 'run on empty' or remain 'up in the air'. On the understanding that we've concluded this mutual contract, we can proceed with our subject.

2

We will begin our presentation of philosophy with just any theme. That is a profoundly philosophical decision with nothing arbitrary about it. But to declare from the outset that one can begin philosophy with just anything brings philosophical reasons into play that immediately divide philosophers among themselves, opposing some to others. This is the first of the indications which give us reason to suspect that philosophers are very sensitive sorts.

For we find, in the history of philosophy, one whole tradition firmly upholding the idea that philosophy, far from being able to begin with anything at all, has, quite the contrary, to begin with an object or term *that rightfully constitutes its absolute beginning.*

To take just one example,[1] repeated in scores of other outwardly very different forms: everyone knows that Descartes requires us to follow an absolutely rigorous order if we are to succeed in conquering the truth. This order apparently begins with recognition of what everyone regards as true, the truths of common opinion (Plato calls them truths of the *doxa*),[2] those that Spinoza breaks down into truths acquired by hearsay and others drawn from vague experience.[3] But Descartes begins with these truths only to go on to remark that they constantly mislead us (errors of the senses), thus calling them into question. *Descartes begins with them only to rule out beginning with them*: not that some might not be true, but, inasmuch as we cannot be absolutely certain that they always are, we have to assume, if we wish to avoid scepticism, that *they are all doubtful.* We have, that is, to go on to subject them to systematic, hyperbolic (= excessive) doubt, supposed to provide an absolute guarantee against all falsity. The result of this first doubt is to accept as true everything that cannot be doubted: not 'composite' truths, but absolutely *simple* truths, the 'simple natures' that are not subject to the confusion of a combination whose elements might be false, but are, rather, given in the transparency of intuition: namely, mathematical truths, including the truths of mathematical physics. Such simple truths are invulnerable even to the vertigo of dreams, for *a geometer can invent a truth while sleeping*, if it is simple and clear!

It might be supposed that this is the absolute beginning of philosophy for Descartes: the simple ideas of mathematics. But this is a feint, because the mere fact of self-evidence is not enough: for the philosopher, it does not establish right [*ne fait pas droit*]. To call this semblance of 'right' into question, Descartes hypothesizes an 'Evil Genius', that is, a God so powerful that he can deceive me even about what I perceive as being obviously true, by arranging for two plus two to be four for me, although two plus two is actually five; or by arranging for me to believe in the existence of bodies, although only the idea of bodies exists in my mind and so on. Hyperbolic doubt thus becomes metaphysical doubt. I have to extend my doubt to even that which I conceive of as true; that is, I have to doubt even the truth of mathematical essences and the existence of the bodies that I know thanks to mathematical physics. If there is absolutely nothing that cannot be doubted, then what can I be sure of? I can be sure of the absolute condition that makes possible this doubt itself, namely that *in order to doubt, I have to think*, and that *in order to think, I have to be*: 'I doubt, therefore I think, I think, therefore I am.' *Here, then, is the absolute beginning, which we have now apparently reached.*

This beginning, however, would be an end if I could not leave the prison of the cogito. I have therefore to go back to the God whose presumptive evilness allowed me to acquire this one and only certitude and, setting out from my idea of him, and from the being that I am, a thinking substance affected by this idea, I have to demonstrate his existence and discover his perfections. I will then have a guarantee that *deception, since it is pure nothingness, cannot belong to this God, who is wholly being*, and perfect; and I will not be able to doubt that all the mathematical truths that I possess are true, or that the external bodies of which I have a simple idea in my understanding exist. The mathematical knowledge that I have will thus be guaranteed as *both* true, *and* as being well and truly knowledge of the world of bodies.

This distinction between mathematical certainty and metaphysical certainty (that of God's perfection) is crucial. For it allows Descartes to affirm both that a child can conceive of all the truths of geometry (even if it has not subjected them to hyperbolic or metaphysical doubt), since they are true, and also that 'no atheist can be a geometer',[4] since to be absolutely certain, metaphysically speaking, of the validity of these truths, we have to recognize the existence of God as well as his omnipotence and supreme perfection. It would follow that there are truths in the natural state, accessible to all men, and that there is, at the same time, philosophical truth, which, by way of the detour of the Evil Genius, rightfully founds all natural truths. This last truth, however, is accessible only to the philosopher who has followed the order of reasons and, by means of a constantly renewed, that is, constantly recalled meditation (for the moment of self-evidence is evanescent), has reached the absolute ground of all truth.

All this seems to go without saying. We should, however, note the altogether paradoxical nature of the requirement that philosophy have an absolute beginning. For, when we carefully consider the way Descartes proceeds, it becomes apparent that the absolute beginning never ceases to recede before the requirement that there be one. We begin with the most common truths, but only in order to call them into question in favour of mathematical truths alone, which are absolutely certain because they are simple. This 'fact' of their self-evidence, however (and, let us not hesitate to say: of their fecundity in the practice of an existing science) is itself called into question, as if a supplementary guarantee were needed. We therefore hypothesize an omnipotent, deceptive God capable of deceiving us about even these self-evident certainties, which we call into question in their turn. We thereby attain the absolute certainty of the 'I think, therefore I am', the certainty of the existence of a thinking substance, which is, however, so entirely the prisoner of this certainty that, to provide it with the guarantee that it does in fact possess objective knowledge, we have to displace the absolute beginning yet again, proceeding from the cogito to God.

Thus, in meditation, philosophy's absolute beginning constantly recedes, until it is at last discovered in God. Between the requirement that there be an absolute beginning and the way (written) philosophy *actually begins*, there is, therefore, the paradox of an inevitable displacement. This first paradox then reveals a second: it is that the God whom we have finally reached behind the false beginnings *only guarantees the validity, without changing anything about its contents*, not of the first beginning (the ideas everyone has), but of the second (the objective truth of mathematics and the existence of the object of mathematical physics), *and even of the first* (for, if bodies exist, the sentiment that connects my body to the world contains some truth). We shall see what the function of this whole 'big apparatus' is, the one that that Gassendi already criticized in Descartes:[5] formally, it might seem to be pure artifice, *a machine that*, literally, *produces nothing*. Yet this philosophical nothing plays an important part in the defence of certain ideas that must be guaranteed in this way so that one can impose them in a world dominated by completely different ideas: by the idea – what a coincidence! – of God.

It should also be noted that this requirement that there be an absolute beginning does not assign philosophy exclusive possession of the truth, since, quite the contrary, the philosophies which invoke it acknowledge the existence of truths common to all men – directly accessible truths, because they are handed down by history, tradition, habit, and empirical practice. This is, moreover, a feature common to all philosophical schools, which do not grant themselves a monopoly on truth that would leave ordinary men deprived of all knowledge – elementary, common, pre-scientific, scientific, or even philosophical. All philosophies take account, even when they seem to abstract from them, of the reality of the real world and the practice of the people who live in it, as well as the truths that they possess in it. This apparently strange fact requires our attention. We shall have to look for the reasons that a considerable number of philosophies present themselves as exiled from the world, when the fact is that they all take the fullest possible account of its existence, and also of the different human practices.

Let us adduce just one example, but an eloquent one. Plato's philosophy, one of those that claim to be at the furthest remove from the sensory world, is also the philosophy that, in his *Dialogues*, brings the greatest imaginable number of practices on stage: that of the blacksmith, who works fire, that of the craftsman, the oarsman, the seaman, the angler, the rhetor, the politician, the slave, the priest, the artist and so on. We shall explain this extraordinary paradox when the time comes. Absolute beginning or not, philosophy is obsessed by the world.

3

Over against the tradition which claims that philosophy has an absolute beginning, there stands another. It affirms that philosophy has no absolute beginning and, consequently, that it can and even should begin with just anything.

This is a principle of Hegel's philosophy. Hegel starts philosophizing by setting out from just anything; at the limit, as appears at the beginning of the *Logic*,[1] from the vaguest and emptiest of notions, Being, which, he shows, immediately reveals itself to be identical to Nothingness. Being is nothing; we can, therefore, and we must, therefore, begin with Nothingness, with nothing. Hegel carries out the same operation in the *Phenomenology of Spirit*,[2] where he starts with that which presents itself to me and which I perceive – with just anything, 'this', the 'this' that I see here and now. Hegel demonstrates that what is thus perceived here and now is merely an abstract generality, since it is just anything, hence nothing. Once again, philosophy begins with nothing.

This idea was taken up by Lenin in his *Philosophical Notebooks*, in which, commenting on Hegel, he writes: anything at all, a grain of sand, the leaf of a tree, a commodity, in short, 'the simplest thing', contains all of philosophy and the whole dialectic – in other words, the ultimate truth of the whole world, at least potentially.[3] From this, Lenin drew, in my opinion, erroneous conclusions about Marx's mode of exposition in *Capital*, where Marx does indeed declare[4] (wrongly) that he starts with 'the simplest thing', the ultimate 'cell' of society, by starting with the commodity, the 'theory' of which he develops in Chapter 1 of Part 1, where he writes (and this is no accident) that here, as in every science, the 'beginning is difficult'.[5] It is odd to see this philosophy, which sets out from just anything, that is, from nothing, or from every thing that is accessible to anyone, thus forced to admit that this beginning is difficult. What is in question here is not the difficulty of choosing an object (since one can start with just anything), nor the difficulty of philosophical abstraction, since the just-anything with which one begins is, as Hegel and Lenin themselves admit, abstract by nature. What is in question is a different type of difficulty, which we shall have to examine in due course.

This examination is all the more necessary in that, to go back to Marx and materialist philosophy in general (if we can agree to leave aside the vulgar materialism that begins with matter), it is striking that the deepest requirement of this philosophy is likewise to start with just anything, but with the additional stipulation that *this just-anything must be in motion*. If I may make a comparison, it can be said that the other philosophies board the train at the departure station, take their seats in it, and stay on board until the train reaches its terminus, whereas materialist philosophies always board a moving train.

This comparison, which resembles a parable, has a very profound philosophical meaning. For it indicates that, for the philosophies we discussed first, the beginning is really only an apparent beginning, since the beginning designated as absolute (the cogito, the sensory, the idea and so on) is inscribed, in advance, in a *system of categories that precedes it*. And these categories are not arbitrary. We have spoken of the departure station and the terminus. Philosophically, we can translate these expressions as the categories of origin and end [*fin*], and say that, for these philosophies, philosophy must always begin at the origin and move towards that which is its end. Thus we see that the categories of origin and end form a complementary pair, as very frequently happens in philosophy (categories come in pairs); we even discover that, in this pair, each of the two categories contains the other's meaning: if there were no end, there would be no origin, and if there were no origin, there would be no end. Philosophy calls this process that leads in this way from an origin to the end a *teleological process*, from the Greek word *telos*, which means 'end': an oriented process, a goal-directed [*finalisé*] process, a process that pursues an end or goal; and, since pursuit of a goal seems peculiar to consciousness, it calls it a consciously oriented, consciously goal-directed process. We shall see, when the time comes, what consequences must be drawn from these few remarks.

If we now consider the materialist philosophies, which, we said, always board a moving train, and if we translate our parable into the language of philosophical categories, we must say that, for these philosophies, the beginning of philosophy presupposes neither a departure station nor a terminus, hence neither origin nor end. In this case, everything we just mentioned (the pair origin/end, teleology, orientation, movement towards a goal, and even consciousness) disappears, as categories lacking all philosophical validity. In its place, there appears a new category which seems rather strange at first sight, yet accounts nicely for what is at issue in the parable of the moving train. This category is the category of *process* (the train's forward motion), but a *process without origin or end* (without a departure station or a terminus), hence without consciousness. Since we nearly always relate consciousness to a subject capable of saying 'I', this category may be called the category of the 'process without a subject'.[6]

What, concretely, does that mean? It means quite a few things, which there can be no question of inventorying or examining here. To provide us with some idea of them, however, here are a few examples. It means, first of all, that the philosopher who believes he can begin with the cogito (with the affirmation of the 'I think'), or sense perception, or the idea, etc., in fact always begins with a notion that did not wait for him in order to begin, a notion that has a long past; not just a philosophical past (Saint Augustine 'discovered' the cogito well before Descartes),[7] but a long historical past as well (humanity has always had sense perceptions and, on the basis of these sense perceptions, has constructed a practical mathematics, followed by a theoretical mathematics, well before this or that philosopher, Plato or Descartes, decided to 'begin with a true idea'). It means, consequently, that the philosopher who proceeds in the way just described engages, before our eyes, in a *feint*. He pretends to believe that the beginning from which he makes philosophy begin is absolute, whereas we know very well (and the most surprising thing is that he too knows this) that this beginning is relative. Why does philosophy, or, at any rate, this kind of (idealist) philosophy, need such a feint? We shall discover that a little later.

4

But that is not all. For at issue is not just that with which idealist philosophers *begin* their philosophy. They are philosophers before they write their philosophy down, and it is also as philosophers that they propose to begin something important. We need only transpose the terms we used a moment ago to discover what they think. They think that *philosophy as such is the absolute beginning*, the absolute. With that, they divide the world into two parts: on one side of the divide is everything non-philosophical, on the other is philosophy. On the one hand, then, we have philosophy, which is absolute beginning, which is absolute – absolute meaning, absolute origin, absolute end – and we have everything non-philosophical on the other, which is to say humanity's entire existence, concrete, material, scientific, social, affective, religious and so on.

When we put things that way, we seem to be stating an almost monstrous proposition. All those with experience of idealist philosophers, however (or of vulgar materialist philosophers, who, from this point of view, are on the idealists' side) know that this proposition is true, and that the characteristic feature of idealist philosophy is to claim to possess the truth, not just of things, but of all existing truths. Such possession can take various forms, but it is universal. To give only one example here, we may say that, for idealist philosophers, philosophy possesses the truth of a science, but of a superior Science (rendered rather well by the Greek word *episteme* as well as the German word *Wissenschaft*) which is, in itself, above all the other sciences, and founds not just their truth, but their existence as well. This can be seen in Plato, for whom philosophy, which is a-hypothetical (in other words, does without hypotheses), is superior to the sciences (mathematics), which, however rational and abstract they may be, need hypotheses in order to exist, but are unable to found those hypotheses, which philosophy founds in their stead. This can be seen in Descartes, who uses a different metaphor: he says that metaphysics resembles the trunk of a tree, the different branches of which comprise the different sciences. It can also be seen in Hegel, who declares that philosophy is the science of Reason (*Vernunft*), which assigns the different known sciences their object and method, since those sciences begin with objects that are simply *given*, not founded, lost as they are in the abstraction of the Understanding (*Verstand*) and so on.

If we go further to consider not, this time, the function of absolute beginning that idealism confers on philosophy, but the relationship between this philosophy and real, concrete history, we see the same reasoning repeating itself. Idealism quite seriously thinks that history begins with philosophy; and since, in this conception, philosophy and history never *cease* repeating themselves, idealism quite seriously thinks that philosophy is always in possession of the absolute truth of everything that happens in history: not just in the history of the sciences, but, obviously, in the history of every other human practice: economic production, ideological (religious, moral, etc.) conflicts, and political class struggles. Idealist philosophers have not always gone as far as to write this black on white, but they have always taken this claim as their premise, and some *have* gone as far as to state and develop it in their works. I shall cite just one example: Hegel, who in his *Philosophy of History* explains lengthily and rather clearly (for he shows his hand here) that it is well and truly philosophy, and philosophy alone, which is in possession of the truth of history, since the different periods (the moments of universal history) are simply realizations or incarnations of moments of the *Logic*, itself identical to philosophy.[1] At this point, it is no longer quite possible (although this possibility cannot be absolutely ruled out) to maintain, as we have just done with regard to the feint, that what is involved is a mere trick and that, in actual fact, idealism does not believe what it says, since one has to be mad, in the proper sense of the word, to believe that concrete history, the history in which people work, fight, love, and die, is the incarnation of philosophical truth. One has to be mad, or religious in the sense of the believers who take literally the dogmas of the creation of the world and the incarnation of Christ, his resurrection, and the redemption of the world through the forgiveness of sins. For to be religious in this sense, whether one is Catholic or Protestant, presupposes that there exists somewhere, outside the world or in it, outside history or in it, an absolute consciousness, that of God, who created everything and arranged it all in such a way that history follows the divine plan of redemption down to its last little details, as Bossuet sought to show.[2] That, however, brings us to an important question: the question of the relations between philosophy and religion. We shall examine it in due course.

We can already glimpse everything that is at stake when the non-idealist, materialist philosophers throw over the whole categorical apparatus that we have just passed in rapid review. The materialist philosophy which refuses to believe that there is an absolute beginning in philosophy obviously also refuses to consider philosophy as such to be an absolute beginning, hence the absolute truth of the sciences and everything else that occurs in history. It holds, however, that everything that comes about in history, while it has *origins* (that is, a cause – or, rather, several causes – and effects) and a *tendency*, has neither *an origin* (absolute beginning, absolute subject, absolute meaning) nor *an end* (absolute end [*fin*], absolute subject, absolute meaning and destination). It believes, accordingly, that to know what happens in history, one has to jettison all these illusory categories and 'devote oneself to the study of actuality' (Marx)[3] in order to discover the rational logic of this concrete process. At the same time, it shows that scientific knowledge of this process, which is different and original every time, is impossible without the help of the category of the 'process without a subject' (without origin or end), a category indispensable to philosophy when it wishes to think what philosophy itself is. For it is not just a matter of rejecting the pretension involved in conceiving of philosophy as possessed of the truth of things, the sciences, and history. Rejected along with it is the pretension involved in declaring that the world and history are nothing but the realization and incarnation of philosophical truth. The fact is that if there is neither origin nor absolute end in history or philosophy, it makes no sense to attribute to philosophy the exorbitant power of creating the world (whether it is a matter of the truth of Logic, as in Hegel, or of an all-powerful being called God) and creating history, on a plan so organized, down to its last details, as to ensure men's salvation or perdition. That is why materialism is necessarily an atheism.

If it is hard to deny all that has just been said, we have to draw the conclusion it implies: philosophy presents itself to us in paradoxical form. On the one hand, all philosophies have a number of basic features in common, having to do with the nature of their terminology, the systematic relationship between the abstract terms known as categories and so on. On the other hand, philosophies can be ranged, at least on a first rough approach, in two great camps, the idealist camp and the materialist camp, which are opposed to each other term-by-term on crucial questions. It is quite as if the adversaries faced off in philosophy, but on the basis of a reality common to them both – philosophy itself – thus realizing a figure of the philosophical dialectic known since Hegel and, above all, since Marx and Lenin. It is called the unity of opposites.

5

To delve more deeply into our subject, and because, as materialists, we can begin with just anything, let us pause briefly to ask ourselves about the words we have been using to designate the problems or the questions of philosophy.

We have been employing the term 'problem' and the term 'question' by turns. There is always something somewhat arbitrary about choosing one term over another, especially when their meanings are quite similar. Let us therefore agree (I admit that this decision is to a great extent arbitrary) to talk about philosophical *questions* rather than talking about philosophical problems.

If we drop the term 'problem', it will not be lost for everyone in our little world of language. . . . In fact, this choice implies a philosophical decision, a philosophical thesis. We are agreeing to talk about philosophical questions in order to reserve the term 'problem' for the sciences. Thus we shall say that there are questions and answers in philosophy, but problems and solutions in the sciences.

I consider this distinction, which we shall of course have to refine, to be essential to understanding philosophy. Anyone who wishes to be initiated into philosophy has to know, first and foremost, that *philosophy is not a science*, and that it therefore does not pose problems as the sciences do, nor, as the sciences do, discover their solutions, which constitute concrete knowledge [*connaissances*]. Philosophy is *a very different practice* that asks questions and answers them. These answers are not knowledge like scientific knowledge.

Nothing about all this is simple or easy to explain; that is why I ask for the reader's attention. I repeat, however, that this point is altogether essential. Anyone who fails to grasp it is lost in philosophy.[1]

I shall, therefore, put the same thing differently, repeating certain expressions that I have already had occasion to use.[2]

I shall say: philosophy is not a science. Philosophy *has no object* (no external, objective, materially existing object, even if that object's mode of existence is abstract, as in mathematics) in the sense in which a science is said to have its object.

From whatever angle one approaches the matter, these theses are hard to dispute.

I have said that every science has an object. It must be added that this object is limited. Everyone will grant that a science has an object. But that each science has a limited object is a proposition that is much less widely acknowledged. It is, however, crucial to understanding both the sciences and their history. I have said elsewhere that the foundation of a new science 'opens up a new continent to scientific knowledge', citing, as examples, the continent of mathematics opened up in Greece by a perhaps mythical figure known as Thales; the continent of physics opened up by Galileo; the continent of history opened up by Marx; and the continent of the unconscious opened up by Freud.[3] In talking about a *continent*, I intended to suggest that the objects of mathematics, physics, history, and the unconscious are *limited territories*. That does not mean that the search for their properties is not infinite (for every science is infinite as far as both its practice and the investigation of its object are concerned: 'the atom is infinite' – Lenin). It means, rather, that the object of each of these sciences is finite and has limits distinguishing it from the other finite objects of the other sciences.

This proposition seems trivial, yet its philosophical and scientific consequences are not negligible. For what do we see in the history of the sciences? We see how 'science', in the proper sense of the word (a discipline that demonstrates the properties of its object) emerges somewhere, with mathematics, thus opening up a finite continent to scientific knowledge. Later, another continent emerges somewhere else: physics. To be sure, this physics is mathematical – I mean that it is treated mathematically – but it is not pure mathematics; it involves motion affected by gravity, hence by speed and acceleration, motion that is irreducible to the analytical geometry of a Descartes. Thus it bears on *material* nature, which is, in principle, an object completely different from the space and numbers of geometry and arithmetic. And so on. Yet what do we see? Within the continents, once they are constituted, we see relatively autonomous regions taking shape; or again, outside these continents, we see, surging up out of the sea of human ignorance, new uncultivated lands that scientists clear and gradually come to know, until, gradually extending their surface, they end up quite closely attached to the old, existing continents.

Thus it is that chemistry, born independently of physics, has been attached to the continent of physics; that probability theory, born independently of mathematics, has been attached to analysis; and that, in our day – a very impressive result – biology, born independently of physics and chemistry, has been attached to biochemistry. Note that this is not yet the case for all sciences. If formal logic has, for fifty years now, constituted a branch of mathematics, we cannot say the same about either psychology or linguistics, their commendable efforts notwithstanding.[4] What shall we say, then, about historical materialism? In spite of all the attempts to attach it to either physics (by connecting the tendential law of the falling rate of profit to the tendential law of the decrease in energy, or the second law of thermodynamics), mathematics (the mathematization of economic models), biology (evolutionism of a Darwinian type), pyschosociology (functionalism), sociology (structuralism) and so on, this continent remains isolated to the present day, and we cannot see how a bridge might be built to rescue it from its enforced isolation, except perhaps in the neighbourhood of psychoanalysis. We shall see, however, that this isolation may have its reasons.

The stipulation that *the object of a science is finite* is thus not without consequences. It allows us to shed light on a certain way of philosophizing about the sciences. For philosophy – or, at any rate, idealist philosophy – likes nothing better than to philosophize about the sciences. And, in the illusion that *the object of a science is not finite, but infinite*, it finds good reason to indulge this passion. Concretely, this means that idealism imputes to a science, to its theory, concepts, method, and results, the claim that it is capable of expanding to cover all existing objects without exception. It is not idle to note that this claim was first put forward early in the seventeenth century by a physicist, Galileo, who wrote that 'the great Book of Nature is written in mathematical symbols',[5] a thesis that Descartes took up in order to confer on it the form of a mechanism generalizable to every reality: everything is so constructed that we can break it down into its parts, which are either material (the bodies of physics) or mental (ideas and perceptions); and the relations between these parts are always simple and mechanical. As is well known, Descartes derived from this thesis the theory of machine animals,[6] conceived on the model of the automatons that people constructed in his day; he expected his generalization of mechanical thinking to produce decisive results in medicine and morality (a branch of medicine, as he saw it), which goes to show that this philosopher had a good imagination. Leibniz found fault with Descartes' imagination, declaring that his physics was a 'novel'; but he himself went Descartes' mechanistic thinking one better with a divine formalism that made the mind something much more accomplished than Descartes' 'thinking soul' had been, since he defined it as an 'automaton'![7]

I shall leave there this first example *of the exploitation* (for what is involved is well and truly arbitrary exploitation, from a to z) of *a science presented as the truth of all existing reality*, in order to move on rapidly to others. For if this was the first example, it was unfortunately not the last. From first to last, the history of philosophy and the sciences abounds in examples of this kind. We may cite the physical experimentalism that, in the eighteenth century, achieved dominance on the basis of Newton's experimental method and theories. We may cite, somewhat later in the same century, the probabilism that took its inspiration from the work of Pascal, Fermat, and Bernouilli, and was applied even (Condorcet) to what was to become the core of the future 'human sciences' (political economy, demography, game theory and so on). We may cite early nineteenth-century spiritualist psychology, a weapon in the war to quell working class revolt. We may cite Comte's and Durkheim's sociology, which came along to reinforce spiritualist psychology. We may cite political economy, which was extraordinarily influential throughout the century, serving Freud himself as a model, to say nothing of physics, chemistry, and biology, which were also contaminated by it. We may cite the energetism of an Ostwald, who conceived of everything in terms of energy, first and foremost matter, but also (naturally!) social relations. Later, with the proliferation of scientific discoveries and scientific impostures (those of the self-styled 'human sciences': political economy, sociology, psychosociology, psychology), various other sciences came forward, or were put forward, as capable of unifying knowledge of the world under the aegis of their theories: among those that thus claimed to be universal, all at the same time, in an impressive ballet, were mathematical logic, linguistics, psychology, sociology, psychoanalysis, physics, chemistry, biology, mathematics, political economy, and even – Marxism.

The fact is that historical materialism itself is not immune to the universal contagion. Most of the time, let us add, it was cast in this role by non-Marxists who mistook the science founded by Marx for a philosophy capable of explaining everything. But there were also Marxists who lent a hand to this imposture. The result was twofold. On the one hand, this putative Marxism intended to account for everything, from the phenomena of the unconscious (Reich) to aesthetic phenomena (Lukács), philosophy (Plekhanov), and even mathematics (Casanova) and physics, when it was not linguistics (Marr, severely reprimanded in his day by Stalin),[8] or even medicine. On the other hand, the very same Marxism was at so great a remove from historical materialism that this science may legitimately be said to have 'disappeared' (as matter had earlier, according to an early twentieth-century physicist).[9] The result was a generalized confusion of the sciences, their object, theory, methods, and terminology. Each science spoke the other's language. It was a veritable Tower of Babel, and everyone was at sea. There were, of course, philosophers who carved themselves a niche in this confusion and drew fashionable philosophical effects from it, thus aggravating, in philosophy, the confusion that held sway in the sciences, and ever more frequently confounding them with whichever ideologies happened to come along. As always when a Tower of Babel is erected and collapses, it is God who triumphs, and then his prophets can be heard lifting their voices, Clavel,[10] or Boutang,[11] or some other fundamentalist. The sad thing is that these prophets do not preach in the wilderness, but to a public opinion overwhelmed by the confusion from which they draw their edifying eloquence. The materialists alone, for their own reasons, and the true believers, for theirs, want no part of this God, sprung up on the dung-heap of human history.

Let us get back to our subject: the fact that every science has an object, and a *limited* object. To say so is not to make a vague statement that applies to everyone and everything; it is to state extremely precise conditions. To say that every science has a limited object of its own means that it has succeeded in identifying that object; this identification is inseparable from an elaborate technical, material *experimental* set-up that affords it a real hold on its object (German admirably says that the concept, the true notion of an object or a reality, is a *Begriff* or a grasp; French says the same thing, if less vividly, when it talks of 'seizing' or 'conceiving' [*saisir, concevoir*] reality), enabling the science involved to bring theoretical hypotheses about its object's 'intimate' reality to bear on it,[12] and to verify (or refute) them in demonstrative or, if one prefers, conclusive forms.

Let me underscore this possibility of being refuted or contradicted in the case of hypotheses subjected to testing in an experimental set-up. For no scientist can know in advance whether the hypotheses he puts to the test will be verified or not, that is, whether they will be verified or refuted, invalidated. The possibility of invalidating or refuting hypotheses is part of every scientific practice and, consequently, of every scientific theory. In contrast, non-scientific theories (theoretical ideologies) manage quite well without the 'criterion' of verification and, at the same time, that of refutation or contradiction, since they aim, not to know reality, but to impose their truth on it, which has to be its truth.

It is around this simple distinction, which is in fact quite shallow, that a philosophy currently enjoying considerable favour with scientists and certain philosophers[13] has been developed for the last forty years: the philosophy of Karl Popper. Popper is right to fasten on the feature of experimental refutation or contradiction[14] (which he calls the 'criterion of falsifiability'), but wrong to affirm that we can, in advance (thanks to some mysterious principle internal to theory; for who, unless he is God, can pronounce *in advance* on the ultimate nature of a theory?), declare that such-and-such a theory is scientific (because it *accepts* the 'criterion' of falsifiability) and that another is non-scientific because it "*fails to accept it*." Historical experience shows, on the contrary (examples abound), that it is never possible to decide in advance whether a given theory is scientific or not, that is to say, whether it will be validated or refuted (contradicted) by experimentation.

It is even possible to maintain that there exist theories, such as psychoanalysis and Marxism, bêtes noires for Popper,[15] who has produced the whole of his philosophical *œuvre* to combat them, which are apparently not subject to the 'criteria' of experimental verification or refutation because the experiments performed in them cannot be repeated under exactly the same conditions. That is perfectly correct: the conditions of experimentation in psychoanalysis (the tête-à-tête between patient and psychoanalyst in the solitude of an office), quite like the conditions of experimentation in the class struggle (which change completely with the conjuncture), do not conform to the classical model of an experiment in mathematics, physics, or chemistry, which can be repeated any time anywhere by any scientist, and always produces the same results, unless a parameter has been neglected.

What, however, requires us to believe that the conditions of experimentation must be reproducible, that is, must be always and everywhere the same? We already know, and have known for a long time, that the conditions of mathematical demonstration are not reducible to the conditions of experimental proof, because mathematical 'objects' are not material, because the dispositive of mathematical demonstration consists exclusively of written signs and, finally, because the question arises as to whether mathematics, that 'science ignorant of what it is, what it says, and what it speaks of', has an object or not – unless we understand, as Pierre Raymond has very recently explained,[16] that mathematics takes as its object the mathematical results produced by the prior practice of mathematics itself, which thus works on itself; unless we understand, accordingly, that the object of mathematics, if it is not material in the sense in which the matter that physics or chemistry works on is material, is no less real for that; and unless we understand that the demonstrative dispositive of mathematics is no less real simply because it consists of signs and figures, and that it produces real proofs, proof and demonstration being, for this reason, indistinguishable.

If we turn this hardly debatable observation to account, and agree to extend its consequences to the cases of psychoanalysis and historical materialism, we have to grant that there can exist theories that are well and truly experimental, although the conditions and forms of their experimentation differ from those of the experimentation we are familiar with in mathematics and physics-chemistry. We have to grant, since it is a question, in both psychoanalysis and historical materialism, of singular conjunctures (for the psychoanalyst, the unconscious, and for the political party, class struggle), that *the theory of the conjuncture* must necessarily figure among the conditions defining these original kinds of experimentation. This naturally presupposes a whole new conceptual elaboration.

Not enough attention has been paid to the fact that both psychoanalysis and Marxism, far from dodging the debate, have taken into account what distinguishes their singular experimental set-ups from those of the natural sciences – namely *the conjuncture* – and have not only developed a theory of it, but have also integrated that theory into their practice. In the case of psychoanalysis, the 'conjuncture' is defined by the relations between the psychoanalyst's and his patient's unconscious, which 'focus on' and work on each other; it is under the domination of this 'transference' that modifications of the patient's fantasies are produced. In the case of Marxism, the 'conjuncture' is defined by the power relations resulting from the confrontation between classes, and it is under the domination of these relations of struggle that social transformations are produced. What distinguishes the experimental set-up of the natural sciences from that of Marxism and psychoanalysis is the fact that the former is constructed from scratch as a function of *universal* elements that are perfectly well defined *from the outset*, whereas, in the psychoanalytical cure and the class struggle, the experimental set-ups are *unique* and are only *gradually* discovered and defined in the course of the cure or the struggle. But since this difference is taken into account and is theorized, we can, at least in principle, assume that it is cancelled out. I say 'in principle', because it is easy to see that psychoanalytical theory and Marxist theory, unlike other scientific practices, are inseparable from the direct transformation of their object.

Let us get back to our subject. If every science has an object, and a limited object, *philosophy has no object* (in the sense in which a science has an object). And the difference leaps immediately to the eye, because there is no philosophical experimentation and no technical experimental set-up in philosophy. Hence there are also no hypotheses subject to experimental verification or refutation. There are no problems posed about a limited, finite object, problems philosophy could be said to be expecting to solve. Philosophy never expects solutions; that is to say, it never expects knowledge of its object, for such knowledge is not its goal. It confines itself to asking philosophical questions about an 'object' X the modality of which is exhaustively defined by the question asked, and it states the answer to this question itself, exercising remarkable precaution: for the philosophical question is always already (by virtue of the teleological process origin/end) the answer to the question itself. This means that philosophy is finite or limited, that it confines itself to always repeating the same question and, in the same question, the same answer, prepared in advance; for the question is simply a feint (here we once again encounter a theme essential to all *idealist* philosophy – we shall see the reason for this restriction, notwithstanding the fact that we are talking about philosophy in general).

Note that when I put forward the idea that there is never any experimentation in philosophy, I am interpreting. For, in history, there exist philosophies (idealist philosophies, precisely) that claim to provide or to produce experiments,[17] and to be based on them, exactly like the experimental sciences. We can cite practically every[18] philosophy as an example, from Plato through Descartes, Kant, and others to Husserl and Heidegger (notable exceptions: Epicurus, Spinoza, Hegel, and Marx). What is quite remarkable in these experiments or so-called experiments, however, is *the absence of any experimental set-up*. They are less experiments (which always suppose such a set-up) than 'experiences' (Kant), and 'interior experiences' at that (Descartes, Bergson), or, as Malebranche rightly said, 'experiences of simple sight'.[19] The instrument of these experiments-experiences is in fact a very simple, very pure and transparent *sense*, whether it is sight (Plato, Descartes), taste, touch, or smell (the eighteenth century), the heart (Rousseau), or the inner sense of effort (Maine de Biran) or duration (Bergson). On this basis, these philosophers produce extraordinary effects of religious eloquence and dramatic gesticulation; yet it is impossible to avoid the conclusion that what is involved is a new imposture that exploits the crucial element in the real sciences' experimental practice to philosophical or religious ends, by mimicking it.

6

Philosophy, then, has no object and does not produce knowledge in the sense, I insist, that these terms have where the sciences are involved. And this way of looking at things is coherent. For there is a close relation of opposition between the condition of a science, which, while it has a finite object, possesses an infinite activity that allows it endlessly to discover new properties in its object, to the point that we may say, paradoxically, that this object is 'infinite' (infinitely rich in objective properties) – and philosophy, which, while it has no object and is therefore unable to discover properties in an object ad infinitum, and while it is itself finite, since it confines itself to repeating the same question, containing, in advance, its answer about an undefined object, nonetheless lays claim to knowing 'the whole' (Plato, Leibniz, Hegel).

What might this 'whole' be? For idealist philosophy (the reader will have understood that we have been talking the whole time about idealist philosophy, even while talking, legitimately, about philosophy in general), this 'whole' is the ensemble of existing realities: the world, the self, and God, and also, let us add in its stead, philosophy itself. The question as to whether this 'whole' is finite or infinite, limited or unlimited in its being or its properties, is, in general, the object of an answer that is resolved *by infinity*, which is, consequently, the infinity of a BEING (the self, the world, God), not of a process (the infinity of process defines materialist philosophy, as we shall see). Of course, the thesis that the 'whole' is infinite creates tremendous difficulties for idealist philosophy, since the here-below, in which we have 'life, the word, and movement' (Saint Paul),[1] is manifestly finite. Philosophy has therefore to conceive of a mediation between infinite Being and finite beings, a mediation incarnating the infinite in the finite. This is an absolute theoretical necessity.

This necessity is met, in Plato, by the theory of the demi-urge; in Descartes, by the theory of creation, including the creation of eternal truths;

and in philosophers of Christian inspiration generally speaking, by the theory of incarnation, which has the advantage of making the infinite exist in the finite itself (in Christ or his surrogates) – unless one assumes, with Hegel, that the infinite is simply the reflection of the finite upon itself, philosophy being the supreme example. We find essentially the same theme in Heidegger, in whom the difference between Being and beings serves as a mediation between the infinite (or the indefinable, the ineffable) and the finite (or the definable, that which can be said). The same difficulty, whose destiny it is never to be resolved, but to be endlessly deferred, reappears in connection with death, in which idealist philosophy is rooted (from Plato through Kant to Heidegger).

Death is what cannot be avoided and must therefore be accepted; but one resolves the contradiction either by supposing a mediation (salvation through the different forms of merit and grace) or by making death something on the order of the very truth of life, an idea which, paradoxically, converges with certain materialist propositions advanced by doctors who were Hegel's contemporaries (Bichat) and, later, by Freud himself: that is to say, one resolves it by once again making human finitude (death) the locus of true infinity. If death and, therefore, finitude are the truth of human existence, however, they become its ultimate meaning, and the human world, since its destiny is death, ends up being divested of all meaning, unless it is acknowledged that this radical absence of all meaning is the very meaning of human existence: either non-meaning (nihilism, according to Nietzsche) or a total absence of meaning, triviality, since the peculiarly human consists in being this 'singular reality' (Heidegger's *Dasein*) which has the power to confer a meaning upon that which by definition cannot have one, itself included – in short, the power of forging a 'destiny' (Heidegger) in order to be able to experience it [*le vivre*, literally, to live it]; and the best way of lucidly experiencing a pointless pseudo-destiny is to sing it or dance it (Nietzsche, Heidegger), since that is, at the limit, the only way to enjoy it. Which means: Let us overthrow all gods and all values! Let us make a huge bonfire of their remains, around which young men and women crowned with flowers will sing incomprehensible songs and dance the wild dance of the mad, accompanied by frenetic music, while the bell of destiny tolls ever more loudly (Derrida).[2] I am of course evoking a mix of themes here; their destiny is not fixed by the mere mention of them, and they can diverge or converge, depending on the authors, their texts, and the moment.

From all the foregoing remarks, in any case, we shall single out the idea that idealist philosophy cannot exist without aspiring to utter the truth about the Whole. When the Whole is infinite, the consequences to which philosophy exposes itself are clear. When it is finite (or when it is an infinite that can be thought by an infinite mind which has mastery over it, such as Leibniz's God,[3] making it to all intents and purposes countable by that infinite mind), one has another way out. If the whole that philosophy thinks is finite, *then it is countable*; all the connections can therefore be demonstrated, analysed, and exhibited; the whole can therefore be exhaustively divided into its parts and thus *classified*.

Here we encounter another grand tradition of idealist philosophy. We can call it *formalistic* or taxonomic (from the Greek *taxein*, which means to classify, to order). This obsession with domination by means of classification has a long history, running from the Platonic procedures for division into pairs, or dichotomy (see the famous division of *The Sophist* with regard to the angler)[4] through Aristotle's classifications (the different meanings of the word being and their consequences),[5] Descartes' distinctions, Leibniz's universal characteristic[6] and the whole formalist tradition it inaugurated (down to the havoc wrought in the so-called human sciences by mathematical logic today), to the structuralist taxonomy of a Lévi-Strauss. That there are obvious distinctions in reality – that the object of one science, for example, is distinct from that of another, even neighbouring, science – is certain. That there are filiations and genealogies is clear. That horizontal classifications can be combined with the vertical effects of genealogies is something no one would dispute. But what is still another imposture is the philosophical ambition to constitute what Lévi-Strauss calls, with the jubilation of the self-taught philosopher, an 'order of orders',[7] and an order which, encompassing all subordinate orders, encompasses itself in the order that it puts in order. What is a still shrewder imposture – harking back to the Leibnizian dream of the universal characteristic – is that this order automatically orders itself, automatically establishes itself, and assigns every being its place and function so as to ensure that order will reign.

Combined in this view of things, which outwardly resembles materialism (process without a subject), are the twin pretensions of functionalism and structuralism, in which place and function go together like hand and glove – and it is not by substituting the logic of forces for that of places, à la Badiou,[8] that one can escape the logic of Order, whoever happens to state it: whoever, that is, gives men this order, in the full sense of the word, on the strength of his own authority, whether he is a professor in the Collège de France or Secretary of a political organization.[9] Be that as it may, these dizzying exercises are not neutral. If they do not have an object, they have objectives or, at the very least, well-known stakes. Since they talk about order, they also talk about authority, and therefore about power: and since there is no power but established power, that of the ruling class, they plainly serve its power, even if they are unaware of it and especially if they think they are combating it. From which it follows that innocent is the last thing philosophy is, as will appear more clearly in a moment. Its world, its real world, looming up on the horizon of all these dazzling subtleties, is the world of men and their struggle: the world of class struggle.

7

If philosophy has no object (from now on, I shall dispense with the phrase 'in the sense in which a science has an object'), what *does* it have, behind the appearances of the undefined object about which it claims to speak the truth? It has objectives and stakes. Before we come to that, however, we have to begin again at the beginning, and ask: *What kind of proposition does philosophy use to express itself?*

I said that science confronts difficulties, poses problems, and produces their solutions, which constitute objective knowledge. This knowledge is expressed in propositions whose essential terms are concepts. What is a concept? It is a word or several words that produce an effect of abstraction and reflect a property or a cluster of properties of the object of a science.

In contrast, philosophy poses questions and provides the sort of answers to them that we have seen. What form do these answers take? The form of *theses*. What is a thesis? It is a notion that is hard to define, because, while philosophy expresses itself in theses, it has very rarely expressed itself about the nature of these theses.[1]

We already know, however, that the terms philosophy uses are categories, not concepts.[2] We shall therefore say that a thesis is a proposition that combines a certain number of categories. For example: 'I think, therefore I am.' We can single out the categories in this proposition: I, think, am, therefore. These are words of ordinary language, but they function very differently in philosophy. The 'I' of the 'I think' is not a psychological, but a metaphysical 'I'; the 'think' designates the thinking substance (and that a substance exists and is, in addition, a thinking substance, obviously gives rise to philosophical questions which, we know, are so many anticipated answers); the 'am' designates a form of being which, albeit peculiar to man (part Being, part Nothingness), nevertheless has the force of an indubitable existence; finally, the 'therefore' points to something self-evident, the self-evidence of the conclusion revealed by an intuition. All these categories in the one short sentence 'I think, therefore I am' are accordingly laden with philosophical meaning. It is well known that even the comma has a meaning, since, in a rather heavy-handed joke intended to bring this out, Lacan has suggested that we write: 'I think: therefore I am'. The colon changes everything.[3]

A thesis thus puts forward a certain number of categories combined in a proposition. But should we say that it is a proposition of the kind that occurs in ordinary language ('I don't think that Georges Marchais dreams, because he said he doesn't on T.V.'),[4] or even of the kind that occurs in scientific language (1+1=2)? Precisely not. We must speak of *position* in the full sense of the act of positing or posing; that is, precisely, the translation of the Greek word *thesis* (thesis). What is thus posited? The affirmation in question: 'I think, therefore I am'; 'God is the being who is sovereignly perfect and omnipotent'; 'matter exists' and so on.

This simple linguistic nuance, which I have merely repeated after the philosophical tradition, provides us with an interesting lead. For when we pose, we pose *something somewhere*, in a place belonging to a certain space. When a philosopher poses a thesis this way, the fact is that he always poses it somewhere, in a defined place belonging to the philosophical space. What philosophical space? The space of his own philosophy, to begin with; then that of the philosophy of his day and age; and, finally, that of the whole past history of philosophy.

But when a philosopher 'poses' a thesis this way, we should not be fooled. He never 'poses' just one.[5] For a thesis never stands by itself: it is always com-posed, that is to say, posed along with the whole set of theses comprising the philosophy of the philosopher in question. We shall see later that – paradox! – there is an infinite number of these theses.

For the moment, let us content ourselves with making a few observations about what goes on here. When a philosopher 'poses' a thesis somewhere – let us take the extreme case, that of his relations with another philosophy that he is combating – he cannot 'pose' it without 'opposing' the theses that he wishes to combat. Every thesis is also an anti-thesis. And this comes about automatically. By no means does the philosopher have to declare war on his adversary. He poses his thesis the way one poses a mine in the adversary's territorial waters: he leaves and the mine explodes later, when an enemy ship (an enemy thesis) approaches it, at which point the whole body of the ship flies to pieces. This kind of *delayed action* is characteristic of all philosophical theses, which is to say that they are always in advance of the moment when they explode. A strange practice! But what is quite remarkable is that even if the thesis is 'posed' by a philosopher who concocted the explosive mixture quietly in his corner, in the neighbourhood of a philosopher friend of his (to help him understand better what he hadn't quite got), there is always, on the horizon, the presence of the Other, the Philosophical Foe who not only surveys the whole situation, but dominates it, forcing our philosopher to put himself permanently in a state of *preventive war*, as Hobbes would have it.[6] Things are so constituted that the philosophical situation is structured by a basic antagonism that traverses the whole philosophical field and commands philosophers' every act: not just their acts of war, but also their acts of friendship and peace. Hobbes demonstrated this well: it is not the villains who start the wars, for they are too stupid for that. Decent people do, if they are smart. For if they reflect and calculate the future, they realize that they cannot avoid war and are at the mercy of the first imbecile to happen along; he can be someone who wishes them ill, or someone who simply shows up at the wrong address. Hence they know that they have to be 'ahead of the game' and attack first so as not to be taken by surprise and defeated. Philosophy is much more radical than social life, which has its moments of respite and its cease-fires, its Matignon Agreements and Grenelle Accords,[7] its popes who preach peace in the wilderness, its Vietnamese who pursue their Tet truce and, finally, its children who say 'uncle' or its Olympic Games, in which the late Baron de Coubertin exercised his talents as a pacifier of minds and legs. Philosophy is a rather more serious business; it knows neither respite nor truce. And when, à la Kant, it preaches 'perpetual peace' among philosophers (and secondarily among nations),[8] it's all just talk; it simply wants the other philosophers to leave it in peace so that it can cultivate its own *Critique of Pure* or *Practical Reason*. It has, however, no illusions at all: it knows it is preaching for others' benefit, that is, in the desert – for, as Sartre wrote (more or less), the desert (and not the dessert) is the others.[9]

Obviously, what is properly speaking beyond belief in this perspective is the state of this philosophy that is in a universal, perpetual war of all against all, against the background of the Great War, the Thousand Years' War between idealism and materialism. What is beyond belief is the fact that this war not only never ends, but has always begun, that is, has no beginning, and has been pursued uninterruptedly down through the centuries. In our time, Plato and Aristotle are as present as ever, and there are philosophers ready to fight them even today, to the death. In our time, Democritus and Epicurus (*et al.*) are as present as ever, and there are philosophers ready to fight them even today, to the death – or to espouse their cause, naturally so as to draw from them the strength to fight the others.

You will reply, and it is true, that not all philosophers are armed and determined to this extent, and that they do not always so clearly see where their enemies are. I am happy to concede the point, but this concession changes nothing fundamental. For take a philosopher who, far from claiming to 'think the whole', sets about seriously analysing what was going on in one or another small region of one or another scientific continent in one or another historical period or in a given small detail of ideology; who sets about, for example, studying the mechanisms by means of which Aristotle[10] constructed his theory of monsters.[11] He will not escape the law of universal, obligatory antagonism. For he thinks in certain forms, using certain categories, and he projects certain 'ends' that he does not invent, even if he imagines that he does, but necessarily borrows from one of the two great camps that make up the field of philosophy, and with it the field of the history of philosophy, structuring both as antagonistic fields. Take even someone who (such people are found all the time), throwing this antagonism and these enemies overboard, declares, as Nietzsche does, that existing values must be overturned – all of them, even the value of truth in which all idealist philosophers take refuge, and even the value of matter in which materialist philosophers take refuge. This philosopher will never be anything other – in the nice phrase coined by Nietzsche, who, unbeknownst to himself, knew himself rather well – than a 'reactive' thinker,[12] in other words, a thinker determined by his reaction of refusal, and thus by the whole philosophical system already in place and, more subtly, by the idealism that never ceases to dominate it. Nietzsche said, or could have said, that it is infinitely preferable to be a reactionary philosopher (for this reaction can be creative) than a 'reactive' one (for, in the latter case, the reaction is purely negative). We shall see that the only philosophers who are reactionaries in this sense – that is, creators – are the materialist philosophers, for they are the only revolutionaries – that is, creators.

8

We may therefore, pending further information, consider this point sufficiently well established for us to go further: that is, to delve a little more deeply into the nature of philosophical 'theses'.

Everything we have said about them so far suggests that they are not serene, objective, 'gnoseological'[1] propositions ('gnoseological' is a monstrous word derived from Greek that means 'of or relating to knowledge') but, quite the contrary, *active, operative propositions*. This goes without saying, given that they are declarations of war and designate their enemy, even if only tacitly. Better, they are not mere declarations of war, but theoretical *acts* of war that can take the most cunning forms of trench warfare, with its ruses, detours, saps, and connecting trenches, or the most overt forms of frontal warfare, with its charges, brass bands, drums, ladders, tanks, diversions, and elephants, its foot soldiers and cavalrymen, its trumpets and banners, its 'rally round my white panache'[2] and 'Father, on your guard to the left, on your guard to the right!',[3] its portable hen-houses and Mütter Courage. All of which suggests that philosophy does indeed act, albeit in a non-material because abstract form, the way an army at war acts against real adversaries; and that clashes take place on the philosophical battlefield (*Kampfplatz*, Kant)[4] which, while categorical (occurring between categories, between Theses), are no less bloody for that – if not immediately, then, at any rate, in the medium or long term.

Acts of extreme violence occur on this battlefield. They begin with the violence done to categories and concepts, and culminate in that done to individuals (think of Giordano Bruno, Galileo, and others) or even whole peoples (enemies reduced to slavery in Antiquity, peoples colonized by capitalism, the victims of fascism familiar to us and so on). And should someone take it into his head to ask, in amazement: 'By what right do you draw this extreme, far-fetched conclusion? Not only do philosophers work exclusively on ideas, as everyone knows, but, what's more, they don't understand anything about the political course of the world, and pride themselves on not getting involved in it,' it is easy to reply: 'Plato didn't get involved in Sicily? And Hobbes, under Cromwell? And Spinoza, in the Netherlands, and all the Enlightenment philosophers of eighteenth-century Europe, including Kant? And Marx in the workers' class struggle? And Bergson in the Union sacrée during the first World War, and Husserl in the crisis of the Western sciences? And Heidegger in Hitler Germany?'

And if someone were to object: 'Yes, *those* philosophers, to be sure, but how many others never got involved?', it would suffice, to convince oneself that these other philosophers' political innocence was merely feigned, to go take a closer look at their work in order to see which theses concluded a political pact, from a distance, but concretely and most effectively, with the philosophers who *did* get involved. This brings us back to the presence of the feint in idealist philosophy: the feint that war does not reign among humankind; the feint that people do not really have a body, but only a soul, or that, if they do have a body, it is a machine without the drive of the muffled, unconscious desire that makes them sexed beings; the feint that 'the heavens are above the roof' (Kant, Verlaine) and the moral law is in the heart;[6] the feint that, if my aunt had two wheels, she would not be a bicycle.[7] We shall see, however, that between aunt, wait, tent, latency and so on [*la tante, l'attente, la tente, la latence, etc.*; these words all sound similar or the same in French], the wheel, the castor, trickery [*la rouerie*, a word etymologically related to the French word for 'wheel'], the bike, the circle, and recycling, there are relations that no idealist philosophy can admit. We shall not be afraid to admit them when the time comes, and we shall see, at that point, what feint means, namely shut up – terribly [*taire – tair-riblement*: *taire* means to shut up and sounds like the first syllable of *terriblement*, terribly].

Let no one accuse us of *playing* with words here. Either we are not playing, which is not very likely, or we are playing, as the greatest philosophers always have – either to amuse themselves (Plato) or, quite the contrary, in order to be serious – when they assigned incredible meanings to already existing words (soul, substance, self, eye, light and so on), or again, when they invented, created out of whole cloth, words that had never existed (a priori, transcendental subject, intentionality of consciousness, différance and so on). Nietzsche, that anti-conformist of conformity, was, with Mallarmé and his epigones, a past master in the art – not a master of materialism.

9

But let us go back to our definition of theses in order to add a very important proviso. If philosophy puts forward propositions which, rather than stating knowledge, state theses, these propositions bear no direct relation to knowledge, hence to what is true, since it is generally agreed, in the ideology of knowledge, that knowledge should be designated as true (or false, or confused and so on). If we are thus accustomed to saying that knowledge (scientific or not) is 'true', what adjective is appropriate for theses? I have suggested that we qualify them as a function, not of truth, but of *correctness* [*justesse*].[1] Thus they will be called correct or false ('false' being, here, the equivalent of *non-juste* [incorrect], a word that does not exist in French,[2] although it exists in other languages. The whole question then comes down to properly conceiving the idea of *correctness*.

It leaps to the eye that correctness [*justesse*] has nothing to do with justice [*justice*]. To evoke justice brings not just the whole court apparatus on stage (courthouse, judges, jury, witnesses, trying a defendant guilty of violating a law), but also a legal and moral idea which sanctions the functioning of this state apparatus: the idea of the just and the unjust, of which Aristotle, among others, elaborated the theory, in order to conclude (this is not every philosopher's position) that the just, far from being the whole or the absolute, is simply the 'golden mean' [*le juste-milieu*] that makes it possible to put things in due perspective – that is, gives the state much more than its due [*fait la part des choses, c'est-à-dire la part belle à l'État*].[3] To take an example that is interesting, because we will take it in the opposite sense in a moment, Saint Thomas defends the idea that there are just and unjust wars, but distinguishes them in the name of justice and injustice, which are religious-moral-ideological principles.[4] Thus it is clear that correctness has nothing to do with this moral and legal idea of justice – let us say, with the legal-moral ideology of justice.

What then is correctness, the word that is called for in connection with theses? It is a notion that can be clarified by starting out from a certain *quality of practice*, when it is properly carried out by the practitioner. If, in a tradition that goes back to Plato and the Sophists, we consider, for example, a tradesman who 'works with fire', like the blacksmith, or wood, like the carpenter, or iron, like the metal-worker, or complex mechanisms, like the mechanic, all these tradesmen, when they do their work properly, can be called *adjustors* in the full sense of the word, inasmuch as all their movements are adjusted to a definite end, and they know how to adjust each piece to fit the others so that they succeed in producing the useful object we expect them to. The operation they perform can accordingly be called *adjusting* or *adjustment*, a name for the complicated kind of labour involved in choosing, burnishing, adapting, and combining the parts required to produce the desired mechanism.

If, however, we turn from the simple field of the crafts to go straight to a completely different field, that of political action, what do we see? We see the same practice of correctness at work. The politician who is conscious of his 'duties' towards the polity, and feels an obligation to fulfil them, is concerned less with the true than the correct, less with uttering the truth or acting in accordance with it than in taking, at the right [*juste*] time and in the proper [*juste*] forms, measures and decisions that are *correct* [*juste*], that contribute to the welfare of the polity.

Here too, correctness is a form of adjusting or adjustment. It consists in taking exact account of all the elements, all the power relations in play, and proving able to dispose them in such a way as to produce the desired political effect: the victory of the polity, the defeat of the enemy. Just as a bill is said to be correct when it is properly drawn up, or the decision to make a surgical intervention is said to have been correct when the operation is a success, so a statesman's or army commander's intervention is said to be correct when it produces the desired result thanks to judicious adjustment of the available means to the ends pursued, in the framework of the existing balance of power. It is plain that nothing in this practice of correctness recalls the legal-moral idea of justice. Quite the contrary: correctness points in the direction of the most realistic, concrete, materialist practice (material or not). To return to our classic example, it is in this sense that politicians as well as materialists will, using the same terms, call a war 'correct': correct not in the sense of justice, but in that of correctness and of the adjustment of motives and means – taking account, accordingly, of the relation of forces in the struggle of the classes, and the general tendency that dominates this relation.

It is in this sense that Machiavelli, Marx, and Lenin talk about a 'just war'. A war thus defined by the correctness of the political line pursued can, of course, be just in the sense of justice too, which is to say in that of legal-moral ideology, in which case those who wage this war have an immense advantage over the enemy, that of fighting for justice as well, something that, as a rule, multiplies their forces many times over. But there are other 'correct wars' that are not just in the sense of justice, and there are political decisions that are correct without also being just in the sense of justice. In such cases, correctness and justice diverge (something that tormented Pascal), making it much harder for the combatants to fight the war or for the rank-and-file to accept a decision: the Communist militants the world over whom Stalin confronted with the Molotov-Ribbentrop Pact are a case in point. It sometimes even happens that circumstances prevent anyone at all from distinguishing correctness and justice. To mention just one example, the imperialist wars of 1914–1918 and even of 1939–1941, although they were experienced as being just by those who took part in them, were neither correct nor just, inasmuch as they were purely and simply wars between imperialist states, blind powers subject to the law of capitalist accumulation, which they were by no means capable of controlling. It is still an open question whether Nazi Germany's 1941 invasion of the USSR changed the 'meaning' of this war, whether the war waged by the 'Allies' became, at that point, a merely correct war, or a just war as well. This brings out the complexity of certain cases, in the face of which philosophy itself must keep silent for lack of information. But that is because the science of history, in other words, the science of the class struggle, itself keeps silent. Why? We shall see, perhaps.

We must, consequently, keep this whole set of practices in mind in order to form an idea of the meaning of correctness, and thus of the meaning of the word 'correct', which it seems to me necessary to apply to philosophical theses.

Our review of these points, if it is convincing, only reinforces the idea that *philosophical theses bear a relation to practice*: to a very particular practice, that of adjustment, and thus of work on pre-existing elements (which we shall have to define) which must be fashioned and then burnished if they are to be adapted to each other and employed to turn out a product answering to a defined end or use. What are these elements? What is this fashioning and this burnishing, what is this adaptation, what are these ends and this use? We shall leave these questions in suspense for the time being.

We do, however, have some idea of the field in which this operation is carried out. It is, first and foremost, the field of philosophy itself. This is so emphatically the case that I have upheld the paradoxical idea that philosophy only ever intervenes in philosophy, and that it can intervene outside philosophy only on the absolute condition that it first intervene in philosophy, in other words, in itself.[5] Yet the field in question is not that of philosophy *alone*. It is also (the order matters little for the moment) the field of the sciences and their practices and, as well, the field of the ideologies and their practices; in short, the field of all human activity without exception, from economic production to political practice and the ideological practices (moral, political, legal, aesthetic, religious, familial and so on). *The adjustment which is carried out this way in philosophy and which results in the production of theses has repercussions on the ensemble of human practices.* If words mean anything, this means, at the limit, that the ensemble of human practices finds itself, more or less, if not adjusted, then at least adjustable by the theses of philosophy, if not directly (that is the exception), then at any rate indirectly. Thus there is nothing surprising about Gramsci's little remark to the effect that 'everyone is a philosopher', since everyone finds himself directly (if he is a philosopher) or indirectly (if he is not) affected by the philosophical adjustment contained in philosophical theses. But we have a long way to go before we can set about demonstrating this point.[6]

10

We have to begin at the beginning again (something we can agree to do now, since philosophy has no beginning for us materialists) in order to examine not the category of correctness that we just sketched (rather – we shall see why – the *concept* of correctness), but the category of *truth*.[1]

For we have opposed correctness to truth. Where does this idea or category of truth come from? Spinoza, in 'On the Improvement of the Understanding', writes: 'for we have a true idea',[2] an idea of the truth. This idea of the truth, which serves us as an absolute standard, is provided by mathematics. Where does mathematics come from? Spinoza gives no answer. We possess it, full stop, and it is mathematics that provides us with the idea of the true that we have and so on. This shows us that the idea of truth is dependent on the sciences, which provide us with objective knowledge.

Let us note that Spinoza never talks about truth, but only about the true: 'the true designates itself as true, and, at the same time, the false as false.'[3] This was not unimportant in a day and age in which every philosopher talked about truth – not just the truth of the sciences, but that of philosophy as well – and talked about philosophy as a search after truth. Why these nuances? Because, if we question practitioners of the sciences, we will see that they never talk about truth, never say that they have discovered this or that truth, never say that this or that theorem is true, or that this or that experimental proof is true. They say so, of course, but only when replying to those who accuse them of fabricating a false demonstration or proof, in other words, of lying. In sum, they do not reply by referring to the truth unless they are charged with lying. In their practice, they do not give a fig about the truth. They simply take note of the fact that one or another theorem has been *demonstrated*, full stop, or that one or another experimental result has been proven, full stop.

What business does truth have here, then? It is forcibly imported into practices (the scientific practices) to which it is alien. If it is imported into them, where does it come from? From somewhere else: very precisely, from fields of ideology that *do* have an interest in the idea of truth: philosophical, legal, moral, and religious ideology, among other kinds. Thus it is quite as if a scientific result obtained in the field of a given scientific practice were transposed into a field of ideology and invested in this field with the attributes of truth. To what ends? We shall discover that when we examine the nature and diversity of the ideologies.

But this simple remark leads the way, perhaps, to an understanding of why philosophy – if not all philosophy, then, at any rate, idealist philosophy – has traditionally taken so deep an interest in what is known as the theory of knowledge, as method and so on.

For the theory of knowledge is nothing other than a philosophical theory that claims to explain what truth is. For the moment, it does not matter whether or not it takes scientific knowledge as its starting point in doing so. What does matter a great deal, however, is the philosophical dispositive deployed by this simple question. Is there any need to repeat here what we said earlier, namely that idealist philosophy asks questions that have no existence in the form in which it asks them, and that these questions always contain their answers in advance, because they are nothing but their answers in inverted form? Yet this simple inverted tautology produces phenomenal theoretical effects, observable in all the different varieties of the theories of knowledge that idealism has to offer.

What, to begin with, is the basic philosophical dispositive in which the question of the theory of knowledge is posed? Simplifying to an extreme, here is what we find.

Philosophy poses, face-to-face, *the object* to be known and *the subject* who is to know it. These are two beings distinct in every respect, and the big, thorny question then runs: how can these two totally distinct beings ever maintain a relation, and a relation that is a relation of knowledge? To answer this imaginary question, idealist philosophy has devised all sorts of ploys, some of which are extremely simple (monism: these two realities are one and the same reality, whether mind or matter), while others are extremely complex (reminiscence in Plato, substantial forms in the Aristotelians and Thomists, the pineal gland in Descartes, the occasional cause in Malebranche, the thing-in-itself in Kant, the dialectic in Hegel, duration in Bergson and so on). Let us note that a philosopher such as Spinoza, who does not seem to call himself an idealist, proposes an answer, parallelism, that literally does away with the question. . . .

Whatever the response to this secondary question, the face-to-face between the knowing subject and the object to be known must necessarily produce an identity: knowledge itself. If we call the knowing subject S and the object to be known O, we have the fundamental equation of every theory of knowledge:

S = O.

Read: the knowledge produced in the subject by the act of knowing the object is identical to the object known. It is plainly the knowledge of *this* object (and no other). Thus there is no mistake about who is who, no mistaken identity. This presupposes, moreover, that the subject and object remain the same, do not lose their identity in the course of the act of cognition; or, if they do change their identity (for example, in a historical development), that they do so in the same sense, maintaining their respective identities and, as well, the identity resulting from the equation

S = O.

But that is not all. For this relation of knowledge can be conceived of as either an immediate act (the seeing or intuition of Plato, Descartes, Bergson, and others), or as a process (Hegel, Marx, and others) which, for one thing, takes time and, above all, modifies the characteristics of the terms of the equation in the course of its development. In the latter case, the term 'equals', which indicates an equivalence in the formula S = O – that is, the equals sign – must be modified so as to signify a movement towards equivalence, a movement towards identity, a movement towards a 'reflection' (Lenin). We can then talk, as Saint Thomas does, about an 'adequation', which is an expression that takes account of this movement-towards. And we can write the famous formula:

veritas adaequatio rei et intellectus[4]
(truth is adequation between the thing and the intellect).

In this formula, however, very curiously, we see truth reappear, although we had done perfectly well without it previously. We had, in fact, accounted for the act or process of cognition by bringing just two terms into play, the subject and the object, and an equivalence, but not truth. Yet truth surges back up here, as if it were 'the truth of' what we said. What business does truth have here? It simply reproduces the common sense justification that affirms that the result of the adequation of the object to the subject or the subject to the object is a piece of knowledge which, since it exactly reflects the object, is clearly the object's truth. Thus it is a purely tautological formula, except for the fact that this common sense justification is, as we have already seen, the justification of a value stemming from certain fields of ideology. We shall come back to this.

We may, therefore, write our modified formula as follows:

$$(S = O) = V.$$

Yet this formula is not quite enough to satisfy the philosopher – say, our Descartes – who, even when he is in possession of a truth that he clearly and distinctly sees is true, sets about doubting it, that is, sets about demanding a supplementary guarantee to eliminate all possible risk of doubt. The idealist philosopher who elaborates a theory of knowledge thus has not only to think the adequation of the subject to the object, $(S = O)$, but also to say that the result of this adequation is a truth: $(S = O) = V$. Still better, he feels the need to affirm, either by way of the fiction of the hypothesis of the Evil Genius of an omnipotent God who would deceive us, or in order to lay his opponents' objections to rest (like Plato confronting the Sophists, or Kant confronting Wolff), that this truth produced by the process of adequation, $S = O$, is indeed true, and that the ensemble of relations involved in this process is indeed true. In short, he feels the need to add an affirmation of truth to the truth that has already been obtained, and to write the new formula

$$V (S = O) = V,$$

by which he means that *it is indeed true that the adequation of subject and object produces a truth.*

This reduplication of truth by itself is one of the major constants of idealist philosophy. We have already seen it in connection with the distinction between philosophy and science, when philosophy both distinguished itself from the sciences and posited itself as their truth, as the science of sciences or the truth of scientific truths. This position can take widely varying forms, from those of the ontology of a Plato (where it is a being superior to all other beings) to the forms of Kantian critique, where a certain subject, the transcendental subject, which we can grasp in the unity of the 'I think', as in Descartes, but which plays a completely different role, is charged with ensuring the transcendental unity (that is, the pure, non-empirical unity, not bound up with the contingencies of the 'spatio-temporal', but, rather, necessary) of the multiple brought together in all concrete knowledge. We would find the same function in every idealist philosopher.

The question is: Why this reduplication of the truth? The facile answer is that it merely registers, reproduces, and thinks an *intellectual division of labour*, which most certainly exists, between the scientists who produce scientific knowledge and the philosophers who think about it, thinking and stating its philosophical truth. But this answer is illusory, because it merely defers the question. To track this answer to its last refuge, we have to ask it: But why this intellectual division of labour? This comes down to asking: But why are philosophy and the sciences not one and the same thing? Or again: Why do the sciences and philosophy exist, either the former or the latter or both?

We can here state the principle of an answer, but it obviously goes beyond the framework of the sciences and philosophy and their relations. This answer is very simple. It consists in taking seriously what goes on in this reduplication. We have already noted that the philosopher feels the 'need' to say: what I have just said (namely that the adequation of the subject to the object produces the truth) is the truth. In sum, a little *supplementary need* that would seem to be peculiar to the philosopher. We have to indulge his little needs. The fact is, however, that it is not a little need, that it is not a need, and that it is not a need of the philosopher's. It is the major manifestation of an intervention which, at the limit, concerns the equilibrium of society as a whole. Let us examine this a little more closely.

When the philosopher declares that what he has just said is the truth, he puts all those who might accuse him of lying on their guard in advance (a preventive action), and he bolsters the convictions of all those who share his convictions by providing them with the guarantee of what he has said and by providing them with the guarantee that he speaks the truth. We have pronounced the crucial word: *Truth is a function of guarantee.* And it is announced in a form that offers all possible guarantees, that puts the truth above all suspicion: the most rigorous form of demonstration there is, inspired by the practices of mathematics in its unadorned rigour (see Descartes, Spinoza, Kant, Hegel) or adorned with the most refined rhetorical effects (see Plato's dialogues) or a deeply personal experience of meditative conviction (see Bergson). In short, depending on the 'objects', talents, and times involved, the philosopher chooses the best of what is available in the way of arguments and argumentative forms, the object of the whole being to arrive at the most persuasive show of truth that he can. Thus he has every chance of putting the guarantee, or as solid a guarantee as possible, on his side. Opponents or adversaries can show up if they dare, but they had better get up pretty early in the morning, for he is ready and waiting for them.

What purpose does this whole fantastic *mise en scène* of the guarantee by way of the truth serve? It serves the philosopher, to begin with, who needs, like everybody else, to assure himself that he is definitely in the truth as he plies his philosopher's 'trade' in the division of intellectual labour and the division of mental and manual labour; for, philosopher though one may be, one is no less human for that, and one has one's moments of doubt (think of Descartes, think even of Spinoza, think of Pascal), one's moments of gloom and anguish; and, even when one has been seized by the flame of truth in a dark night and has seen, one can be afraid, afterwards, that one has dreamt or been deceived by an evil genius, so that one must endlessly trudge back up the slope. And it is not just the wavering of this miracle that makes the philosopher tremble: there is all the world's grief, the wars and the massacres, which make him ask whether it is worth even an hour's pain to adjust thoughts in one's head while the world is starving to death; which make him ask, even when he believes in divine Providence: 'Why does it rain upon sands, upon highways and seas', when that rain falls to no purpose (Malebranche)?;[5] which make him ask: Why this gigantic mental effort, when it cannot prevent a child as pure as the dawn from dying in agony? We could make books of this doubt and this anguish of the philosophers – of the greatest among them – in the face of their vocation. One of them devoted his life's work to it; his name his Kierkegaard. For, in the depths of his soul, the philosopher trembles at the thought that he has usurped this function of universal guarantee that he performs before scientists and all the other members of his society, and even before universal history. That, moreover, is why he goes about it with such fury: in order to ward off the risk, which he knows he is taking, that he might prove unworthy of his task. By dint of argument, he sometimes manages to convince himself.

That, however, is not what really counts. For whether or not the philosopher is convinced is a question for his conscience, his friends, and his personal diary. For the others to whom he addresses himself orally or in writing, there is no problem: he is always convinced, since he is a philosopher, since he says so, and since it is one and the same thing to be a philosopher, to be convinced that one is in possession of the truth of truths, to speak the truth, and to do so convincingly. The reduplicated philosophical guarantee of the truth works this way for the outside world, always. *Truth is for the others.* Great, supreme feint! It is enough for the others to believe in it, and to believe that everything is for the best; to believe that, if there are philosophers, it is to tell those in possession of the truth the truth of their truth and so on. Yes: everything is for the best. The division of the world between those who know and say so, and those who do not know and listen, is for the best. The division between those who work and produce and those who do not work, but have the leisure to think the truth and utter it, is a good thing. The division between those who govern and those who are governed is a good thing, between soldiers and civilians, between men and women, between freemen and slaves, between Greeks and Barbarians (or slaves or immigrants), the division between adults and children, the division between the gods and men, the division between priests and laymen, the division between seers and the blind, the division between sacred prostitutes and secular prostitutes: all that is a good, is an excellent thing. See Plato, who explains this in detail throughout his work. It is a good thing, because this division is simultaneously a division of labour that produces the unity of its result: the unity of the community, precisely, and peace among its citizens. Marx, because he is a troublemaker, explains that this whole system, including the philosophy that sanctions and guarantees it, has just one function: perpetuation of the dominant class's domination of the dominated class, a perpetuation that necessitates, precisely, these divisions, these multiple functions and, as well, the guarantee that all is for the best in the best of all communities, since the priests, the politicians and, ultimately, the philosophers guarantee that it is so for all those who might entertain doubts, or be looking to make trouble by attacking the order of the prevailing class dictatorship.

With that, we begin to see that philosophy is less and less innocent, since it plays its role in perpetuating (or overthrowing) the established order and is, consequently, tied in with politics.

We have not, however, finished with the theory of knowledge. Purely imaginary though it may be in the form (I insist) in which idealist philosophy conceives of it, it nevertheless produces both questions and answers, and thus new categories and theses as well as theoretical and practical consequences.

For once the philosopher has written his new equation

$$V = ((S = O) = V),$$

he cannot help asking a new question, since he is, as a philosopher, curious by nature (Aristotle): *Where does that truth come from?* To put it differently, he asks himself a question that we have already encountered: the question of the origin, which can also be called the question of the first principle (Aristotle), the question of the foundation, the question of the sufficient reason or first and last reason on which everything else depends (Leibniz). In other words, the philosopher asks himself a very simple question, which will finally allow him to rid himself of all his subjectivity, that is, all his doubts and anguish, which he had, until then, kept to himself in the silence of his heart (for it was imperative that he not lose face in front of all the poor souls who needed him and his certitude). This question is: *But what founds the guarantee that I am in the process of providing?*

This is clearly a legitimate question if ever there was one, if the philosopher wants to escape the human condition that makes him a contingent individual, born in such-and-such a country, in such-and-such a year, to such-and-such parents, with such-and-such little foibles: for example, this love for cross-eyed women and taste for Swedish princesses (Descartes), this yearning to go walking alone every day out by the trees and piss there (Kant), this need to go contemplate Being in the sap of the oaks of the Forest of Fontainebleau (Lachelier), this desire to haunt the woods of the Black Forest in order to break one's nose in the paths the lumberjacks blaze there (Heidegger). But you know about all these peccadilloes; allow me to move on. In a word, the philosopher who wants to exempt himself from what Feuerbach calls empirical determinations (having a pointy or a stub nose) and who wants, above all, to exempt the truth he utters and the guarantee he provides from these contingencies, so that they are valid and guaranteed for everyone for all time – this philosopher feels a legitimate need to answer the question: How are the truth I state and the guarantee I establish *founded*? (That is: How shall I found them?) Or, generalizing: How are the truth philosophy states and the guarantee it establishes founded?

And, as always in idealist philosophy, no sooner said than done, since the answer is always there in the question. The philosopher will, therefore, once again reduplicate the truth he has attained, but by conferring higher status on it: a status that is no longer personal and empirical ('you can believe me because I say so, and provide you with proof to boot'), but universal and absolute. He will, consequently, 'produce' – that is, in the etymological sense of Sartre's waiter,[6] bring us on a platter – the superior truth (truth number 3) that he needs to found everything he has so far 'proven'. This truth is, accordingly, the absolute, radical *Origin*, the one it is impossible to go beyond, like certain train stations in Paris, Marseilles and elsewhere that are dead-ends (like Heidegger's *Holzwege*), because the rails end at the buffer and one can go no further, although one can set back out for all the other train stations in France. This absolute truth is at the same time the absolute Principle, the one that goes furthest back in time (before it, there was no time), and the one on which all consequences will depend, although it depends on nothing. This absolute truth is also the foundation, the base on which every edifice, whether being or reason and reasoning, is based for all time; it is that which bears without being borne by anything, the Earth that nothing supports, or the originary Giant of mythology who supports the world on his back, although nothing supports him, or God, who sustains everything with his strength, but, as is well known, needs no ground, no *Grund*, on which to plant his feet (indeed, he does not have feet, which make man what he is, on which see Leroi-Gourhan:[7] it is his feet, not his hands or skull – his feet, in other words, his upright stance, which allow man, as Freud shows in *Totem and Taboo*,[8] to piss on the fire, which is not very nice for women). This absolute truth is, finally, the sufficient reason, the *ratio rationis*, the reason for every reason on earth, the ultimate or final reason that accounts for everything existing in the world, for the radical origin of things (Leibniz)[9] and their *raison d'être*, that is, their end, their destination, their goal, which is established outside them but for them, or for the greater glory of God, the beauty of a world realized as economically as possible, or man's salvation (or the order established by the dominant class).

The reader will have noticed in passing that, setting out in search of *the origin*, the principle, the foundation and the sufficient reason, the philosopher has inevitably encountered, by the same stroke, *the ultimate end*: the ultimate ends, the destination of Being, and the 'destiny' of Being (not of beings: Heidegger),[10] and that if he wants to write the radical origin into his equation, as the ultimate reason for all that exists and the guarantee of the guarantee, he must also, and simultaneously, write the ultimate reason for, and the ultimate end of, this whole process into it. And he must, at the same time, make this very simple, because tautological, observation: *the ultimate, radical End of things is identical with the primary, radical Origin of things*; the end is in the position of a mirror vis-à-vis the origin, and the origin is in the position of a mirror vis-à-vis the end, one sending the other its own image and vice-versa, one constituting the truth of the other and vice-versa, as we have already noted about the questions that philosophy asks.

This gives us a definitive equation, which is written as follows:

$$O = (V = (S = O) = V) = E.$$

I say 'a definitive equation', but that is just a figure of speech. For the philosopher may still be uneasy, and ask himself: 'But just what grounds *this* equation?' Then he will perform the same operation on the preceding operation, and so on, ad infinitum. This is not just a fanciful image intended for didactic use. We find, in history, philosophies that indefinitely repeat the same operation of guarantee on the guarantee – Hegel's, for example. We even find philosophies which, setting out from the paradoxes of set theory (can a set of elements contain itself as one of its elements?), attempt to take this circular repetition into account in order to forge the theory of it, in either a formalist sense (Russell)[11] or an ontological sense (Heidegger).[12] Finally, we find a philosophy that attempts to draw the critical, and therefore materialist, lesson of these sophisticated theoretical attempts, and to think what this philosophical circle with no outside might be, hence what this non-philosophical-philosophical outside of philosophy as margin might be

(Derrida).[13] With that, however, we find ourselves at idealism's limits (a philosophical category par excellence, by means of which idealist philosophy begins to become aware of its own imposture); that is, we find ourselves at the extreme point at which idealism no longer has anything but materialism before it.

11

We have, however, still not finished with the theory of knowledge. Let us go on to say a word about its function. It is intended, as we have come to realize, to perform the function of *guaranteeing the truth* (the truth of all that exists). But, paradoxically, it performs this function of universal guarantee (of the established order) by way of the function of guaranteeing *the truth of knowledge*. This means that it uses the reality of knowledge as a prop in proposing its services of universal guarantee. From the standpoint of truth, its services are imaginary, but they are very real from the standpoint of scientific, ideological, political, and social reality.

Yet the knowledge that the theory of knowledge uses as a prop, the knowledge that it takes as its pretext, is not itself imaginary. People know things. They know them by very diverse means, and their knowledge of them is very diverse. They know things from practical observation, which is always more or less closely connected with natural transformation in the things observed (stars, plants, the tides) or human transformation of things (hunting, fishing, the domestication of animals, construction, destruction, production, consumption, the transformation of raw materials into tools and so on). Such knowledge is never purely passive, even when it is a question of simple observations. For knowledge is always dominated and guided by a certain number of pre-existing ideas, social, religious, or both at once, as study of the most 'primitive' of observable societies shows. People live in society, even if that society is rudimentary, and they have language at their disposal.

This double condition, which is in fact just one (society and language), as Aristotle clearly discerned, affects what may be called the forms of perception and representation of the first human beings. This is not a matter of decree or caprice. If they are to survive, human beings cannot afford not to take account, in their relationship to nature – which means, as well, their knowledge of nature, their only source of subsistence – of the social and sexual relations reigning among them. This is easy enough to understand where social relations are concerned. But sexual relations must also be taken into account; they command the biological reproduction of the human species and, interwoven with the social and ideological relations which reflect them, play a primordial role at this stage. Scientific knowledge properly speaking comes into play only later, after the first general and generalized empirical knowledge. What conditions made it possible for scientific knowledge to irrupt, with Thales, in sixth-century Greece? This is a still obscure question, in which the Pythagoreans' ascetic religious ideology seems to have played a part[1] by compelling people to regard numbers, hitherto simple empirical objects or operators, as ideas, that is, as universal, necessary realities abstracted from any empirical content, on which operations could be performed independently of all concrete reference. But, whatever the truth of the matter, an irreversible step had been taken and a point of non-return had been reached, on the basis of which it was possible to pronounce Spinoza's formula: we have a true idea, that of mathematical knowledge, and this idea can serve us as a standard for judging ideas and producing other true ideas.[2]

Although all philosophies acknowledge the reality of this distinction between practical and scientific knowledge, idealist philosophies and materialist philosophies do not treat it the same way. And although it is common to all philosophies to canonize this distinction by 'drawing lines of demarcation' between the two types of knowledge, they do not all draw it the same way. For what interests idealism is to safeguard, demonstrate, and guarantee scientific knowledge's superiority to practical knowledge, even if it is by way of an acknowledgement of the temporal priority (when such priority exists) of practical or empirical knowledge to scientific knowledge. What interests idealism is to show that scientific knowledge is, by rights, completely different in nature from practical knowledge, that it is the object of a completely different faculty (understanding or reason), infinitely superior to the merely sensory or empirical faculties. It is also to show – the ultimate ploy – that the truths of scientific knowledge, for example, are already present in practical knowledge itself, albeit only implicitly (Plato), or that their a priori forms or 'passive synthesis' form the condition of possibility for all sensory experience (Kant, Husserl). At the limit, idealism thus upholds a thesis which, albeit paradoxical, is in perfect conformity with its objectives: it consists in the claim that, in the form of miscognition, all sensory experience is already, by rights, scientific knowledge that is simply unaware of its true nature.

Thus when idealism, making allowances, in fact recognizes the existence of practical knowledge alongside that of scientific knowledge, or, going to extremes, takes all knowledge to be by rights scientific, it invariably arranges for scientific knowledge to triumph over empirical, practical knowledge. Hiding behind and expressing itself behind this triumph is, naturally, the triumph of philosophy, which alone possesses the truth of scientific knowledge's domination of practical knowledge. We know a little something, by now, about the purpose that this justification and this self-justification serve.

Naturally, recognition of the distinction between practical and scientific knowledge is always more or less falsified by idealism. This falsification is indispensable to it if it is to be able to ask the philosophical 'questions' near and dear to its heart, the answer to which it holds in advance. For when idealism declares that scientific knowledge dominates practical knowledge, it does not state anything that is obvious or true. Quite the contrary: it merely gives expression to the accomplished fact of the real domination not of scientific over practical knowledge, but of the intellectuals who practice science over the workers who produce and, behind these two human groups, the dominant class's real domination of the exploited class.

Affirming this reality, however, does not release one from the obligation to produce evidence showing how this falsification works. For the sake of brevity, I shall take just one example, the Kantian theory of experiment and experience. Kant has the merit of distinguishing these two realities, thus taking account of the existence of the experimental physics of Newton, who carried out experiments. However, even as Kant distinguishes experiment and experience, he ultimately manages to conflate them under the unity of the category of experience, which he uses to account for the unity of the different forms of possible experience (from the simple perception of a boat sailing down a river to a Newtonian physicist's experimentation) under the unity of the transcendental subject. Scientific knowledge's domination of practical knowledge (perception) is ensured in this way, and the difference between practical experience and scientific experiment is 'erased'. In the same general connection, we might also cite the examples of Plato, Descartes, Hegel or Bergson. The forms of falsification undoubtedly differ, but the falsification is in principle the same; it invariably serves the 'greater glory' of scientific knowledge and, behind it, of the philosophy that possesses the secret of this whole business.

It is a very different story in the materialist philosophies. Here, we must first take the precaution of issuing a warning. Because the history of philosophy has been not simply dominated, but crushingly commanded by idealism, materialist philosophies have always been subject to the crushing domination of the adverse party; they have been influenced and contaminated by it, and have usually been reduced to fighting on the adversary's ground, to the point of using, not just his arguments, but his theses as well – while skilfully diverting them, it is true, from their original idealist meaning. One has to know how to decrypt these philosophies, quite simply in order to see behind the mask that they were forced to borrow so as to be able to express themselves openly in a day and age in which materialism and atheism fell under the jurisdiction of ecclesiastical and state courts and were punishable by death (thus Giordano Bruno was burned at the stake for his ideas, while Spinoza was excluded from Amsterdam's Jewish community, a draconian measure at the time, one that made him a sort of prisoner in his own city). If we know how to decipher, in this way, not just the philosophies that declare themselves to be materialist (we often discover that they are, under the mantle of a declaration of materialism, philosophies influenced by idealism, as were most eighteenth-century 'materialists' and also Feuerbach), but also those that declare nothing or are even sometimes forced to give the impression that they are idealist (for example, Spinoza, a great materialist[3] philosopher and, in my estimation, the greatest philosopher of all time), we expose ourselves to surprises that are sometimes pleasant and sometimes disappointing.

We must add another determination to the foregoing. In the Marxist historiography of philosophy since Engels,[4] it is customary to say that the history of philosophy comes down to a struggle between idealism and materialism.[5] This formula is correct, in its generality. But if we apply it mechanically, setting out to identify, for each period, the materialist philosophers who opposed the dominant idealist philosophers, and if we assume that every idealist (or materialist) philosophy represents idealism (or materialism) one hundred per cent – in other words, is one hundred per cent idealist or materialist – we end up understanding nothing at all, even on a straightforward reading of the philosophical texts. For we discover the paradox, when we undertake such a reading, that every idealist philosophy contains, despite or perhaps even because of its idealism, elements of materialism, and that every materialist philosophy contains, despite or perhaps even because of its materialism, elements of idealism.[6] We have to take this fact into account and think it, without abandoning Engels's idea. But we can think it on only one condition, which comes down to the idea that every philosophy (the work of a philosopher or philosophical current) is contradictory, and contains within itself, in its problematic, categories, theses, and justifications, idealist and materialist elements alike, which interact to constitute the philosophy as it exists. If and only if we have properly deciphered these different elements in their contradiction can we decide whether a given philosophy is 'idealist' or 'materialist', that is, whether idealist or materialist elements dominate it.

What is in question here is not a contingent fact. For, to take an example that is a limit case, an idealist philosophy does not contain materialist elements simply in order to 'take account of' a reality that all philosophers must supposedly acknowledge. Since it is dominant, it obviously does not contain them because it is subject to the influence of materialism, which is too weak for that. It contains them, basically, for a different reason (I say 'basically' because exceptions to this law can be found) having to do with the war of all against all that reigns in the philosophical domain, as we have seen, between the philosophies associated with idealism and those associated with materialism: for a *preventive* reason. For, since every philosophy is in a state of war, at the limit, with the other philosophical tendency, materialist or idealist, it must necessarily take preventive action against the enemy in order to get the better of him; in other words, it must preventively occupy its adversary's positions, even if that means cloaking itself in its adversary's arguments.

It is no accident that the word 'positions' has cropped up again at this point in our discussion, for positions are theses, and theses are occupied positions, including the adversary's positions. I am even tempted to say 'especially the adversary's positions', since, in this war, one only ever occupies, at the limit, positions that one has taken from the adversary, hence the adversary's positions, which one occupies, naturally, in order to convert them to one's own purposes. Yet something of the adversary's positions always remains. It is, moreover, good colonialist method to leave the indigenous leaders in place: they know much better than the occupiers how to exploit their own compatriots, as the British method has shown. That is why, since antagonism is to be found everywhere in philosophy, it is necessary (not mere accident) that an idealist philosophy contain, contradictorily, materialist elements, and that materialist philosophy contain, contradictorily, idealist elements.

This explains – but this is just one example that we would have to extend to the whole history of philosophy – why materialists such as Marx and Lenin were able to turn Hegel's philosophy of absolute idealism to good materialist account, a discovery that amazed Lenin and had him exclaiming in surprise when, in 1915, he read Hegel's *Science of Logic*. But this also explains, to consider the matter from the opposite angle, why philosophers who declare themselves to be materialists, such as the great eighteenth-century materialists or even Feuerbach, whose materialism Lenin commends, contain elements of idealism – to the point that we may even ask whether, dominated as these philosophers were by feudal and bourgeois idealist philosophy, idealism does not largely outweigh materialism in their work.

We can conclude these remarks with the affirmation that Marxist materialism itself, albeit sharply critical of every vulgar or mechanistic materialism, will never be able to claim that it is one hundred per cent materialist, but will always, inevitably, include elements of idealism. Indeed, if we consider dialectical materialism today, as it exists in the productions precipitated by the effects of the 'Stalinist deviation',[7] we have to go much further, and say that the idealist elements are largely predominant in it. That, however, unfortunately or fortunately, is a non-fortuitous accident in the history of Marxism, which we shall examine elsewhere.

After these preliminaries, which warn us how hard it is to come up with a correct expression of the positions of materialism, to say nothing of a comprehensive one, let us turn to the materialist conception of the theory of knowledge.

It must be said that, in principle, materialism does not grant, or should not grant, that this is a philosophically valid theoretical *question*.

We shall begin by noting an apparently strange fact: in the history of philosophy, the place and importance of the theory of knowledge have varied. After occupying a subordinate place in Greek and medieval philosophy, the theory of knowledge began to hold an increasingly preponderant one from the seventeenth century on. Since Hegel, it has been losing this preponderant place, despite Husserl's attempt at a restoration. How are we to explain this phenomenon?

One could propose a very simple explanation based on the history of the sciences. Because the sciences were poorly developed in Antiquity and the Middle Ages, this explanation would run, the theory of knowledge found itself pushed into the background. The significant development of scientific discoveries since Galileo, however, contributed to the new philosophical prestige of the theory of knowledge, which held centre stage in all seventeenth-century and eighteenth-century philosophies, with very rare exceptions. But this explanation, while plausible as far as Antiquity, the Middle Ages, and the Classical Age are concerned, is untenable for the modern period. How are we to explain the decline of the theory of knowledge in a philosopher such as Hegel, a contemporary of very great discoveries in mathematics, physics, chemistry, and political economy? How are we to explain the spectacular attenuation[8] and ultimate evacuation of the problem in modern philosophers, contemporaries of the greatest discoveries in the history of the sciences that humanity has known? We must advance another explanation.

For my part, I would look for it in a history other than that of the sciences (the importance of which I certainly do not deny): the history of legal and political ideology.[9] For it is no accident that the rise in the philosophical fortunes of the theory of knowledge coincided with the return of Roman law, brought up to date, naturally, and therefore altered, by the birth and development of the capitalist mode of production in Western Europe. We spoke, a moment ago, of philosophy's function of guarantee. *Only rights can be guaranteed*, the guarantee of a state of affairs being a question of force, which, as Rousseau very nicely puts it, 'does not make right';[10] and, in philosophy, it is always a question of a theoretical guarantee, hence a guarantee of the very special kind of facts known as rights, which can be guaranteed only by a foundation of right, a reason of right.

Thus it is quite as if, in this period in which the bourgeoisie had to conduct an uncertain class struggle against the dominant nobility and, in order to do so, had to rely on scientific discoveries capable of developing the productive forces and intensifying the exploitation of a waged labour force, and had to conduct this class struggle against religious ideology and its philosophy, which made every guarantee of truth dependent on God – it is quite as if this ascendant bourgeoisie felt the need for a guarantee independent of the feudal God and, above all, for a guarantee that put the truths of the natural sciences within simply human reach, in forms that simultaneously made it possible to guarantee the freedom of individual subjects: subjects of productive labour, subjects of capitalist enterprise, moral subjects and political subjects – in short, subjects of right. To that end, it had to put forward a theory of knowledge, a theory of knowledge that functioned in terms of right; it had to establish what Kant would call, in a miraculous phrase, the 'Tribunal of Reason',[11] so that it could call before this Tribunal both the human subject (what can he know?) and everything purporting to be knowledge. (Which knowledge is true knowledge, scientific knowledge? Not the reigning metaphysics, not rational psychology, theology, and cosmology; but mathematics, physics and perhaps, some day, chemistry; not, in any case, either psychology or history.)

If this hypothesis is well-founded, it also provides us, perhaps, with an explanation for the decline of the theory of knowledge in nineteenth-century philosophies, beginning with Hegel. For, sure now of its real power, newly hegemonic, and increasingly confident of its ideological state apparatuses, the bourgeoisie no longer needed this philosophical guarantee that had only recently constituted its first and last theoretical recourse. The sciences existed, were producing results, and no longer had to fear interference or condemnation from the Church. Bourgeois right was an established fact, recognized by one and all, including the exploited. It was no longer a question of justifying either the right to know or the right to dominate. It was quite simply a question of organizing the established power and deriving from its organization, and the exploitation that it protected, a means of fighting the tendential fall in the profit rate.

The number one political, but also philosophical, task was to organize established fact, to observe fact, and to deduce the laws of its optimal organization from it. Even if this task did not impose itself from the outset, it was not long before it had begun to do so ever more insistently on men of all social conditions. The Saint-Simonian dream of replacing the government of men with the organization of things was translated into fact, and reinforced by the tasks assigned to the government of men: to bring the exploited under the sway of the dominant class's 'spiritual power', a power exercised – what a surprise! – by the special sort of priests known as positivist philosophers. Positive, positivism: the reigning capitalist bourgeoisie now let loose its rallying cry, which would never again loosen its grip on the bourgeoisie's imagination. The question of right, all questions of right, and even the Tribunal of Reason were things of the past. It would be enough positively to organize the reign of positivity, to learn the laws of process, whether it was dialectical à la Hegel (who still bore the marks, ambiguous to the end, of the struggles of the French revolution, only to end up in the Restoration) or dialectical à la Comte: subject to the law of the three stages, thesis-antithesis-synthesis, which, sure of what it was about, that is, of its effect [*de son fait, c'est-à-dire de son effet*], that is, of its goal ('enrich yourselves!'), reigned serenely over a society that no longer needed any guarantee at all beyond that of its police (very positive men) and its philosophers (very positivist men).

To be sure, there were (and still are) a few scatterbrains who dreamt of the old theory of knowledge, such as Husserl, alarmed by the crisis of the sciences in a Western Europe that fascism would soon engulf, dragging the hatred of reason in its wake,[12] or a few philosophy professors who repeated the old masters' lessons. Ultimately, however, that is not where things were happening. After Comte and positivism, they were happening in the great movement which, under the influence of the great modern discovery, Mathematical Logic, swept ideology towards the new forms of *logical neo-positivism* that found their warmest reception in the human sciences, in functionalism and structuralism. This time, there was no role left for philosophers, to whom Comte had still entrusted 'spiritual power'.[13] The machine now ran all by itself: all one need do was install a good programme in the computer, which ran conjointly on electricity and formal logic, and everything would emerge from it: not just the plan, but the decision as well. Man, who no longer needed right, no longer even needed freedom or thought. The machine thought and decided for him. It even programmed the costs of class struggle into a firm's investments! Under these conditions, bourgeois idealism had no use whatsoever for the theory of knowledge. The only people to continue to concern themselves with it were the handful of eccentrics and the traditional professors I just mentioned, and also, paradoxically, a redoubtable battalion of Marxist philosophers in the Eastern European countries or of the Eastern European school, who, prisoners of bourgeois ideology, trotted out in their turn, on the basis of a total misunderstanding, 'the theory of knowledge', as if it were essential to Marxist materialism. Their influence had only to reach a country such as France – which its philosophical traditions have left, like a 'pocket of Royan',[14] untouched by the global neo-positivist invasion – for these Eastern European philosophers to find emulators who run on as seriously as can be about 'gnoseology' (theory of knowledge) and, gnoseology *oblige*, about 'ontology' as well, as we shall see in a moment.[15]

12

If, as we have seen, materialist philosophy, unlike idealist philosophy, cannot pose the question of the theory of knowledge, how *does* it broach the reality that is, however well disguised, at issue in the idealist theory of knowledge? We may put it simply: it broaches it by doing away with the question – not by passing it over in silence, but by producing and putting in place the philosophical means that allow us to do away with it. Theoretically, this comes down to producing a category or categories which, in the equation we have discussed,

$$(S = O) = V,$$

reduce the equals sign (=) to zero.

Tendentially, the answer to this question can be said to come down to the affirmation that the equals sign (=) is itself equal to zero, in other words, is nil. Let it not be supposed that this is pettifogging on the part of the individual who is striving laboriously to provide an initiation into philosophy, or pettifogging on philosophers' part. Since, for philosophers, everything happens *in* philosophy, it is only to be expected that such important questions should be subjects of extended elaboration and, naturally, abiding dispute.

To say that the equals sign is itself equal to zero means that the equation tends towards the identity of its terms, and thus that the subject and object are one and the same thing. That is the monist position, which, we have said, can be spiritualist, if this thing that is one and the same is mind, or, equally, materialist, if it is matter. (Let us note in passing that this is not the only occasion we shall have to observe a strange kinship between spiritualism, a variety of idealism, and materialism.) Thus materialism here presents itself as a monism of matter; this realizes the identity between the subject and the object. Now, however, monism must account for the difference between this subject and this object, without which the question of monism could not have been asked in the first place! Materialism consequently looks for alternative categories with which to think this identity in a form that respects the difference between subject and object. The classic form, the matrix of all other alternative forms, has been provided by the Aristotelian tradition, which may be said to have a certain affinity with materialism on this point. We are already acquainted with this form: *veritas adaequatio rei et intellectus* (Saint Thomas), truth is adequation between the thing and the intellect. In sum, the thing and the intellect are almost the same thing, since their adequation tends towards unity, in other words, towards suppression of the distinction between them.

But the most famous, because the most categorical and scandalous form of the suppression of the problem by materialism has been provided by the *Leninist theory of reflection*. This theory consists in the claim that knowledge reflects the object – a thesis of objectivity – and that this reflection reflects an object that is in the last instance material – a materialist thesis. However, in its abruptness, the thesis of knowledge-as-reflection throws up problems. We can confront them by declaring, as do all of Lenin's commentators, following hints thrown out by Lenin himself, incidentally,[1] that reflection is not purely passive, but active, productive, etc.; this is a shamefaced way of recognizing a certain officially denied difference between knowledge and its object. Yes, knowledge is active; yes, people have to act and have to transform the real object in order to acquire knowledge of it; yes, reflection, which is apparently 'passive' when conceived on the model of a simple mirror, must therefore be declared to be active. But a declaration, which can be issued by the first responsible official to come along (and the first irresponsible official as well), is one thing; knowledge of the fact itself is quite another. The philosophical justifications for the theory of reflection, the objectivist and materialist principle of which is correct, fall short of the mark.

Another astounding theory has been proposed in history in order to abolish the difference between knowledge and its object even while conserving it: the Spinozist theory of *parallelism*. For Spinoza, all reality is constituted by a single substance, God or nature (paradoxically, God is for Spinoza the same thing as the nature that emanates from him: what political dexterity, to know how to put one's adversary, God, in one's own camp!), which has an infinite number of attributes, of which we know only (that's just the way it is) the attribute extension (or matter) and the attribute thought. Thus we have, face-to-face, knowledge (thought) and its object (extension or matter). These are two obviously different attributes, although, insofar as they are produced by God's active omnipotence, they are in a certain way identical. Yet the fact is that they are given in practice as different. The question then becomes: How can their difference be reduced to unity in a materialist way?

Spinoza answers with the theory of *parallelism*. Everything that happens in the attribute extension has its exact correlative in the attribute thought: '*ordo et connectio rerum idem est ac ordo et connectio idearum*':[2] the order of things is identical to the order of ideas (of their ideas, hence of the knowledge of them). Since, in Spinoza, every being is power [*puissance*], we have to do *from the outset* with an active parallelism, an active correlation, an active reflection. Spinoza does not confine himself to declaring this. He shows it and proves it in his 'theory of knowledge' (which is no such thing, as the reader can well imagine), in which there exists a certain play and, consequently, the possibility of real activity between the 'first kind of knowledge', which is purely practical, 'the second kind of knowledge', which yields our 'common notions' or the general laws of all objects, hence scientific knowledge, and the 'third kind of knowledge', which produces knowledge of the singular, whether what is involved is an individual or a given historical conjuncture – say, that of Moses and the Jewish people during the exodus, which is analysed in the *Theological-Political Treatise*.[3] Thus we have to do here with a form of consistent materialism that annuls the difference between the object and knowledge of it, while acknowledging – abstractly, it is true – the difference between them; while acknowledging, in other words, the possibility of play and of a dialectic that allows us to make the transition, in three moments, from one to the other via the different kinds of knowledge.

We find something similar in Hegel, who considered Spinoza to be the greatest of the philosophers.[4] For there is no theory of knowledge in Hegel; there are simply 'figures' of consciousness comparable to the kinds of knowledge in Spinoza. We also find in Hegel, as in Spinoza, both acknowledgement of a difference between knowledge (consciousness) and its object, and the requirement that this difference be abolished. This abolition is the result of considerable 'labour', the 'labour of the negative',[5] which confers the leading role on the dialectic, while defining it, for the first time in the history of philosophy, as labour, albeit formal labour. For at every moment (degree), we find a lack or a negation at work, one that carries the moment under consideration beyond itself and towards the next moment. In Hegel, however, the number of moments is not limited to three, as it is in Spinoza, although, when we consider the process as a whole, it too is limited to three moments: sense perception, understanding, and reason. Most importantly, each successive moment is the 'truth' of the previous one for Hegel, which means that the previous moment already contained, 'in itself', the next moment, which becomes 'for itself' what the preceding moment was 'in itself'.

It must be admitted that this is an extremely simple way of annulling difference, because it is, in the proper sense, tautological; because every result is contained in advance in its premises or causes; and because difference is, in consequence, only ever recognized by a feint (once again!) that pretends to posit difference when it has in fact annulled it from all eternity. That is why we may say that absolutely nothing happens in Hegel's philosophy, apart from this change in form known as the dialectic, since the dialectic is nothing other than the logic of this change in forms or figures, and since absolute logic, whose science Hegel writes in the *Science of Logic*, is the dialectic, the dialectic of reason – ordinary logic, yours and mine, having been demoted, like that of the sciences, to the level of the logic of the understanding, which dwells in separation and abstraction.

Thus we find in Hegel, behind the façade of an enterprise bolder and more consistent than Spinoza's, a veritable regression behind Spinoza towards a conception of the 'labour' of science and of the difference between the object and the knowledge of it that brings us back to the essence of the religious conception of the world. This conception makes everything depend on Providence, its designs and its ends, while assigning God a priori knowledge of everything that will happen. For it is God who creates the world and makes everything in the world and, as well, gives man knowledge of all things. This knowledge is adequate knowledge without distance or difference, and without labour, without toil or risk: the knowledge that Adam possessed before original sin, according to Malebranche,[6] the transparent knowledge characteristic of the epoch before Adam and Eve sought to acquire knowledge of the difference between good and evil (identical to sexuality), an act that cast humanity into the consequences of sin: labour, suffering and so on, including the labour required to acquire knowledge of things, which had become opaque and sombre, as if they were now out of reach. All of which once again shows that, as soon as a teleological conception comes into play (a conception according to which the things of the world, men, their objects, and their acts are, from all eternity, governed by an End and destined for an End [*telos*]), philosophy not only lapses into idealism, but also defers to simple religion.

A consistent conception was reached only with the advent of Marxist materialism, a conception that lapsed into neither the abstraction of difference (Spinoza) nor the teleology of the labour of the dialectic (Hegel). Marx has left us, in the chapter on the method of political economy in the famous Introduction to *A Critique of Political Economy*,[7] all we need to reconstruct the essentials of his theses about the reality that is disguised in idealist philosophies' theory of knowledge.

Marx begins by ruling out (simply by his silence) all question of right, which constitutes the idealist theory of knowledge as a theory of knowledge.

Just as Spinoza points out, with no comment whatsoever, that 'we have a true idea' (that of mathematics), and writes, tersely, '*homo cogitat*'[8] (man thinks, a phrase that forever distinguished him from Descartes: 'I think, therefore I am',[9] since Spinoza deduces absolutely nothing about existence from the fact that man thinks), and just as Kant, in his turn, speaks of the 'fact of Reason' to sum up the whole of his critical reflection,[10] so Marx sets out from the *fact* that knowledge exists, some of it scientific and some not. To set out in this way from the facts (as both Spinoza and Marx do) is obviously to reject the question of right (what can man know, his faculties being what they are?). It is to reject the idea that we should put the question of its titles of legitimacy to the fact of knowledge (non-scientific and, later, scientific knowledge): for example, the question as to whether or not metaphysics, rational psychology (which deduces the properties of the human subject from his faculty of thought and his freedom), and rational theology (which deduces God's faculties and intentions from his all-goodness), or rational cosmology (which deduces the world's properties from its unity) constitute scientific knowledge, and the question as to what scientific knowledge humanity may one day legitimately aspire to (in chemistry or psychology, for example). This is – let us not close our eyes to the fact – a very powerful idea. It comes down to acknowledging the primacy of fact and the derivative nature of right, and thus *rejects the possibility of a prior legal question* about the facts, the question of truth not excepted.

It is on this negative, yet very positive basis that Marxist materialist theory develops. Marx does not, however, content himself with this thesis. He adds to it another, of the highest importance: that of *the primacy of practice over theory*. This affords us a glimpse of what 'thesis' might mean. For, on a rough first approach, the categories of primacy, theory, and practice seem clear enough. When we go into detail, however, we discover an extreme complexity, which shows us how a thesis functions. Doubtless the first form of functioning of a thesis is to function as an anti-thesis: the materialist thesis of the primacy of practice over theory stands in opposition to the idealist theory of the primacy of theory over practice, which it rejects without appeal. At this level of abstraction, however, we have not got very far. For the categories can be extremely equivocal, can tend in one direction or the other, can take on one meaning or another. What is theory? What is practice? An endless effort of definition is required to confer meaning on these categories; an endless train of theses is required to exhaust the meaning (and that is impossible, since the variety of cases exceeds every definition) of the general thesis of the primacy of practice over theory. The grand line of demarcation that Marx drew between idealism (the primacy of theory over practice) and materialism (the primacy of practice over theory) is less a line drawn once and for all than *the constantly recurring demand to return to and redraw this line of demarcation on the occasion presented by each theoretical or concrete case*, whether it is a question of the theory of knowledge, as here, or, as elsewhere, of political theory and practice.

In the 'theory of knowledge' (or, rather, what replaces it in Marx), the primacy of practice over theory means, to begin with, *the primacy of practical over theoretical knowledge*, in the historical sense (humanity began with practical knowledge, no one can claim the opposite) and, simultaneously, in the logical or theoretical sense (every time, even when it is a matter of scientific and, therefore, theoretical knowledge, it is practical knowledge which is determinant in the last instance; and, behind practical knowledge, it is the practice of production and social relations, hence, in class societies, the class struggle, which is determinant in the last instance). This naturally implies a whole social and historical theory of this determination, which allows us to escape radically from the opposition and solitary confrontation of the terms of the equation $(S = O) = V$; it implies a whole theory of the development of the productive forces under the domination of the relations of production, and their combined effects in the field of scientific discovery. Here too, history is a witness for the defence of Marxist materialist theory, since, as we have seen, the great scientific discoveries have always stood in close relation with the development of social classes, the development of the bourgeoisie above all; this is so emphatically the case that many scientific discoveries were precipitated by episodes in the class struggle between the bourgeoisie and the proletariat.

Thus when Lenin declares that all knowledge has its origin in *the senses*,[11] he finds himself in a direct line of descent from Marx. Doubtless we can criticize him, at most, for trailing slightly behind the 'Theses on Feuerbach', which talk about not the senses, but human 'sensuous practical activity', since the senses are passive only at the limit and when abstractly considered;[12] in fact, they come into play in the 'whole' of a sensuous practice, which orients and guides them in accordance with not just human individuals' needs, but the 'interests' of the primitive social group, intent (unawares) on maintaining a favourable equilibrium with the nature from which it draws its subsistence. Here too, however, everything depends on the analysis of its material and social conditions, hence on the science known as historical materialism.

The second moment of knowledge is that of the 'concept' (Lenin) or 'theory' (Marx) and, eventually (for there exist pre-scientific and non-scientific theories), of scientific theory. Between these two levels, Marxist theory observes the existence of a 'leap', a 'qualitative leap' that illustrates one of its dialectical theses. Thus there is a transition, as philosophers (even idealist philosophers) have clearly seen, from the order of empirical observation and calculation to that of necessary abstract theory. At this level, knowledge of the object comes not through observation of its empirical variations, but through knowledge of its 'essence' (its deepest reality, conceived as hidden and 'internal' or 'intimate' because it is discovered after the fact), and this knowledge presents itself as (to humour Kant) 'a priori' knowledge, since it seems to precede its results. The fact is that people no longer go out to meet nature the way one goes out to meet a stranger. They go out to meet nature as they would go out to meet an acquaintance about whom they already have enough ideas to ask him questions, to 'put him to the test' of their questions (Kant).[13] That was Galileo's method, extolled by Kant. Descartes criticized Galileo for going out to meet nature without having sufficiently firm ideas about it; for Descartes had a different idea of nature, that of the 'novel' that Leibniz criticized him for fabricating.[14] Kant, in contrast, commended Galileo for having good ideas about nature and for asking it questions stemming from those good ideas in order to verify them.[15] That is how any science proceeds: it is not a science unless it has succeeded (even if the science involved is mathematics – we have already seen why – or physics) in forging *a theory of its object*, on the basis of which it asks questions of its object in order to see whether they will be verified or refuted: this is what is known as the practice of *experimentation*, which, despite the claims of certain idealist philosophers with an interest in putting mathematics and the human sciences in a category apart (mathematics because it is superior to the sciences, the human sciences because they are inferior to them), is universal in the sciences we know.

Is there a third level? Idealist philosophers say there is: philosophy. We, however, know enough about the matter to reject this answer as an imposture. Philosophy is not superior to the sciences (nor inferior to them, for that matter), because it is not knowledge, but a universal form of intervention-without-intervention that produces its effects everywhere, in the sciences, to be sure, but also in the ideologies and practices: in the whole range of human activities. We shall see how in due time.

If, however, we confine our attention to knowledge, what becomes of our famous little equation $(S = O) = V$? It disappears and it doesn't: it is transformed in an altogether unexpected way. For, in the Marxist materialist conception, there can be no question of denying the difference between the object and knowledge of it. All the terms and their relationship must, however, be conceived of differently. To begin with, it is clear that the subject is not a psychological subject. When an individual makes a scientific discovery, he does not act in his own name or use means all his own. He is not necessarily the one who has posed the (scientific) problem, for, usually, the problem has been posed long before him (consider cancer). Nor is he the one who has defined the conditions of the problem; they have been defined by all the past work of the researchers who have preceded him. Nor is he the one who has worked out the scientific theory on the basis of which such-and-such a question is put to nature; his predecessors have. As for the means he employs in his research (laboratories, instruments, mathematical formulas), they do not originate with him, either. And even if he comes up with a new theory or new analytical instruments, he owes them, although he may not always be aware of it, to old theories that have proven insufficient and, no less, to philosophical or ideological questions that are in the air – when what is involved is not a 'commission' from business or industry. The researcher who thus 'discovers' a new piece of knowledge is just one link in a chain without origin or end, only a moment in a process without origin or end, an agent who is, to be sure, active, but in a 'process without subject or end' that points back, in the last instance, to a society's process of development. The subject accordingly disappears, replaced by an agent in a process without subject or end. It is on this condition that it becomes possible to satisfy a requirement to which idealists are extremely attentive when they wish to safeguard the objectivity and universality of scientific knowledge: the requirement that one not lapse into what they call 'psychologism' (a conception which has it that individual subjectivity, whether psychological or historical, sustains the validity of scientific knowledge).

But what becomes of the object? It is real, and 'continues to exist outside the subject just as it did before' the process of knowledge, that is, the work of research (Marx). Marx explains: when the relation to the object is purely 'speculative' (a relation of pure knowledge), when it is not a question, in the process of knowledge, of modifying or transforming the object, the object obviously remains the same, 'just as before' the process of knowledge, which takes place outside it.[16] These affirmations give expression to a fundamental materialist thesis: that the object (or being) exists outside knowledge (or thought).

It is good method to consider the limit case of a 'merely speculative' form of knowledge, for if we can move mountains, we can move molehills, which is to say that this limit case will also shed light on knowledge that is not 'merely speculative', but 'practical'. In the case of 'merely speculative' knowledge, then, in which the object continues to exist unchanged outside the subject of the process of knowledge, 'just as it did before', what happens? For something happens, after all, this something that is known as scientific research, scientific work, or theoretical practice. What happens? *The object is reduplicated.* The scientist does not work directly on the object that he wants to know; if he did, he would transform it. He works on something else: on his provisional representation of it. Provisional, because if he intends to acquire knowledge of the object, he will transform his representation of it: it will not remain what it was, it will change. But can it be said that the scientist *works*? It can, because he applies to his object, as if it were raw material (which I earlier called Generality I), the theoretical instruments of production, the theoretical tools that he has in his provisional theory of his object (I called this theory Generality II). And all this work, all this 'theoretical practice', has but one goal: knowledge of a new property of the object (which I called Generality III).[17]

In any case, I used the term 'generality' deliberately, to make it clear that the scientist never, but never, has to do with the object as such, with its peculiar individuality, impossible to confuse with any other. He has to do with a mixed set of more or less abstract generalities, partly scientific and partly non-scientific – ideological or practical – which designated the object only by means of their abstract generalities. Scientific work then comes down to proceeding, as Marx himself puts it, not from the 'concrete' (the supposed object as such) towards the abstract (knowledge of it), but from the abstract (these generalities) to the concrete (the object and knowledge of it). Since this process is a process without an end, one always remains within the realm of generalities, without ever arriving at the object's concrete individuality. That is why I thought that I could also use the term generality, Generality III, to designate the provisional concrete result which is the knowledge that this process produces.

It was, accordingly, necessary to draw the conclusions implicit in these premises: to recognize the difference between two objects, that is, the existence of two objects. The first was *the real object*, which it was a question of knowing; the second was a complex, provisional representation of this object, on which the scientist works (since he does not work on the real object). Taking my cue from Spinoza, who had understood all this very well, I called this second object *the object of knowledge.* Thus we had two objects: the real, immutable object, and the object of knowledge on which the scientist works and which is therefore a changing object, changing to make it possible to attain knowledge of the real object. Spinoza had already said all this, and Marx may have been aware that he had. That is, however, of no importance. (We have an 1840 notebook of Marx's full of notes on Spinoza.)[18]

Spinoza said that the Big Dog, a glittering constellation, is one thing, and that a real dog, which does not glitter, is quite another; that the concept of a dog is one thing, and the dog that barks quite another. The concept of a dog does not bark.[19] A circle is one thing, and the idea of the circle is another and so on. Thus Spinoza distinguished between the real object (the *ideat* in his terminology) and the object of knowledge (the idea or the concept of this idea). We know that he did not establish a relation of adequation or reflection between these two objects, but a relation of *parallelism*, a subtler and more accurate solution. Marx went still further. Not only did he do away with the idea of the object in favour of the idea of a *process* of which such-and-such an object is never anything more than a moment, a link in a chain; he also abolished the difference, which he had noted, between the two objects. For him, there is immediate identity, *but in the process of knowledge*, between the object of knowledge and the real object. When we know a thing, the knowledge of this thing is the thing itself, known. It is in this sense that we should understand the use that Marx makes of the notion of 'economic category' in his discussion in *Capital* of the economic categories discovered by the economists of classical Political Economy. A category is at once the concept of something real (capital, wages, surplus value, commodities, money) and the thing itself. Marx's materialism is thus based, in the pseudo-'theory of knowledge', on monism. There is only one reality, only one process. It is, at one and the same time, a real process and a process of knowledge, and nothing else, and every dualism is idealist.

I remind the reader that what is involved here is a philosophical thesis, which produces no knowledge, but is intended to guide practice. Otherwise, we would be at a loss to understand the fact that Marx both acknowledges the existence of two objects, and also abolishes it. The truth is that Marx poses this thesis (as is the case for all theses) in order to oppose it to the idealist theses he is combating. He espouses some of their authors' arguments, but only in order to turn those arguments against them. Like Lenin, he 'bends the stick in the other direction' in order to straighten it out.[20]

But, it will be objected, is it not a different story when, rather than 'merely speculative' knowledge, we have to do with practical knowledge, which transforms the object in the process of knowing it or in order to know it? And is this not the general case, since every science, being experimental, puts its object, in the proper sense, 'to the question' [*torture*] (Kant) of its experimental set-up?[21] Do we ever see anything other than the effects of these deliberately induced transformations in the objects we claim to know?

This objection is not very serious, since we have already cleared all the space we need to refute it by introducing the concept of *process*. In the case of knowledge that transforms its object, we still have to do, appearances notwithstanding, with the distinction between the real object and the object of knowledge. The sole difference is that the nature of Generalities I and

Generalities III varies, but as a function of the variations affecting Generalities II. As for the real object, if it is transformed, it is transformed as a function of the action of Generalities II (the theory and its instruments), which, since it can be exactly measured, can be taken into account in assessing the relation of difference. Hence this relation of difference does not substantially change.

For the case to be radically different, the real object and, as well, the transformation to which it is subjected by the theory and instruments (Generalities II) would have to be completely unknown and unknowable; but that is absurd, and takes us far from science, into mysticism. Thus the hypothesis of knowledge that is not 'merely speculative' ultimately changes nothing at all about what the other example has taught us. In every case, we have to do with a process in which an agent intervenes: the specialist in the division of social and intellectual labour known as the researcher. It is, however, a process without a subject or an end, without a subject or an object, in which knowledge, while it presupposes real labour on this agent's part, is nevertheless identical with its object.

In fact, Marx, when he invoked the case of 'merely speculative' knowledge, was most certainly thinking of something quite different from the arguments of idealist philosophers of science, who refer to the transformation of objects in experiments which, they say, never allow us to perceive anything other than the experiments performed on the objects, not the objects themselves. For this whole idealist plea has only one objective: to show that the subject, at any rate, does not change, because he continues to be the one who produces and records changes in the object, and never knows anything but his own activity carried out on an object that he transforms in order to know it. We have examined the sophistry underlying this argument.

Marx, however, had a completely different idea in mind: knowledge that was not 'merely speculative', knowledge that aimed to transform its object and was capable of bringing this transformation about. Here [in the 1857 Introduction to *A Contribution to the Critique of Political Economy*] he is plainly referring to the kind of knowledge that makes revolutionary practice possible. He had already said so in the 'Theses on Feuerbach': in this practice, it is not just the object that is transformed, but the 'subject' (the agent) of the transformation as well.[22] Here the externality of the agent with respect to the object and the 'merely speculative' transformations of it (scientific transformations in the sense of experimentation in the natural sciences) ceases; the agent is now one of the components of the experimental set-up. And knowledge is now impossible if it does not take the whole conjuncture into account, including, consequently, the activity and transformation of the agent in the course of the transformation of the object. At the theoretical level, this means recognition of the conflictual nature of society and of the class theoretical position required to know a process of class struggle that is already under way and commands its own theory.

Should we therefore say that knowledge changes nothing in its object? No, it changes nothing in its object. But it adds something to a society's culture: superior knowledge of this object that is determined and determinable as a function of this knowledge. Observe, however, the way things happen. This knowledge that, in a first moment, seems to be distinct from its object, enters into it in a second moment, is integrated into it as knowledge *of this object*, as a property of it, as one of its properties. Knowledge of a property of the object thus becomes what it always was: a property of the object itself. This re-establishes the eternal identity, disturbed for a moment by the appearance of the distinction. And anyone who imagines that all this occurs in time, with a before and an after, is mistaken. Of course, there is a before and an after for the researcher; otherwise, we would not understand and he would not understand why he has to engage in all this work and this protracted research. But that by no means holds for the object. 'Just as before', as Marx puts it, the object subsists outside knowledge and possesses all its properties, except that they have not all been discovered yet. The object, however, could not care less about that. All it has to do is wait: it has its whole future behind it.

Marx said nothing else when, in a brief, enigmatic passage in *Capital*, he wrote that, basically, the theory of value had always existed, more or less consciously.[23] This is true, as anthropologists can testify: people have always known everything, about the world, and nature, and society, and above all, perhaps, about sex – with the minuscule difference that they have doubtless not always known that they knew it. Descartes, for example, knew this, and put his God to tremendous trouble to make him create, in a mighty effort of the will, eternal truths that were already eternal without him.[24] Spinoza knew this: he went so far as to write, as the good experimentalist [*expérimentaliste*] he was: 'we feel and experience [*expérimentons*] that we are eternal.'[25] And he wrote this about scientific knowledge. We are in pretty good company. You might as well admit it.

13

However far we have gone in our consideration of the questions philosophy asks about the theory of knowledge, we cannot fail to note that all these questions were asked on the basis of a categorical couple (subject/object) that has not, for its part, been questioned yet. What, then, is there to be said about this subject and object – to begin with, this object?

I leave aside the special meaning of object here, as that which unifies the data of perception or makes it possible to identify the experimental manifold. I am going to look beneath it for the deeper meaning haunting it: Being. I propose the following remark: it is not surprising that a 'gnoseology' should be completed by an 'ontology' that can even perfect it, according to certain philosophies. It may seem odd, after two centuries of critical philosophy, which have, since Kant, radically extirpated ontology from philosophy, to see this theme coming back into fashion. Yet Husserl is not very far from us: we have yet to finish translating him into French. A curious business! We thought that ontology, the science of Being as Being, belonged to the distant past of Aristotle and Saint Thomas; the great seventeenth-century classics, Descartes and Leibniz, had already, even while compromising with ontology, put a serious dent in it, and Kant had given it the *coup de grâce* with his rejection of Being and his theory of the phenomenon. But, lo and behold, it is headed back our way and, what is more, in two forms that refuse to take the least notice of each other: Heidegger's, itself oddly descended of Husserl, that critical philosopher; and in the form it takes in the interpretation advanced by Soviet philosophers and their emulators in every part of the world in which they have gained a foothold, an interpretation that claims, however incredible this may sound, to be faithful to 'Marxist philosophy'. Later, perhaps, we shall see the reason for this singular convergence or mysterious misunderstanding.

For now, let us go back to ontology's philosophical demands. Ontology's crucial question may be stated as follows: *Why is there something rather than nothing?* It will immediately be objected, with good reason, that this question is not really philosophical, but religious. However, before philosophy truly rid itself of religion, let us say with Kant (but did it completely rid itself of it then? – that is doubtful), it still thought in religion or, rather, religion still thought in it, dominating its thinking. That is why all the great religious dogmas (religion has its dogmas as philosophy has its theses): God, the creation, the incarnation, salvation, redemption, heaven, hell, evil, original sin, paradise lost, the perfection and omnipotence of God the creator, his glory, and even Christianity's angels and mysteries (the Eucharist, etc.: Descartes himself claimed to have invented a physics that made it possible to think the transformation of water into wine)[1] – that is why all these dogmas haunt philosophical thought, in forms that are only partly philosophical. This question well and truly figures among the great questions that philosophy inherits from religion: *Why is there something rather than nothing?* Being rather than Nothingness? And the philosophy of this period thinks, as we can see in Descartes, against the background of this extreme opposition: the opposition of Being and Nothingness, with man holding the middle ground, as Pascal too thought, along with, ultimately, all the other philosophers of the day except Spinoza.

Why, then, is there something rather than nothing? To this question, philosophy (quite like religion) offers no answer in the proper sense of the word. It offers illustrations and justifications instead. It shows, by way of example, that there *is* in fact something rather than nothing, hence that Being is and Nothingness is not, something that is obviously tautological. We have, however, been sufficiently forewarned about the tautological character of every philosophical question, even when it is taken from a dogma and transposed, not to be surprised by this by now. And, after all, adults and children ask very similar questions and come up with answers. The one about the ocean, for instance. How come the ocean doesn't overflow, when all the rain from the sky falls on it and untold rivers go pouring into it? The answer goes: for starters, there are big patches of sand on the sea floor, and they absorb a lot of water. Then there are fish of all sizes in the ocean. Like Spinoza said, the big ones eat the medium-sized ones, who eat the little ones:[2] that frees up lots of space. Finally, the ocean is teeming with an endless multitude of fish, the ones just mentioned, and they all go swimming around with their mouths open, which forces them to drink a tremendous amount of water. And since the water is salty, they're always thirsty. There you have a good question and a good answer. The philosophy of ontology can't match it. All it can say is that Being is, and that Being is because that's the way it is and that's all there is to it. Accomplished fact, in its utter speechlessness. One thinks of Hegel confronted by his mountains:

'So it is'; Kant confronted with what he called the *Faktum* (brute fact) of reason; and so many others whom it would be easy to name, beginning with Aristotle, who observes, 'look here, being is expressed in several senses', and he counts them and says 'that's the way it is' – and so on ad infinitum.[3]

It is not the uses to which we can put Being, what we can expect from it, that will ever teach us anything about its reason for being. For Being can be put to every use there is, although it has only a limited number of senses in Aristotle (the categories of language). One can make use of Being to commune with it in religious fusion or ecstasy, or even philosophical meditation (Heidegger); one can even, like Lachelier, find Being in the bole of a beautiful beech in the Forest of Fontainebleau, now a place of pilgrimage, or look for it, like Lequier, who did not know how to swim, in the sea at Palavas, from which he never returned, or look for it in a star singer, sportsman, or actor, or the face of a beloved woman or, again, that of a child. In such cases, however, one looks for it, even if one is Saint Jean de la Croix or Saint Teresa of Avila, only in order to find *oneself* – that is, to save oneself. One can also rely on Being to give direction to one's life or direct the lives of others towards ends in which one happens to have an interest; and if one should, perchance, be the leader of an army or a religion, or the leader of a state, a party, or both, this can produce rather satisfying results – although, when it comes to mobilizing souls, there are ways and means infinitely superior in their class to this ridiculous plaything known as being.

Philosophy does in fact make use of Being, but in a completely different way. The '*that is how it is*' which it utters as if it were an accomplished fact – a fact that, consequently, no longer need be accomplished – serves it as a basis and ground on which to plant all the visible beings in the world, inanimate, animate, or spiritual, in their characteristic existence and determinations. It is thus characteristic of Being to ground existence and the determination of existence. Being is a god of sorts, who, however, stands not in a relation of creation, hence of distance, with the world, but in a relation of presence. Being is presence, as Derrida has very ably shown, and has shown even with respect to Heidegger, whom he judges severely, but does not neglect. Being is being-there, *Dasein*, in Hegel's opinion as well as Heidegger's – in the literal sense, I mean, for the philosophical sense is not the same in the two philosophers. It is because Being is there, present, here and now, from all eternity, that there are finite, provisional, temporal beings, whom Heidegger calls 'beings' [*étants*] (thereby distinguishing ontology as the science or philosophy of Being from the ontic, the science or philosophy of 'beings'); and Heidegger rightly aspires to re-examining, in spirit and in truth, the whole 'history of Western philosophy', which he believes (wrongly, as we shall see), is, in its entirety, locked into the categories of the ontology founded by the Greeks, with Plato standing head and shoulders above the others (for this ontology itself pre-dates Plato, and Heidegger is right to look for it in the pre-Socratics). Thus it is because Being is there that beings exist (you, me, a cow, this or that science or historical event and so on). And it is because Being is what it is (omnipotent as well as omnipresent) that every being is determined as it is, and endowed with the capacity to determine other beings. Thus everything happens in Being, but under the 'law of Being'. We still do not know what that law is, apart from this double function of foundation.

On top of this double function, moreover, comes a third. It concerns *the end* of beings. It too is determined in them by Being, which possesses it in itself in advance, and can either reveal it to human beings (the miracles of religion or of history and nature) or hide it from them, in accordance with the secret design of its calculations and plans.

For we know nothing about Being: about its mode of foundation, mode of action, or the ends it pursues through beings – except that it is, founds, determines, and destines. That is not much, yet that is all. We know, in any case, that we know nothing about it; and that is invaluable knowledge, the *docta ignorantia* (learned ignorance) celebrated in the Middle Ages, when people's views of Being were, for atmospheric reasons, particularly foggy, so much so that certain mystics went about celebrating the dark night of Being as the supreme light, elaborating, to orthodox theology's dismay, what was called *negative theology* after Denys the Areopagite, who denied that we can give God the least human name without first negating it.[4] This smacked of revolt and revolution; it was something like the anti-psychiatry of the day. We cannot, in any case, deny these courageous men the merit of going all the way down a road only gingerly tread by others, faint-hearted souls who deemed themselves quite advanced for having taken a step or two down it.

At all events, there is here, in ontology's typical way of proceeding (whatever differences in meaning we may find between an Aristotle and a Heidegger, and these are very important), a demand that inevitably arises as soon as one puts a theory of knowledge into operation (or the other way around): one cannot but wonder about the nature of this object that is said to be known and, behind it, in the last instance, about the nature of the Being that sustains it in its existence, determines it, and assigns it an end. This demand can be more or less clearly perceived or conceived, and can be thwarted by the irruption of an unpredictable conjuncture; it has its logic nonetheless, which reproduces idealist philosophy's major theses. We already know some of them: the thesis of the foundational origin, here identical to Being, or the thesis of the identity of origin and end. Here they come into sharper focus, and more theses appear: among others, that of the primacy of meaning over existence, Being over beings, content [*fond*] over form, depth over surface, concealment over manifestation and, finally, paradox of paradoxes, the thesis of the primacy of Nothingness over Being, which is logical, after all, since it is clear that Nothingness must be before Being, if one may put it that way, for the existence of Being and its beginning to have meaning.

That is why every ontology – as can be seen not just in negative theology, but also in Heidegger and Sartre (who is more a critical philosopher than a philosopher of ontology) – is in the last instance haunted by a theory of Nothingness as the naked, unveiled truth of the theory of Being that ontology claims to forge. What can a theory of Nothingness – read: universal Nothingness – possibly signify or mean [*vouloir dire*], since, if this theory exists, then at least a little Being (the theory itself) exists, and Nothingness does not devour everything? Yes, what can it possibly mean? For we have already learnt that philosophy, which never means anything [*ne veut jamais rien dire*], nevertheless has a meaning and searches for it, and exists in this search itself. How are we to conceive of or imagine this Nothingness?

The old mythologies, and the religions as well, imagined it as an originary Chaos that was before the world came to be, and they imagined that this Chaos was an utter void or a dispersion of formless elements with no order. Nothingness is thus the originary matrix and originary matter (Plato says the *chora*)[5] of which everything was made when the demi-urge ordered the elements or the god created the world. This extreme example shows plainly that this spiritualist religious philosophy has a little materialism to its credit, since it acknowledges, in this way, a certain primacy of matter.

Nothingness can, however, be something quite different: no longer originary Chaos, but something else originary: that which, in nature, annihilates, says *no*, halts the course of things, refuses, and freely picks its way – in other words, man. From Descartes to Sartre, this view has been forcefully upheld by one whole tradition. Hegel, when he took it up, did so in order to invest it with a deeper meaning, by detaching Nothingness from the human subject in order to make it a moment of the dialectic of any process (without a subject), the moment of negativity, where the 'labour of the negative' takes place. This can also be the labour of the worker face-to-face with an idle master, or the labour of negative history, when it destroys the old forms to bring new ones into being.

Such is ontology's destiny: to begin with a theory of Being only to end up, necessarily, in a theory of Nothingness; hence to contradict itself, but to tarry in this contradiction, in which Hegel would surely see a new form of the 'labour of the negative' – Hegel, who said plainly enough what he thought of Being, which was, in his view, merely empty abstraction, and the emptiest of all abstractions, a word with no meaning at all, and thus nil, and thus identical to Nothingness. Hegel thereby sanctioned, in a philosophical theory that is, it must be admitted, one of a kind, the identity of Being and Nothingness that no ontology ever ceases to celebrate, despite itself or avowedly, depending on the case.

I beg the reader's pardon for discussing, in connection with the question of ontology, a case that is properly speaking trivial; but current events and the means of ideological pressure familiar to all of us leave me no choice. I am alluding to the interpretation of 'Marxist philosophy' in terms of 'gnoseology' and 'ontology' by a good number of[6] contemporary Soviet philosophers and their Western emulators. At the basis of this misinterpretation is, obviously, a total misunderstanding. These authors take the idealist thesis of the primacy of Being over beings and even of Being over thought – and also, as we have seen, of the primacy of Nothingness over Being, at the limit – to be identical to Marx's materialist thesis of the primacy of matter over thought. It will be objected that these are just minor terminological differences. That is not true: for when one mobilizes categories that are translated into the same terms at the literal level (for instance, in order to clarify this comparison or this confusion, the primacy of Being over thought), one must also bring the *system* of those categories into play, as we have seen. The meaning of any particular category can result only from this system, even if the category bears the same name in both cases.

In this imbroglio, it is the 'theory of knowledge' which allows us to clarify things. We saw at length that it is out of the question for Marxist materialism to admit the possibility of a theory of knowledge. The Soviet authors, however, begin by retreating on this point, and set about slapping together a 'Marxist theory' of knowledge, notwithstanding the texts, by Lenin as well as Marx, which rule this out or, at the very least, problematize it. Once this front has been abandoned, all of bourgeois idealist philosophy, in its ontological version, overruns the field and occupies it. It is not hard to reconstruct the whole of this mechanism, but it is ultimately uninteresting; anyone can see for himself what is what by reading the production of these authors or their local emulators. Much more interesting is the question: Why this misinterpretation? The first answer might run: they have moved away from Marx. But why? It will be said: out of dogmatism. But why? It will be said: because of the influence of bourgeois ideology, which has succeeded in investing Marxist philosophy from within (we have already experienced an example, the Second International's revisionism). That is already better as explanations go. But it will be asked: Why did those in the Marxist camp prove unable to withstand the influence of bourgeois ideology? A lack of vigilance? The answer is too subjective. We have to come round, therefore, to considering the social relations prevailing in the USSR, and we have to organize the series of approximate answers just given as a function of those social relations.

Yes, Marxism has 'disappeared' in the USSR; yes, bourgeois ideology largely holds sway there, disguised, for the time being, in Marxist terminology. The reason is that the USSR, although it is not a classic capitalist state,[7] is nevertheless not a socialist state either, although it claims to be. But, at all events, it is a state; and, like any other state, it needs the help and support of an ideology suited to the prevailing relation of forces in the class struggle. Marxist philosophy, interpreted as a gnoseology and an ontology, finally performs, and rather well – at its own level, of course – the role expected of it: because it took more than thirty years for Soviet philosophers to make up their minds at last to produce what was expected of them, what the state of the class struggle expected of them: this deformation of Marx's and Lenin's thought in philosophy. The fact that the product has been exported to foreign countries, like any other commodity, does not find its sole explanation in the contagion of ideas or the power of the Soviet state, and certainly not in the prestige of a philosophy of a rare mediocrity. It finds its explanation in the state of the class struggle in our countries, where the class struggle is waged, with the help of well-known practices, by Communist parties that need this philosophy in their turn in order to maintain their domination over their rank-and-file.

In this philosophy, what matters ideologically and politically is the ontological base. I said a moment ago that the only valid definition of Being is 'that's just the way Being is, and that's all there is to it'. The implication is that changing anything in the established order is prohibited, getting one's orders wrong is prohibited, disobeying one's orders is prohibited. We know that the idea that this pretension is based on nothing (on Nothingness) is not true, for the existence of classes and a class struggle in the USSR (in however atypical a form one likes) is not nothing. Rather, for those who rule and give the orders, it is important, in order to cut all protest short, to make it clear that because things are the way they are and that's all there is to it, there is nothing to go looking for behind the orders they give, no de facto or de jure justification to invoke or discuss: *all discussion is therefore out of order*. That is the meaning of the Nothingness that is identical to Being: there is nothing to discuss, because there is no reason for the decisions taken. Fact reigns supreme. One can put on kid-gloves and go looking for the de jure reasons for this reign of fact in a decorative gnoseology, but that's just for the sake of appearances: the die has been cast, and all the discourse about knowledge is just the discourse of the ignorant, as all the discourse about Being is just a discourse about Nothingness, and null and void. And those who take it into their heads to question these Facts are promptly reminded of the order of their duty, and of the Nothingness of their pretension, by the Nothingness of the courts and the prison administration, the administration of life (and death) that sees to inflicting on them a (be it recalled) 'state of the whole people' which, for its part, is mindful of its duties not just towards philosophy and humanity, but towards the ruling class as well.

Of course, these considerations do not exhaust the questions of ontology, which are infinite. For once we have posed the thesis of Being, we discover that its mechanism is a little more subtle than we have said. Being is not just 'that's the way it is'; this character takes the liberty of going into detail. He is not one of those people who say that 'the practical side of things will take care of itself': he goes out into the field and puts things in proper order, since, after all, the things are his. He establishes order in Being – read, in the ensemble of beings. He puts each in its place, one above the next, in accordance with a carefully conceived hierarchical order guaranteeing, between one being and the next, the organic bond required to ensure that their 'entente', far from threatening the head of the construction site, who is also the chief-of-state, consolidates his domination in the most peaceful possible form.

There we have the reason for the order of orders that we spoke of earlier, this taxonomy that has been haunting ontologizing Western thought since Aristotle and even Plato, the great classifiers, down to Leibniz and modern logical neo-positivism. This time, however, we have found in it the substantial satisfaction of knowing why this Order of orders exists and, therefore, why its orders do: because Being is. This time, this Order is at last founded, which is reassuring; for, earlier, it was unfortunately possible to wonder whether it was not fortuitous and accidental, after all. If tomorrow, as Hume asked himself, the sun failed to come up,[8] if my wife left me, if my workers went on strike, if my Algerians went back home, what a wretched shame it would be! Now we're sure of what we're about.

I know very well that you're going to reply: 'A lot of good that does us, because, Being or no Being, it all comes down to the same thing, since Hegel has very ably explained that Being is a lot of hot air.' But you are speaking for yourself, my friend, you who have a mind free of all prejudice or chock full of prejudice. Think of the others for just a second, those who have no prejudices or nothing but, and ask yourself whether it changes nothing about their lives, their convictions, or their servility to know that things are guaranteed, that that's the way it is and that's all there is to it, instead of finding themselves still in the void and, therefore, exposed to the temptation to change something about their lives.

Being, then, is Order, and is the ordering of beings grounded in Being and determined and assigned their destiny by Being. Of course, given the omnipotence of Being, this Order can be infinitely diverse.

It can be as *flat* as a sidewalk, like Cartesian space or a plain in the Beauce region, and extend to infinity. You know that our friend Descartes was logical enough to explain, in a day and age when the earth was no longer covered with forests, that a man lost in one need only make up his mind to walk straight on in any direction he liked in order to end up, perforce, in fields, where he would have a clear view of things.[9] What an advantage to have a flat Order for promenades in the countryside or flights from captivity!

Order, however, can be *round*. Kant had noticed this. But it wasn't just the roundness of the earth that brought it to his attention.[10] It was on account of private property. One couldn't, said Kant, extend it infinitely: since the earth was round, property-owners who settled alongside previously established property-owners would necessarily end up meeting the others at the poles, and then curtains! 'The end of the frontier' *à l'américaine*, no more totally free enterprise; nothing for it but to compromise, and then, lo and behold, the social contract is rapping at the door again, and physical possession along with it. Note that Kant had a fall-back different from this Round Order, because he had the star-spangled heavens above his head and the moral law in his heart: in sum, a Round Order rounded off by an above and an inside, if one may put it that way. Kant looked for the relationship between all three his whole life long, and thought he'd found it in the *Critique of Judgement*,[11] which Heidegger confirmed in his fashion.[12] Before Kant, however, there had been Rousseau, and after Kant, Hegel, who are both a great deal more interesting.

Rousseau too knew that the earth is round, by God! But, contrary to Descartes, he thought that in the beginning, in the days of the 'first state of nature', the earth had been completely covered with forests, with no clearings or open fields.[13] Thus there was no way to end up in the great open spaces of the plains by walking straight ahead, and likewise no way of arriving at the antipodes, like Kant, and then returning to one's starting point by following one's nose (this is a precept of moral law, but it also holds for voyages around the world in 1789 days: this date left a deep impression on Kant, who didn't churn anything out that day). The man of 'the state of primal nature', who roamed through the forests without even being aware that they *were* forests, since he'd never seen and could never see anything else, above all not the plain, and had only just barely glimpsed the sky, and who never encountered anyone – this man had, literally, no chance of ever getting out of the woods. This was plainly Rousseau's opinion, for he wrote: without an accident of the ecliptic, things would never have changed.[14] It follows that they changed because of this accident or others (collapsing continents, upwelling islands, and the like), which forced humanity to emerge from this fabulous, comfortable mindlessness; and since the seasons had emerged from it as well, he had to go to work clearing the forests to grow a little wheat and make some dough, with the result that the whole dialectic was set in motion.

However, this time, at least, it was clear why Descartes had told us his story about the man who can walk straight through the forest: it's because it's ringed round by cleared fields. Naturally, things took the course, if in somewhat modified form, that Kant was to discuss: the earth is round, private property is to blame; property is private, blame the earth, which is round. A round order, once again, but with the difference, this time, that this round order that divides the earth up into private properties that have limits, but whose value can go to infinity, rests on a base of bloody disorders, unless someone such as Machiavelli or Hobbes, Marx or Rousseau himself, incidentally, or even Kant, who talks about 'unsociable sociability', comes along to explain to us that this disorder has its own order, which we can know: the proof is that they explain it to us in terms of human passions, which are oblivious to the laws of reason and morality.[15]

What disorder there is in this Order, then! We might well ask whether the affirmation of this Order, flat, round, or whatever you like, is not there in trompe-l'œil, to make people (those who must submit to this Order, including you, my friend) believe that this Order exists or, let us say, should exist so that order may reign, the simple order (the two hundred families are not overly demanding) of the (poorly) established order, which, because it is poorly established, must be consolidated by a *supplement of order*. But when you strike down these Cartesian paths, since they go somewhere (they're not Heideggerian, not *these* paths!), beware of a backlash, for you smack a little too heavily of heresy. This leads not to Swann's way, but to Marx's.

In Hegel, things are more radical. Order is round, no problem there, since everything is a circle, and the Whole is a circle of circles and so on, ad infinitum. Better, there is no longer this opposition between Kant's and Rousseau's round Order (the earth is round) and that other dimension, which has no curve to it, but has to do with high and low: the star-spangled heavens and the moral law in Kant's vertical dualism. Hegel is consistent. There's no getting out of the roundness of a circle or sphere once you're in it. Are you in the world? You want to add the Heavens to it? Fine: you're in this round world, then, rounded off by the Heavens above the roof, and also by the moral law with which you've clearly been impregnated, since it's inside you. We are, therefore, in the absolute sphere. How do we get out of it? It's impossible to get out of it.[16] As a matter of fact, the question of getting out of it makes no sense, since it's impossible; it's a 'verbal word', as they say at the *Canard enchaîné*,[17] the philosophical level of which is underrated. One is where one is, and nowhere else. That may well be, you will say, on account of the fences, the barriers, the limits, the barbed wire, the borders, and the boundary-stones. But beyond the boundary-stones is the plain; all prisoners, even if they haven't run away, are aware of that. Under the paving-stones is the sand, said the rebellious dreamers of May 1968.

No, says Hegel; there is nothing beyond the limits, for a simple reason: *there are no limits*. Otherwise, you lapse back into the inanities of a Kant, who, like Descartes with his forest, never stops thinking in the category of limits. Besides, you know very well what the meaning of this category of the limits is in Kant. Popular wisdom puts it crudely: 'once people have crossed the limits, they know no bounds', which is the sort of thing that all chiefs-of-state and of Churches, of political parties, unions, and families like to say. That made a lot of sense to Kant, who was none of the above, but had a damned good sense of his secular responsibilities. He had a nice example at the ready for you, fresh with freshly spilt blood: the Terror in France. Not that Hegel was for the Terror, by no means; but he was for logic, after all, and that lent force to his remark that there are no limits, for, otherwise, aberration knows no bounds. If there are no limits, it is, firstly, because one is no longer in the finite, as Kant would have it, but in the infinite. Secondly, it is because *the outside isn't outside, but inside*; you have to look for and find your own limits in yourself, finite-infinite man, for they're nowhere but inside you. If there's no outside because it's inside, nothing more need be said.

Nothing, except the question that has not ceased to haunt all philosophy since Hegel: If there is neither outside nor limits, then why continue to talk about limits, and the circle of circles, and the round Order?

We must accordingly find the means, and it is not easy, to think, simultaneously, the Order which is round, and thus limited by its curve, and the not-outside, that is, the absence of curves and limits. A limit that is, in sum, a non-limit, a circle that is a circle, but with no outside. One thinks of Rousseau again, of those islands that have surged up out of the sea and are connected to no other land mass;[18] one thinks of those scientific continents that have surged up in the sea of practical ignorance. One thinks of the appearance of a saint in a world torn asunder by egoism: one thinks of the impossible love that Géraldy sings: 'if you loved me, if I loved you, how I would love you!'; one thinks of a chief-of-state who would put cultivating the family's eggplants in command, as Cato did; one thinks of a scientist who would look for women with sorrel-shaped ears, a bird that would make red-currant jam on André Breton's head, and what else? We all know enough about such things to know, in any case, that this question is damned serious, that it may even be the question of questions, and that we must treat it as it deserves, even if it is handed to us on a platter by, first and foremost, our friends the idealist philosophers.

Heidegger has his idea about this question, in the sense that he was the first, together with logical neo-positivism, to take it seriously. But logical neo-positivism, as befits a respectable ontology, has a way of treating this question that is by no means encouraging. It says – and it does so despite all the respect it has for set theory (which is deeply interested in the question of the limit, for when a vase is full, everybody knows that a drop is enough to make it overflow)[19] – that it does not want to hear anything about the limit, that that is a religious, metaphysical, psychoanalytical, and Marxist question (wham!), and that it is interested in *the facts*. And that that is the way it is and that's all there is to it (a familiar phrase). And if you don't like it, you can go pick daisies or take a trip to the moon. It adds that it's a crying shame to be so poorly understood and held in such contempt by the philosophers of our day, but that, given the universal decadence (it is not very easy to see where it is, in these times of rising productivity and the liberation of women and homosexuals), it's the usual thing, after all, and that it's enough to wait and, even if things fail to sort themselves out, God will recognize his own (pardon! 'God' is a figure of speech, for we don't believe in him: too bad).

Yes, Heidegger is far more interesting, for he takes the question into account and wonders how to settle it. He gets out of trouble by clouding the issue, erasing the limit, and referring it, simultaneously, to its short-of and its beyond, the result being a language that is all but impossible to read, for just try to go and say these things clearly! In sum, he acknowledges the issue, but thrashes around in rather than resolving it, since, instead of maintaining a healthy balance, he assigns Being primacy over beings, like the good spiritualist that he has basically continued to be. Unfortunately, I cannot, in a few words, be any clearer about this thought that has won a reputation for profundity by dint of obscurity, and I prefer to move on, without delay, to the one who has clarified all this and provisionally settled the question, and in very comprehensible terms at that: my friend Jacques Derrida.[20]

Derrida has very convincingly shown that we must to look to the *margin* for the answer to the question of a limit that is not a limit.[21] Everybody knows what a margin is: there is one on this very page, an empty space alongside a full one. You would think that fullness could not do without emptiness, and the other way around. This presupposes a limit between the two, of course, but a limit that is not an Order or, at any rate, does not derive from an Order, since we can vary the margin, and thus the limit. It makes no difference whether the margin is two centimetres wide, or three; it's enough to come to an agreement with the compositor, and you're all set. Derrida has seen, then, that this 'play' matters to the margin, quite as much as the margin matters to the limit. But this 'play' of course changes everything, since it is free, not constrained; thus it frees itself and frees us of all Order, flat or round, monist or dualist, or even twisted.

This margin is now beginning to sustain our hopes, after being subjected to our despair. For what is in the margin is marginal: the mad, children, deviants, philosophers, the mentally ill, deranged or normal artists, the abnormal and so on. And it turns out that, once normality has been demystified (Canguilhem has done a great deal to help us understand this,[22] after Spinoza and Nietzsche), one suddenly realizes that interesting things go on in the vicinity of the margin: on the margin of official society, where the exploited workers and the immigrant workers are, together with children, from whose mouths the truth has long come, and artists, from the greatest to the humblest, with Breton and his friends in-between, and the poor in spirit when they are saints, even if they don't know it, and the mad, and certain prisoners, Soviet and Latin American prisoners in particular and so on. The margin is also the beach, the one on which everyone will alight to enjoy the sun after we have at last crossed this terrible river of socialism in the boat of the dictatorship of the proletariat. And then we shall have the free reign of the margin on the beach of communism: there will be no more written texts, no more written right, no more written law, no more written orders, no more writing, nothing but living traces, traces of the spoken word, exchanges of words and goods without money, without (written) accounts, exchanges of looks and voices,[23] of love or hate, with no dishonest descriptions of the merchandise. This will be the end of the dictatorship of writing, the end of the dictatorship of language, the reign of the universal margin and the universal family, I tell you, the reign of whiteness, which one will see in the whites of people's eyes, the universal reign of whites, that is, of the white race, but all the races will be white [*blanc*], that is, all colours, and only the wise guys [*blancs-becs*, literally, white beaks] will have to watch their behaviour, unless they turn into Prince Charmings [*merles blancs*, literally, white blackbirds]. What is more, all blackbirds will be white: black will be suppressed, along with all the mourning and suffering it is possible to avoid.

What is encouraging – for I know you, you're going to say I'm raving – is that the margin is no utopia; it exists today, well and truly, in reality. Witness not just Derrida's theory, but the existence of all the marginal sorts, in the official statistics or not. It exists and is developing in every country – yes, in every country, even the USSR.[24] I shall explain that to you some day;

unfortunately, I don't have the time today. If that isn't a way of saying that Derrida hasn't missed the mark in putting the question of the margin[25] in the command post![26] The interest of Derrida's research resides in the demonstration that philosophy and politics are, in a certain regard, the same thing. The fact that a theory of the margin such as his leads straight to an encounter with the theory of politics[27] and, from a certain angle, anticipates communism, proves this, quite obviously, with no need for comment.

It must nevertheless be said that, from the theoretical standpoint, this reflection on the limit introduced by the notion of the margin takes some liberty, serious liberty, with Forms tout court: not just those of the geometry we know, the flat or the round, but the (differential) limit or, again, the twisted (the Möbius strip dear to Lacan),[28] or even the soft and the viscous, with which the physics of solids has begun to concern itself, after Sartre.[29] It must be said that, when it comes to Forms, all the known sciences, especially since falling to their knees before Mathematical Logic, are woefully impoverished in the face of the forms observable in human relations, in 'inter-subjectivity' or the unconscious, where the Formless [*l'Informe*] of fantasies holds sway. As a rule, however, the sciences do not care to know anything about all that; it diverts them from the Forms in which they think their own affairs – which are, consequently, the Forms that suit them.

This does not mean, however, that the sciences have not invented surprising Forms in their turn, beginning with Newton's action at a distance (the attraction one planet exerts on another and, generalizing, that one body exerts on another, whence gravity, the tides and so on), which wrought no little havoc with the old Forms in which thought had gone on since Aristotle: the distinction between *natural motion*, thanks to which a body tends towards its place (a stone towards the bottom, smoke towards the top) or a man towards his (a slave towards the bottom, a prince or a man of means towards the top), and *violent motion*, which counters natural motion with an unexpected impulsion, thanks to which it is possible to shoot arrows or cannonballs that kill the enemy; thanks to which, praise the Lord, it is also possible to force slaves, who might otherwise believe that they are free men, to submit.

This notion of action at a distance, which Einstein's physics and the modern physics of particles have at once abandoned and renewed, is not – would you believe it? – without interest for philosophy, because philosophy, remember, only ever acts within philosophy, acting in the world outside only on condition that it act only in philosophy. This, however, is not the place to pursue the present enquiry, for we would risk – however great the progress the so-called natural sciences have made in the way of creating novel forms – running up against the formlessness [*l'informel*] that reigns not just in the human unconscious (which ignores – would you believe it? – the principle of contradiction!), but also in certain margins of political, aesthetic, familial, moral, and even (my word, where will it all end?) religious practice. We shall, therefore, leave this chapter unfinished, sure that the work of the sciences, the reflections of the philosophers, and the imagination of artists and politicians will know how to pursue it and make it more precise.

14

The time has come to discuss another category that has been waiting for us kindly to concern ourselves with it, since we have summoned it to appear before the 'Tribunal' of our limited reason together with the object. I mean the subject, S.

Obviously – we have already realized this about the object, which we have evoked by way of its truth, namely Being – these categories are of interest not just to the theory of knowledge, but to philosophy as a whole. It is in this spirit that we shall say a few words on the Subject.

The subject can be what one is talking about even when one talks about the object. At all events, the subject is then *identified*. The subject can be the one who speaks and says 'I', as he says 'you' to an interlocutor who is present and 'he' of a third party who is impersonal and absent. 'He is the one who is absent': the absent person, the impersonal person, as Benveniste very nicely puts it.[1] This is a way of saying that language, especially verbs, cannot be employed without identification, hence without the *identity* of *subjects*, which designate the one who speaks, the one to whom one speaks, and the one of whom one speaks, in the singular and plural. Identification, identity: it is plainly I, it is plainly you, it is plainly he; there can be no question of an error about who is who. Otherwise, all discourse would be impossible, no reality would be identifiable, and nothing would be identical with itself. Nothing would be one, *this* one.

There we have what the subject adds to Being: it is plainly he, not another, this individual who is such because he cannot be cut in half. Thus Hegel tells the story of Solomon rendering a judgement without appeal in the case of two women both claiming to be the mother of the same child: since each of them says that the child is hers, let it be cut in half! This made them cry out in horror, for the concept of the individual, as the word suggests, cannot be divided and is stronger than any putative property that would divide or fragment it. We have to go back to what is prior to [*en deçà de*] every subject, the unconscious, in order to acknowledge, as Freud had said and as Melanie Klein showed with respect to very young infants,[2] that there exist fantasies of partial objects, hence that fragmentation can be a form of existence, and that the non-division [*l'indivis*] of the subject presupposes this primordial fragmentation as that which it must go beyond in the Oedipus complex in order to attain to the existence of the subject: one and indivisible, like the Republic or God. For the fact is that, in philosophy as well as politics, all division is deadly.

It is plainly he, not someone else, and he is one and indivisible: such is the subject, in principle. Thus it is the subject that makes it possible to identify every object or reality as being identical to itself in space and time. The subject is, then, the self (it is plainly he, not another), that which Hegel calls the *Selbst*, capable of saying 'it is plainly I, not another', one and self-identical, identity being reflection of the one upon itself as subject.

This category of the subject (which we are defining by its philosophical function), even when it does not have the same name it does in our language – which is terribly contaminated by bourgeois legal ideology, we shall see why – even when it has a different name, is obviously indispensable to every philosophy, whether it adopts this category or rejects it.

For how is one to proceed, once Being has been posited, to bring it to manifest itself in such-and-such forms, one and indivisible, and capable, if they could speak, of saying: yes, it is definitely I, I am indeed this stone, this dog and so on (for we can count on beings endowed with the power of speech, with the reservation that, inasmuch as they can speak, they can also lie, that is, not just be deceived, but also deceive) – how is one to proceed once Being has been posited, if not by positing the subject or its equivalent in order to think particular beings in their *individuality* and *identity*?

Thus it is that Plato – to take just a few examples (for examples abound) – proposed the theory of participation.[3] Every concrete, self-identical individual exists only through participation in the idea that is its idea: a beautiful boy, a beautiful girl are beautiful only through participation in the idea of the beautiful. That, however, is not enough, for such participation confers only the generality of beauty on them, not the singularity of the existence of subjects. At this point, Plato imagines his theory of the *mixture* [*mélange*], with mixing paradoxically founding the individual distinction between subjects in order to account for even their most singular individuality.[4] What is combined in this way to constitute such singularity? 'Kinds of being' (the *Sophist*), being and not-being, the general and the particular, the beautiful and the ugly, the same and the other and so on: kinds of being that anticipate Aristotle's celebrated categories.

For Aristotle realized that Platonic theory was not just contradictory (because the mixture is intended to found, and thus to guarantee, the not-mixed, distinction, the subject's singularity), but was also incapable of producing the intended result: it is not by combining general ideas, even ad infinitum, that you will ever reach *concrete singularity*, the singularity of 'it's plainly he, not someone else'.[5] Aristotle accordingly set about analysing matters the other way around: rather than starting out from the Ideas, that is, postulating that there corresponds, to every concrete being, a pure idea that confers existence and determinacy on it (rather than starting, in some sort, from Being conceived as an absolute, unequivocal, full and complete reality), he started out from the concrete, from that which anyone can see and touch here and now, and store in his memory in order to subject it to reflection. That is why Aristotle is rightly regarded as the father of empiricism, which we will discuss later.

Analysing real things this way, Aristotle discovered that they were multiple and distinct, ad infinitum, yet that, in this Being that was their *existence* (the first sense of Being), they displayed not forms, but singular modalities common to all of them: quantity, quality, time, space, place, duration and so on: other senses of Being. Aristotle was surprised to discover, unlike Plato, that there was a *finite* number of these modalities, a finite number that Kant would later adopt,[6] to Hegel's profound indignation. Aristotle called these modalities *categories*[7] (the word is not used in our sense here, although the two senses are related). It was by conjoining the Being of existence and, at the same time, the combination of the relevant modalities of the Being of the categories ('Being is expressed in several senses'), while basically identifying the philosophical categories of being with the linguistic categories of being (the modalities of the declinations and conjugations), that Aristotle believed he had attained the result that Plato had failed to: that he had attained, at last, *the singularity of the existing subject*.

Yet Aristotle too remained in the abstraction of generality, going so far as to declare that there 'is no science of the individual'.[8] For, if you grant that a subject exists, agreed: you have endowed it with Being and thought it under Being. If, in addition, you say that it exists in the modality of quantity, quality, place and so on, agreed: you have specified the modality of this existence. But what guarantees that there does not exist a considerable number of subjects all falling under your combination of categories? Above all, what guarantees that you have attained these subjects' or this subject's intimate *essence*, if what is in question is a singular subject, such as the sun (the only member of its species) or Socrates (irreplaceable, since, after his death, only memory and regret remain)?

Aristotle tries to muddle his way through this contradiction, which he has himself precipitated, with the help of a strange theory that is at once a theory of substance, essence, and individuality. He begins by forging a theory of *substance*, for there must clearly be a subject under the attributes with which the categories affect this or that determinate being: a *hypokeimenon*,[9] something which, literally, 'is stretched out underneath' – a 'support', as Marx will put it in *Capital*.[10] But to say so is still general. Doubtless, it makes it possible to attribute determinations to a subject, to substance. That, quite simply, allows us to talk (an activity that the sophisms of Aristotle's adversaries, who are criticized throughout his work, literally prohibited people from engaging in), and not just to talk, but (for Aristotle is not a nominalist) to attribute real attributes to real beings with words.

Nothing about all this, however, qualifies *substance as subject*. A theory of *essence* must therefore be added to the theory of substance. The most interesting thing is doubtless that Aristotle, from the moment he shifts to the theory of essence, mobilizes the same category, the same word, *ousia*, to designate both essence and substance, which is now no longer the *hypokeimenon*, 'that which is stretched out underneath', the 'base' or 'support'.[11] The reason is that *ousia* attests to another ambition: to succeed in saying what specifically constitutes such-and-such a being and is 'clearly that being's own, individual, essence, not another'. Thus we find, in Aristotle, an elaborate theory of essence which leads us to believe that the goal has been reached and that we now have a definition of the *subject by its essence*. That, however, would be too simple, for essence is still a general notion that is applicable to any being, and the requirement that this essence be such-and-such a being's individual essence is itself general.

That is why Aristotle, despairing, but lucid, goes back to work, and asks himself what *individualizes the subject* (read, here: individualizes both in being and in its definition, since the two theories, of being and of definition, are always combined in Aristotle). He gives, naturally, several different answers, because he is stuck: what individualizes is now *matter* (but what is matter? – matter is ambiguous in Aristotle, who, a few vague, passing impulses notwithstanding, is no materialist), now *accident*, and now *form*.[12]

Is there any need to translate these expressions into ordinary language? If *matter* individualizes, this means not just that such-and-such a variety of matter defines a particular rock, animal, or human being, but also the singular disposition of this matter (that a particular dog has red fur, a particular person has a long nose and so on) and, as well, the time and place of its existence (the dog descended of my bitch, the baker's wife, the mother of my children, the president of the Republic in 1976). If *accident* individualizes, this means, to confine ourselves to the example of human beings, that being cross-eyed made the woman whom Descartes loved what she was, that stuttering defined Jouvet, that limping defined Lesage's devil, that sleeping whenever he wanted to defined Napoleon, that sleeping all the time defined Kutuzov and so on.[13] Finally, if *form* individualizes (Aristotle hangs all his dashed hopes on form, for form is the highest cause and the one that most closely espouses its object), this means that *the end* or goal or destination defines the subject's individuality – the subject's individual end, given that, in particular circumstances, and although 'every graveyard is filled with irreplaceable people', individuals are not interchangeable (as everyone knows perfectly well: I is not you, my wife, thank God, is not me, Aristotle could not be replaced by anyone, Alexander the Great even less) and the world is made up of beings 'whom one will never see twice',[14] whom we must, therefore, either love or eliminate.

When Aristotle speaks of *final form* [*forme-fin*], he does not mean function, because every function can be fulfilled by any functionary at all (one need only recruit him). It is, rather, a question of finality, an irreplaceable finality, for the world is made in such a way that one place cannot be occupied by two beings, that two people cannot sit on the same chair unless one takes the place occupied by the other and literally throws him out, something that is contrary to nature, *physis*, which finally steps in to attempt theoretically to plug the holes in this lacunary system.

Yes, there is a nature (sublunary nature, the here below; the moon and stars are exempt from change, because they go round and round in circles,[15] whereas animals and people are condemned to being unable to go round in circles, which is why they are mortal). Yes, there is a nature, and this nature is an order, the Order of orders, which assigns each individual being its place and function in its organized whole. It is nature which makes some people 'slaves by nature'[16] and sees to it that they will remain slaves for as long as 'the shuttles do not turn (round and round) all by themselves'.[17] It is nature which sees to it that there are chiefs-of-state by nature and, naturally, philosophers by nature to elaborate the theory of this Nature, which is terribly diplomatic in its silence. But, thank God, the philosopher speaks for it, so that everyone accepts the place imposed on him and everything runs smoothly – yes, runs smoothly, because one sees, when one makes the final tally, that this movement and this change that do not run smoothly *do* run smoothly, and that the final tally is always the same. The history of political constitutions proves it: they always go through the same phases, monarchy, republic, tyranny. Aristotle was familiar with heaps of constitutions, having counselled kings and chiefs-of-state on the basis of a theory invariably confirmed by events, barring one or two exceptions, among them the one that saw Aristotle ending up banned without leaving Athens. For the fact is that there are exceptions in nature, although nature does 'nothing in vain' and 'makes no leaps'. These exceptions are, precisely, *monsters*, the theory of which we also find in Aristotle, who was honest and never passed one up (never passed up an occasion, that is: this man also forged a theory of the occasion).

That, then, is how an intelligent person tries to muddle his way through a theory of the subject when it is underpinned by a theory of being and a theory of essence. It can be seen that he did not succeed in formulating a theory of this 'species of individual' Hegel ironically discusses: the subject. All indications are – to judge by the number of bad apples [*mauvais sujets*: literally, bad subjects] haunting his work, from slaves unwilling to accept that that is what they are, through statesmen who are carried away by ambition or do not accept the destiny assigned them by nature, or the bad philosophers known as the Sophists who are unwilling to call a spade a spade, to the passions unwilling to abide by the 'Golden Mean' – all indications are that it was not possible to formulate such a theory on this theoretical basis.

Aristotle, however, consoled himself with the thought that there exists, somewhere, a Being that is the individual par excellence, purified of all matter and all accident, a *Being that is pure form* and far superior to the sun – that individual with the drawback of being nothing but matter (subtle fire) – because he is pure intelligence: God. To avoid getting tangled up in all of Aristotle's problems, this God, far from thinking the world (now there's an adventure for you!), is content to think himself, to be thought that thinks itself, *noesis noeseos*.[18] That way, he has no worries. And, being thought, he contents himself with contemplating both lunary and sublunary nature from afar, and acting on it at a distance (already!) like the good philosopher he is, since he is nature's *telos* and, consequently, exerts (already!) a beneficial power of attraction over it. This is a way, to be sure, of dispensing with God, something that gave Aristotle a reputation for being a materialist, which Averroes systematized among the Arab philosophers in Spain, to the indignation of Saint Thomas, who fought him without respite.[19] But it is also a way of placing God off to one side, far from all opposition, as the supreme category that philosophy needs, despite all, in order to think what it thinks: the world and its own failures. And it is also – this is what is terribly concrete – a way of guaranteeing 'Nature', that is to say, the established order: the order of already acquired knowledge, of course, even if it had to be developed (Aristotle founded the first CNRS[20] in history), but, as well, the social and political order, which desperately needed guarantees in a day and age in which the class struggle kept producing, unpredictably, coups d'état and social upheavals.

15

I would here like to make a simple remark in passing. It is that a true philosopher such as Aristotle thinks, and thinks in a consistent way, on the basis of his philosophical presuppositions. The philosopher is not a man who seizes on the fly whatever presents itself to him. In his fashion, he 'puts to the question' not nature, but his own questions, and carries them to their conclusions. In carrying them to their conclusions, when he is an idealist (the case of materialism will be examined later), he keeps butting up against difficulties engendered by the imaginary nature of his presuppositions and questions and contradicted by the facts of experience. He responds to these difficulties by devising theories that are so many flights to the front, transposing a previously unresolved question into a new one that is insoluble in its turn; and he continues this way until, finally, in order to resolve all the contradictions left in suspense and the contradictory theories of them, he finally goes back home, that is, returns to his point of departure, unawares, of course: to the idea of Being that he pretended to question. In so doing, however, he adds to Being, as an attribute, the tremendous effort of thought that he has made. That is why Being becomes thought, and thought that thinks itself: in other words, an incarnation of the philosopher himself, who produces all of the laboured discourse that he does in order to provide his readers and those they may be able to influence with a guarantee that the natural order, that is, the established order, the social and political order, is 'in conformity with Nature', in other words, is good, and that it would be a crime to tamper with it.

It will be said that this tremendous effort is vain because it is tautological. That is not true. For, as he advances, by asking this or that question, the philosopher brushes up against real problems, unbeknownst to himself. Better, he forges theoretical categories and concepts to help pose these scientific problems and, at the same time, to resolve them. The history of philosophy provides striking proof of this. The fact that Aristotle conceived of the category of action at a distance twenty centuries before Newton and, twenty-two centuries before Freud, conceived of the category of the unmoved mover, which roughly sums up the psychoanalyst's position, shows this rather spectacularly. A Czech mathematician has just explained, for instance, that there are things in Aristotle that anticipate non-Euclidean geometries (this is not surprising in itself, since Aristotle's theory of place is linked to being, not the space of Euclidean geometry). To confine ourselves to less spectacular, more modest examples, we know very well that the categories of substance and essence, which Aristotle rather univocally established in their place in idealist philosophy, dominated all thinking down to the late eighteenth century, not just in philosophy, but in the sciences as well.

We had to make this remark to show in what sense (not only in the social and political field, where this is patent, but in philosophy and the sciences as well) philosophy presents the paradox of being both utterly nugatory, as imaginary speculation, and also concretely quite useful. And I am talking about the most difficult case here, that of idealism, for matters appear more plainly in the case of materialism, since these functions are much more conscious. This explains, among other things, why scientists (and even mathematicians) could not care less about philosophy and seem to manage quite well without it. They consider it to be a superfluous game, although in fact and, of course, without being aware of this, they cannot elude it. It can be an obstacle for them, or an unperceived resource: at all events, it exists in the field of their theoretical practice and plays a more or less important part there, depending on the conjuncture. The fact that they do not suspect it obviously changes nothing about the matter. This would not be the first case of men and scientists being driven by a necessity that they experience as their own freedom, when it is in fact leading them around by the nose. How and how far? We shall see that elsewhere.

16

I cannot turn from Aristotle to bourgeois idealist theories of the subject without pausing over a philosophical event of great importance that clashes with the idealist tradition. It owes its existence to the Stoics and Epicurus.

With them came a philosophical revolution that directly concerns the arduous constitution of materialism. For the Stoics (I am not proceeding chronologically) elaborated an astonishing Logic that did away with the presuppositions of the logic of Being.[1] It has, for this reason, fascinated modern logicians (neo-positivist or not, that hardly matters here). The Stoics chose not to subsume (subordinate) beings and facts under pre-existing categories. They refused, in sum, to begin with the origin and Being. They dared to begin with nothing: with the *absence of meaning* [*ce rien de sens*] known, precisely, as the facts.

Their way of proceeding might be summed up, in its entirety, in one short phrase: 'if . . . then.' If human beings are mortal, then there is no future life; we must, therefore, try to find happiness here below; we must, therefore, struggle to achieve it in the form in which it is possible (for the Stoics, ataraxy and impassibility, which made sense in a world dominated by appalling class struggles and wars) and so on. In sum, the Stoics started out from the facts, studied them, and drew from them the consequences that they contained, without adding anything else. We have become accustomed to this theory and practice in our experimental sciences. We should, however, take the measure of its revolutionary import. No longer did Ideas precede the world as its model, dominate it thanks to their power, and conduct it towards its necessary end. No longer was a definition of the individual subject to be sought by way of substance and essence.

There is just one world (but an infinite number of worlds is possible, and this hypothesis of an infinity means just one thing: it brings out the contingency of all worlds and, consequently, of ours), and this world has neither origin nor end. Men live in it with what they perceive of it and do in it as their sole horizon, and they have to cope with this wretchedness one way or another, with no hope that a god or a master will ever rescue them from their confusion and finitude. That does not prevent them from living, adding to their stock of knowledge by virtue of the principle 'if ... then', or acting in a way that is consistent with this conclusion [*en conséquence de cette conséquence*], but they can hope for nothing from either Nature, which exists, or the gods, who, if they exist, are perfectly impassible. That is how the Stoics dealt with the gods: by exiling them, the way the new tyrants exiled their opponents. An excellent policy, and one which averts bloodshed, as long as one is certain that one's opponents will never regain sufficient strength to set back out on the conquest of power. Weak gods are convenient. This simple idea would give rise, in due course, to phenomenal developments in the sciences and politics, furnishing weapons against religion and despotism as well.

Epicurus went infinitely further.[2] He did not content himself with indicating, by way of the hypothesis of a plurality of worlds, the contingency of ours; he went into detail to show contingency at work by thinking it. He did not set out from an origin, either (which is always an origin of meaning and end: the truth of things in its entirety is wholly contained in the origin, as is, together with their truth, their necessary ends, that is, their destination and, consequently, each individual's role in the state). He set out from a strange 'fact', inspired by Democritus: the fact that, from all eternity (for the world is eternal, a materialist thesis *par excellence*), the world has been composed of atoms, indivisible corporeal particles (perfect because indivisible individuals: this settles part of the question of the subject) falling parallel to each other in the void like raindrops. We find the image of the rain in Lucretius's Epicurean poem *On the Nature of Things*.[3] On this hypothesis, obviously, nothing happens. It is important that nothing happen before all beginning, hence that there reign the Nothingness of events [*le Néant d'événements*], but not the Nothingness of matter, just as it is important that this matter be not formless, but very sharply defined, inasmuch as it is made up of perfectly similar atoms that are subject to gravity in the void and ready, should the occasion ever offer, for the event. Thus, for the world to be, nothing must happen before its beginning, yet all the matter suitable for forming it must exist; otherwise, we would be squarely in idealism. How, then, can the world begin? It can do so thanks to a property of the atoms, *declination or swerve* (the 'clinamen'), which enables them to deviate imperceptibly (by an infinitesimal difference) from the straight line of their fall. When that happens, the deviant atom necessarily encounters the one next to it. From this we see that, according to Epicurus, it is *deviance* or deviation that is at the beginning of the world: deviation, not the norm. This constitutes a radical critique of all norms, logical, legal, moral, political, or religious; it sweeps the stage of the world clear of all such prejudices, and lets things come about by the necessity of deviation and aggregation.

In fact, the different atoms, encountering each other and aggregating, produce the singular entities that we know and that constitute our world, the only one we know. Differences in aggregation produce differences in constitution, form and appearance. This resolves the question of the individual subject in a simple way. The crucial point in this theory, apart from the thesis of deviation-deviance, concerns *the encounter*, which is the developed concept of contingency. For nothing pre-destines any particular atom to encounter any other particular atom, and yet it is from this contingent encounter, which takes place in matter and has matter as its principle, that everything is produced. With the thesis of the encounter, Epicurus introduced into philosophy an idea of phenomenal importance that has hardly been consciously perceived until now, except by Machiavelli, Spinoza and Marx. That everything is an encounter, of either elementary particles or composite bodies and subjects; that every encounter takes place under the domination of [*sous*] that other encounter of time, space and their contents that we call a conjuncture (using a word that repeats 'encounter', but in the form of junction); and that every encounter is, under the conditions stated above, contingent, and necessarily contingent – all this opens up unprecedented perspectives on events, and thus also on history and time.

For an encounter, if it comes about, can also come undone [*si elle se fait, peut se défaire*]. It can quite simply be a missed encounter and not take place (the fourteenth-century Italian bourgeoisie and the capitalist mode of production: a missed encounter). It can be just a brief encounter (a man and a woman; Louis XIV and the Grand Turk; the USA and China), or a lasting encounter (a successful romance, Marx and Engels, etc.). It can also be a premature encounter (Aristotle and non-Euclidean geometry) and thus go unnoticed, or a posthumous encounter (Marx and Spinoza), fertile in this case, futile in others (Léon Blum and Marx).[4]

If, however, we pursue the concept of the encounter further, taking into account the conditions of its failure as well as its success, we must say that an encounter does not take place *unless something 'takes'* [*prend*];[5] the atoms must be hooked in order to hook together. Once the encounter 'takes', it has taken place. Of course, we can define the conditions of this 'take' [*prise*], but that can be done with certainty only afterwards (*nachträglich*, as Freud would later say,[6] repeating an idea of Epicurus's unawares). It is, to be sure, not impossible to do so beforehand, but that is a relatively aleatory possibility, secured only to the extent that we can bring about the controlled, regular repetition of an event that has already occurred under conditions that can be controlled thanks to our knowledge of their variation.

Thus the encounter 'takes' [*prend*] the way water crystallizes [*prend*] to become ice, the way mayonnaise 'takes', the way state power 'takes' in people's consciousness, the way a mode of production 'takes'. That this 'take' [*prise*] should give rise to double takes, mistakes, retakes, un-takes, or take-overs [*surprise, méprise, reprise, déprise, emprise*] etc., as well as to all that which, in German, has to do with conceiving and grasping/understanding (*begreifen, Begriff*) etc., merits attention and examination. What I wish to say, however, is that, with his thesis about *deviation, encounter*, and the *take*, Epicurus has provided us with the means of understanding precisely what the idealists had aimed at and missed: namely the irruption of a subject, *this* particular subject and no other.

17

This conception, audacious in its simplicity and seldom understood, was, with the beginnings of capitalism, soon occluded (as Husserl would have said) by an altogether different idea. It sprang from bourgeois law [*droit*], which had been taken over from Roman law in a conjuncture that, precisely, allowed it to 'take' or 'retake'.[1] The model of the subject now changed, becoming the *subject of law*, and this model triumphed virtually across the board. It did not drive the old categories (subject, essence and so on) from the world of philosophy, of course; they continued to fulfil their functions. But it took over from them, maintaining their work assignment basically intact, while putting them under its supervision.

What, then, was this subject of law? Note that it did not intervene in philosophy directly, as such, but in the form of its surrogate in legal ideology, the subject-origin-owner-author-actor: in short, *man as subject* or, again, the human person. But to understand the fact that man in general was conceived of as a subject, we have to go back to the subject of law.

For bourgeois law, every human individual is a subject of law. 'Subject of' means that he has defined legal capacities: above all, the capacity of possessing property and the capacity of alienating it in a commercial exchange. The subject of law is, then, the owner of his property. To own property, however, he must first own himself and his will, with the result that his will is free. He owns his property in all freedom and alienates it in all freedom by establishing a free contract of exchange with a third party. Since legal *freedom* is everyone's freedom, all men are *equals* insofar as they are subjects of law. This condition has nothing of a utopian dream about it, as has been supposed, since it simply defines the fact of the basic conditions of commercial exchange, which was becoming universal at the time. *Right is a matter of fact, and expresses nothing but fact.* The fact it expresses is doubtless the fact of commercial law [*droit marchand*], but, in this case, right [*droit*] and fact coincide, a property whose mirage idealist philosophy had pursued in vain.

It is this fact of right that is taken up in legal ideology for interesting reasons of principle. For we may legitimately ask ourselves why law, which seems to suffice unto itself, thus duplicates itself or completes itself in a legal ideology. Yet the matter is simple enough: law, while formally sanctioning all commercial transactions, does not force anyone to accept them (a matter for the state and the police) or create an obligation to accept them (a matter of morality). It therefore needs the double supplement of the state and a moral ideology that is not unrelated to religious ideology, at least for as long as religion exists. What one then calls *legal ideology* is this ideology partway between pure law and moral-religious ideology, an ideology that takes up the categories of law, while conferring on them a form acceptable to morality and religion. This operation of transfer and transformation comes about through a displacement of the category of the subject, which ceases to be a simple *subject of law* (with limited attributes) in order to become a *human subject*, capable of being invested by legal categories, but also by moral and religious categories. To the categories of property, freedom, and equality, this new subject thus adds the moral categories of fraternity, generosity, moral consciousness, good intentions, and an upright conscience, as well as the religious categories of the finite creature created for his salvation by way of sin and a redemption that guarantees him eternal life. And since these legal, moral, and religious ideologies obviously affect the ideology of the practices brought to bear on nature, and also those that human beings bring to bear on other human beings (the practices of production and of politics), this new subject becomes, in addition, an active, operative subject responsible for his actions, conscious of his projects, and master (or not) of his acts. And, when everything is over, he pays the reckoning before, not God, but the tribunal of history, which, however, is not a tribunal, except for the unrepentant idealists who maintain that the world has a meaning even when it is secular and capitalist.

As Marx has shown, all bourgeois philosophy has been erected on the basis of legal ideology. Kant can be called its supreme representative, at least in the period in which the bourgeoisie was aspiring to take power. From the bourgeois standpoint, Kant is a true materialist philosopher. He put an end to ontology, pursuing the critique of Being and substance inaugurated, against Leibniz, by Locke and Hume. He drove religion from the territory of science and morality, relegating it to the corner reserved for the postulates of practical reason, the appendage of a morality that could have done very well without it, were it not for the idea Kant had of the purity of moral acts, of which we do not find, he said, a single example on earth: their existence had to be guaranteed somewhere (the guarantee again!), lest one lapse into what he wrongly considered to be empiricism. Kant drove all the pseudosciences, the sciences without an object (the metaphysics of Being, psychological ontology, ontological psychology, ontological theology), from the field of scientific knowledge the way Christ drove the money-changers from the temple. He produced a theory of knowledge (*The Critique of Pure Reason* and *The Critique of Judgement*) which is wholly given over to sweeping Being from the field and defending the idea that it is not Being, but phenomena that are accessible to human knowledge, which is in part a priori – in other words, independent of all experience – in its pure forms, whether they are forms of perception or forms of the understanding and reason. He showed that the cogito is not ontological (Descartes's 'I think') nor, a fortiori, psychological, that is, empirical, but 'transcendental' (in other words, above all experience), since it provides a unity that can only be a priori, binding together all the elements of either a perception or a scientific judgement, whether that judgement is itself a priori (mathematics, pure physics) or empirical (experimental physics).

What Kant had accomplished for knowledge with his pure subject he accomplished for morality with his pure conscience, by showing that no moral act was conceivable without the a priori known as good will: the pure will to do good and nothing else, in the absence of any empirical motive.[2] And Kant showed, surprisingly, since Kant was not Sartre, that this pure good will dragged a whole structure of practical reason in its wake, that is, moral reason, which also has its pure categories, pure judgements, pure reason, and pure ends. This is normal, in a sense, since everything is pure in morality; but it is necessary at the same time, because, since morality is never pure in real life, it was necessary to distinguish the pure in it as a condition of the impure, at the price of tracing this impurity back to human passions and interests, to the 'pathological' that humanity has doubtless 'freely' chosen from all eternity in a kind of original sin, since it is so deeply attached to it that its whole life is – against the purity of practical reason – governed by it.

I shall not dwell on the well-known fact that the same conception of the pure subject also governs, in Kant, both the theory of Art and the theory of society and history. He did not innovate much in any of these areas, because he had been preceded in this conception by the eighteenth-century philosophers, Hume, Locke, and Locke's successors (Hume & Co.).

This conception had the immense advantage of ensuring that the beings existing in the world *were clearly subjects* – pure subjects, and also empirical subjects – and that they were, as such, subjects not just of knowledge, but also of law, morality, politics, taste, and religion. The question as to whether they were 'plainly this subject, and no other' had thus been resolved in principle, except that one question was again left in suspense: it was impossible to deduce the fact of the *singularity* of such-and-such a subject in particular, although one had the assurance that he possessed the form of the subject in general. This is one of the reasons that Kant denied the possibility that psychology or, similarly, history could ever be constituted as sciences; for, since only quantity can be applied to them, and as quality is itself an abstract category, the *quid* (the specificity) of individuality would always elude them. Real history was to show that Kant was mistaken, and that he was mistaken precisely because he had grounded his whole conception on the legal ideology of the subject.

18

Before Kant, however, and while taking diabolically wily precautions, someone had struck down a different path, a materialist path: Spinoza. Spinoza quite simply began with God. 'Others begin', he wrote, 'with thought (Descartes) or beings (Saint Thomas).' He began with God.[1] It was a stroke of unheard-of audacity of a kind rare in history. For to begin with God was to begin with the origin and the end at the same time, and therefore literally to bracket out, from the subsequent course of his ideas, this couple that constitutes every idealism in philosophy. To begin with God was simultaneously to say that nothing other than God exists in the world, and this came down to saying, in defiance of all the theologians, who were not fooled, that since God exists in everything, he exists in nothing and therefore does not exist. Spinoza, however, also needed God so that he could endow him with all the possible attributes (infinite in number) which express his essence, are at one with his essence, and are absolutely indiscernible from, because conflated with it. He needed God, in other words, to account in advance for the singular power of all singular subjects, whether stones, dogs, or human beings. Here too, there was no managing without structure, either, because, since attributes are infinite (the only two that human beings know are extension, or matter, and thought), an intermediary was plainly needed to get from God to the singular individuals known as the finite modes (mode = variation/modality of an attribute). For Spinoza, these intermediaries were the infinite modes (for example, the space of geometry and the understanding), whose overall combination gives rise to arrangements that Spinoza calls, using a curious term that has discouraged all his commentators, except for Martial Gueroult, '*facies totus universi*', figures of the total universe,[2] figures which are, doubtless, the most general laws governing, on the one hand, the ensemble of bodies and, on the other, the ensemble of minds.[3]

It is obvious that, on such a conception, the subject-object distinction goes by the boards, as do the question of right, the question of truth, and the question of the criterion of truth, so that the theory of knowledge disappears from the outset. Its place is taken by a curious theory of the 'three kinds of knowledge', presented as a fact outside the jurisdiction of any question of right. In this theory, we are told about a first kind of knowledge, or imagination; and since Spinoza has already served notice that the category of 'faculty' must be rejected, this first kind of knowledge or pseudo-faculty seems, rather, to designate a world, the immediate world. Spinoza does not say the world of ideology, but we may suppose that that is what is in question, especially after reading the *Theological-Political Treatise*, in which the imaginary [*imaginaire*] is what everybody perceives and believes, including the prophets who man the outposts of the imaginary, since they hear God without understanding what he is telling them, although it is true.[4] For the strange thing about this imagined reality [*imagination*] is that it contains a portion of truth, the true-in-part, the true-as-inadequate, which refers us to the true-as-adequate of the second kind of knowledge, present as such rather than disguised. Here the true wears the aspect of the common truths in which the sciences and philosophy operate.

But what of the subjects, it will be asked. They are imaginary in the first kind of knowledge; they are perhaps known, but only abstractly, in the common truths of the second kind of knowledge. Spinoza held the surprise of a third kind of knowledge in store for them, one that would furnish the knowledge of them, since it provides, precisely, knowledge of *singular essences*. And there can be no doubt that Spinoza concealed, behind his famous example of the different ways of arriving at knowledge of the fourth proportional,[5] other examples of incomparably greater importance: the knowledge of human individuals and the singularity of their histories, or knowledge of the singularity of history, and even the moments and instants of a people's history, as we see in the case of the Jewish people in the *Theological-Political Treatise*. We should bear in mind that the times were against Spinoza, who could not say everything openly.

However that may be, it is not impossible to maintain that something about this astonishing construct recalls materialism. It does so in a negative, critical way above all, no doubt about it, yet in a way that no philosopher before Marx was able to surpass. For there was more than just materialist refusals in this philosophy (I shall not come back to this point, which is obvious); there were also astonishingly fertile theses in it. For instance, the idea of the infinity of the attributes[6] (in a day and age in which humanity was just beginning to acquire true knowledge of arithmetic, geometry, analysis, and physics) left the door wide open to the discoveries of the future. To take just two examples, besides the two known attributes (math and physics), the continent of History, into which Marx would resolutely advance, was opened up by Spinoza himself with his *Theological-Political Treatise*. Formally – I say formally – Spinoza left the door open to another continent, into which Freud would later venture. For example, another idea, parallelism, which can, to be sure, be called idealist in a certain regard, in fact left the door open to the question of the primacy of matter over thought. To cite one last example, the powerful idea of a causality that operates in its effects and exists only in its effects announced, from afar, an idea that Marx would take up in his turn: that of the causality of a relation with respect to the elements that constitute it as a relation (consider the relation of production) or a causality of the structure with respect to its elements (structural causality). Evidently, Spinoza lacked the idea of the dialectic he needed to confer a meaning on these intuitions of genius. It was not, however, Hegel, who rightly criticized him for this absence of the dialectic, who would truly answer the question, unspoken in Spinoza and posed by Hegel. It was Marx.

Yet Hegel seems to have inherited what was best in Spinoza: the critique of all theories of knowledge, the critique of right, the critique of the moral and political legal subject, the critique of the social contract, the critique of morality, the critique of religion as an appendage to morals. Hegel thereby put himself in a position to criticize Kant as Spinoza had criticized Descartes, and in almost exactly analogous fashion. Moreover, Hegel introduced into philosophy precisely what was lacking in Spinoza, *the dialectic*, or the 'labour of the negative'. It was thanks to this that each singular being existing in the world could finally be identified as 'this subject and no other', whatever the forms of singular individuality involved (a particular variation of the perceived world, a particular figure of individual consciousness, a particular historical individuality – that of a human being or a people, etc.). And it clearly seemed that the idealist question of Being, that empty question, had at last been answered because it had been posed differently. Unfortunately, our philosopher had not evacuated idealism, he had merely confined it to – the dialectic itself.

For the old Aristotelian idea of determination by the end or *telos* – teleology – operated at full capacity in the dialectic, and was announced openly, with complete confidence. Thus every being, far from possessing its essence in itself, saw it fulfilled in its end:[7] in another being that was its development and realized its essence in its stead, on the pretext that this second being was 'for itself' what the first was only 'in itself'. Hegel thus restored the finalized order of a material, intellectual, and social nature in which every being was supposed to occupy the place and possess the essence assigned to it by the End of the world (with the being that was its truth serving as a provisional intermediary): the World Spirit that ruled over the whole course of things from the start, despite, and including, the 'incidental expenses' of history which Hegel, as a good theoretician of capitalist production, did not hesitate to acknowledge and enter in the accounts. 'Why does it rain upon sands, upon highways and seas?' Malebranche asked, troubled; but he also said that if God had created valleys, it was to provide a run-off for the water that poured down from the mountains. Hegel took charge of this historical refuse, declaring that it was required for the production of history, although it produced nothing itself. Thus this Nothingness entered into the positive dialectic, with evil, wars, and everything else that is outrageous in theologians' eyes.[8]

An accountant was needed, however; and it was Hegel himself who kept the books, not God, who had been struck from the list of philosophical personnel. This restored the Aristotelian figure of the philosopher who knows everything, the figure of absolute knowledge, whose name Hegel had been the first to dare to pronounce; who is not God, it is true, but his consciousness; who is not the Prince, it is true, but his consciousness, the prince being merely the earthly figure of God. All this happened during the French Revolution and the Restorations, periods rich in events and reflections, from which Hegel drew the lesson that history had ended, because the bourgeoisie still considered itself eternal, since it had just come to power; and since history had ended, the concept existed concretely in the form of the concept, an obscure formulation that should be translated: 'the truth dwells at last among men, all men are citizens of a state, and free, free and equal; they are upright, and never lie when they speak, for that shows on their faces or, if they hide it, there exists a good police force that will make them talk, policemen being – as has been well-known since Brunschvicg, who, poor man, said so before he was forced to flee them – 'representatives of Reason'.

The affirmation that history has ended has been misunderstood. It does not mean that time has been suspended, but that the time of political events is over and done with. Nothing more will happen: you can go home and go about your business, you can 'enrich yourselves', and all will be well; your property is guaranteed. This whole history of the guarantee, this long, painful conceptual history of the guarantee thus culminates, pathetically, in a guarantee of private property. With it culminates, in the same way, the whole long history of the guarantee of the proprietorship [propriété] of things, the properties [propriétés] of things, the specificity [propre] of things and of everyone, hence of the subject, whose hands are always clean [propre], for there are no bad apples or, if there are, there are courts and there are hospitals for the mad to take them in and rehabilitate them. Everyone can sleep in peace, decent folk in their homes, thieves in the prisons, the mad in the hospitals: the state of reason watches over them, this state that is, as Gramsci said, borrowing a phrase from I-don't-know-whom, a 'night watchman'.[9] In the daytime, the state slips away, since the citizens keep watch. An excellent economy: the economy of bourgeois exploitation. Like the prettiest girl in the world, the bourgeoisie can only give what it has.[10] Which is already not half-bad.

19

This was not the opinion of Marx, who said out loud what the proletarians thought, but kept to themselves.

I repeat that Marx has not given us a book of philosophy, but just a few allusions; that Engels has left us only a polemical work, *Anti-Dühring*; and that Lenin has bequeathed us, apart from *Materialism and Empirio-criticism*, nothing but reading notes on Hegel. They had other things to do, and – we shall see why later – they were quite right: philosophy is not the motor of history. The fact is, however, that they have left us in a real pickle, the more so because Marx, who was once young, like everyone else, perpetrated, in the works of his youth, as they are called, a certain number of written thoughts that could only be borrowings, subject as he was, like everyone else, to the influence of the masters of the dominant idealist philosophy, beginning with Hegel and Feuerbach. I too attempted, in my 'youth' (which was unfortunately belated), to sort these possible confusions out somewhat; they had, incidentally, been rather well exploited by all those with an interest in betraying Marx in order to mislead Marxists and proletarians about his thought. Yet, when one reads the *Contribution* (1859)[1] and *Capital* (1867), or Lenin's, Gramsci's, and Mao's works, there can be no doubt about the matter: there exists a Marxist materialist philosophy, whose theses we must laboriously reconstruct, since Marx worked none of them out, a handful of exceptions aside. To which we must add this very easily understandable fact: despite a rupture and a 'break' that are visible in his texts, Marx did not rid himself once and for all of the dominant bourgeois ideology, which, because it was dominant, never ceased to dominate him despite all, and to preserve in him, despite his best efforts, certain old formulations still smacking of idealism. A great deal of work that has not yet been undertaken will be required to settle accounts with these residues and fine points.[2]

Despite all, we may say roughly the following. For Marx, who rejected the whole idealist problematic, and *radically* rejected it, like Spinoza and also Hegel, as far as what Hegel took from Spinoza is concerned, materialism's first demand is to bring philosophy into line with what it really, practically is; in other words, *to ensure, within philosophy itself, the primacy of practice over theory*. This simple idea – to ensure the primacy of practice over theory in the materialist philosophical theory that proclaims this thesis because it is materialist – is itself revolutionary, if it is concretely, practically realized.

For to ensure this primacy means treating philosophy as it is, not in its theory (which varies, as we have seen, from one extreme to the other), but in its practice. But what is philosophy in its practice? It is struggle, a combat that is perpetual and preventive because it is universal. And philosophy is also the battlefield on which this perpetual war unfolds between a great many combatants, all of whom, however, in providing others with supplies and support, or by virtue of the intentions they harbour, ultimately range themselves in one of the two great camps that group together all the philosophers in the world: the idealist and the materialist camp. There may be messengers between these two camps, providers of imaginary or selfishly motivated services who suggest compromises and the formulas to couch them in, people who, like Kant, are from the bourgeois standpoint fairly materialist, but are, from the proletarian standpoint, literally 'shamefaced materialists', 'agnostics' (Lenin).[3] The truth is that no philosopher is neutral, even if he thinks he is, even if he establishes a zone of philosophical extraterritoriality for himself in which he can, what with freedom of trade and duty-free goods, convince himself that he stands above the fray, or even offer his territory as an asylum to battle-weary warriors or those with pursuers on their heels. On the philosophical battlefield, whatever the name under which combatants of the most widely varying kinds range themselves – and the objective meaning of that name (empiricism, nominalism, realism, sensualism and so on) can vary, depending on the way the battle goes – on this battlefield, there can be no neutrality. Every philosophy belongs, directly or indirectly, avowedly or not, to either the idealist or the materialist camp.

The conclusion that materialism draws from this (idealism draws the same conclusion, but, since it does not say so, it helps to maintain the idea that it has not chosen and that there is no choice to be made) is that *one must choose one's camp*, that every philosophy always chooses its camp, and that the materialist, to be a materialist, has to choose the materialist camp (otherwise, he would simply declare himself a materialist while remaining in the idealist camp or its appurtenances). This is what Lenin called 'partisanship' in philosophy.[4] This partisanship has an important consequence: obviously, it cannot be a simple declaration of partisanship, but must be real. A philosopher who chooses the materialist camp in full awareness of what he is about has to reconnoitre the terrain to determine exactly what positions his camp occupies, and he has to reconnoitre the adversary's camp, the idealist camp, the same way: he has to reconnoitre [*reconnaître*] it in detail ('If you want to know your enemy, you must go to your enemy's country': Goethe, cited by Lenin)[5] if he is to know [*connaître*] the adversary's positions well. This recommendation is by no means merely formal, for the camps have not been constituted once and for all, nor the positions occupied once and for all. Philosophy is a millennial trench war in which entrenched adversaries face off; they cannot always see each other, but they never lose touch, even if they are only at shooting distance or in flight range. Moreover, the front line shifts in the course of the fighting; it also shifts as a function of the stakes of the fighting, which vary with the vicissitudes of history and the war. Sometimes it is a hill that must be taken by storm; sometimes it is the hollow of a valley or an old fort which has been armed by the enemy and temporarily shut down, but which, once captured, will be put back into operation.

So it is that, depending on the course of the battles, nominalism changes camps, as does empiricism, and realism, and even the names 'idealism' and 'materialism'; for, in this war as in any other, one tries to trick the enemy with ruses and feints. Thus Spinoza takes God by surprise and by storm and, from the divine heights, dominates the whole battlefield: from then on, no one can drive him from it. Thus, again by surprise, even if we saw him coming a long way off, Heidegger captures the Thing and turns it against Hegel. Thus Marx wrests thought from idealism in order to subordinate it to the primacy of matter, or to that of the (nominalist) difference between the real object and the object of thought and so on.

The history of philosophy resembles that of a protracted war: when the front shifts, it leaves behind, forever engraved in the combatants' minds, the name of a tiny village no less than that of a fortified town. Who today remembers the Thomist impetus? Yet it was the theatre of a bloody war associated with the birth of Galilean physics. Who remembers the pineal gland? Yet it was the name of a place where the destiny of Cartesian psychology was played out. Who remembers the Greeks' and Aristotle's earth, immobile in the centre of the universe, now that Kepler and Galileo have demonstrated that the earth revolves around the sun? Yet Husserl remembered it, and recaptured it, although this fortification had been abandoned and shut down; and he armed it again in his fashion, using weaponry all his own, when he declared that 'the earth as First Principle does not move.'[6] Once again, neither categories nor theses have anything definitive about them, since their meaning is conferred on them by the role falling to them in a given philosophy's categorical system, which is governed, in its turn, by the current conjuncture of the struggle.

The foregoing explains why it is hard to establish an exhaustive list of the theses of materialism (at all events, we know that these theses, like those of idealism too, are infinite in number), since the way they are formulated varies as a function of the adversary and the conjuncture. This does not mean that it is impossible to state some of them. We must keep in mind, however, that formulations of them can vary with the conjuncture and its stakes. More than ever, we have to understand theses as positions, a set of positions.

Besides the primacy of practice over theory (Thesis 1), we should mention a second essential thesis here (Thesis 2): the primacy of matter or Being over thought or consciousness. This thesis allows us to justify all the analyses that historical materialism substitutes for what idealism calls the theory of knowledge. Of course, this Thesis does not determine in advance the derivative philosophical forms required to justify these analyses ('justify' does not have a moral sense here, but must be understood in the sense of 'to adjust', 'to make (more) accurate'), since they depend, to a great extent, on the way the conjuncture develops. It is, however, important to note that this Thesis intervenes in second place, 'covered' by the first, as one says in military jargon, for this cover prevents the second Thesis from drifting in the direction of idealism, and restoring, in the guise of the pair matter/thought, the old idealist pair Being/thought, or subject/object, or even the category of 'reflection' the way we see it functioning in certain passages in Lenin that fall a bit short of the mark and, when they are not equivocal, in many of his commentators too.

Thesis 3, internal to Thesis 2, might be put as follows: primacy of the real object over the object of knowledge. Thesis 3 would pave the way for Thesis 4, taken directly from Lenin, on absolute and relative knowledge: it would affirm the primacy of absolute over relative truth, thus ruling out all historicism.[1] We could go on this way ad infinitum. The reader would benefit from engaging in the exercise.

It is enough, however, to consider all these materialist theses in their interrelations in order to see that they contain theses of another kind, which might be called *dialectical*. The question of how to understand the dialectic is a ticklish, still controversial one in Marxist materialism. Marxists are happy to declare that Marx is a materialist, and they subscribe to the Theses that I have just recalled. However, it seems that the relationship to Hegel, which is ambiguous and hard to break off, has given rise to the idea, as appears clearly in Engels, that what Marx owed Hegel was precisely the dialectic, which he had detached from Hegel's bad, reactionary '*system*', and that he had a right to do so, since the dialectic is, when all is said and done, a *method*, the universal method.[2]

Nothing could be farther from the truth. Every philosophical method is the inevitable by-product of an idealist theory of knowledge, and it is a mystery by what miracle a system as bad as Hegel's could have been thus miraculously paired off with a first-rate, revolutionary and, what is more, universal method. Yet, despite all, the caricatural idea that the dialectic is something other than materialism, that materialism is a theory of Being or an ontology, and that the dialectic is 'its' method, has lingered on. We still find it in the majority of Soviet philosophers and their Western emulators. We even find the idea, unfortunately put forward by Engels in the *Dialectics of Nature*, that the essence of the dialectic is motion, and that motion is the property par excellence of matter, so that Being is matter in motion; this justifies speaking about the laws of Being (materialism) and, at the same time, the laws of motion (the dialectic)![3] This idea of laws of the dialectic, which Lenin also let slip once or twice (we should not be afraid to correct it) is, properly speaking, absurd if the reference to the scientific category of 'law' is taken literally: it restores the idea, which it pretends to found, that there should exist, to counter idealist ontology, a materialist ontology that would provide us with the laws of Being (materialist theory) and its movement, that is, its development: the laws of a dialectic at once objective and subjective (Lucien Sève) that would thus cover all questions, in other words, all imaginary difficulties – I mean the adversary's difficulties.[4]

It must frankly be said that, today (for the front may shift tomorrow), the main obstacle blocking the development of Marxist philosophy resides here, at the very heart of Marxist philosophy. *There are no laws of the dialectic, but only dialectical theses.* The dialectic, which falls under the jurisdiction of philosophy, does not provide knowledge of the pseudo-laws of its object, but states theses. The absurdity of the claim that one can state laws of the dialectic is attested by the problem of counting them. As a rule, one says that there are three or four such laws: the interdependence of phenomena, the qualitative leap, the negation of the negation, and contradiction. Yet Lucien Sève himself, who maintains, in his way, that this idea of laws of the dialectic is correct, reveals other, supplementary laws for us in his research. We know that they are in fact infinite in number; this infinity is due to the fact that they are theses, not laws.

We should therefore say that the dialectic produces theses; in other words, inasmuch as there is no special instance here possessing the right to state certain theses and not others, that there are dialectical theses or, better, *that all theses are at once materialist and dialectical*. The proof is the character common to all the materialist theses we have named so far: they all talk about a relation of primacy, X over Y. Yet what do we see in this relation? A difference, a hierarchy, hence a contradiction. Not contradiction in general, but an always specified contradiction, which has a primary aspect. We may further observe that, in the series of theses, contradictory among themselves, there is always a primary and a secondary contradiction. This merely reflects, at the heart of materialist philosophy, its antagonistic, dominated (or, some day, dominant) relation to the idealist philosophy standing over against it. This is necessarily the case if philosophy is, in the last instance, struggle in theory.

When Lenin declares that the essential feature [*le propre*] of the dialectic is 'to help us (that is what he says: to help us) to conceive of the contradiction in the intimate essence of things', he simply sums up this characteristic, which, insofar as it is stated in the form of a thesis (but that is the essential feature of any thesis), is treated as universal.[5] And he is perfectly right to speak of the 'internal essence of things'. He does not, however, lapse into ontology as a result, because he has taken the materialist precaution, unlike Stalin (see, on this point, Dominique Lecourt's limpid demonstration in his *Lysenko*),[6] of defining the thesis of the dialectic as capable of 'helping us to conceive of' contradiction, rather than saying, like Stalin, that contradiction is the law of the development of contraries. Lenin thereby also affirms a thesis absolutely essential to Marxism – very precisely, to historical materialism, the theory of classes and the struggle of the classes – the thesis of the primacy of a contradiction over the contraries. This thesis is 'justified' by the sequence of materialist theses that we listed a moment ago.

Thus it is clear that, on these bases, the idealist distinctions between Being and thought collapse; that there is only one world and one reality; and that the process of knowledge of this world enjoys a relative autonomy, although it is subordinated in the last instance to the process of nature, as can be seen in the relation between production and the history of the sciences. As for the dialectic, its function, as in Hegel, is to prevent the process of knowledge from coming to a halt on fixed concepts and thus stopping this process. It does not, however, substitute itself for the laws discovered in nature and human history by this process of knowledge. Not only does it clear paths by opening up the space of knowledge in opposition to idealist prejudices, but it also provides the process of knowledge, as materialist theses do too, with categories essential to the constitution, renewal, and pursuit of this process. We shall, however, see that in a moment.

21

For we cannot, at the point we have now reached, avoid a crucial question. It is true that we observe the existence of a philosophical battlefield; that philosophy is a perpetual war; and that there are, in the last instance, two camps in philosophy, the idealist camp (still dominant) and the materialist camp. It is true that the battle follows a shifting front as it unfolds, and that, astonishingly, we see on this front, depending on the conjuncture, old positions of strength that have been abandoned being put back into operation by those who conquer them and so on. But *what explains the fact that one does battle in philosophy?* And what is this conjuncture that is capable of varying and producing these shifts in the front, including the spectacular reversals that we have discussed? We have to get to the bottom of the matter here, to what cannot *not* be the sketch of a scientific theory of philosophy.

It cannot be objected that such a scientific theory is impossible in principle because we have said that philosophy is not a science: the science that we are proposing will not be a philosophy, but a science of philosophy. It might, however, be further objected that, since philosophy is a battlefield, anyone who enters the field to forge the theory of it will be caught in the cross-fire and must himself take sides, for, if he fails to, he will find himself outside the field and thus out of range of his object. This objection does not stand. It has in its favour only the appearances of a confusion: the one that would reduce a science of philosophy to a variant of philosophy, and have us believe that objectivity is impossible in the field of human realities or theories about philosophy. Yet this objection, which no philosopher before Marx was able to overcome, was well-founded then, at a time when there existed no science of the laws of the class struggle (this is how we shall define historical materialism, in the shortest and, at the same time, most accurate way). There could therefore be no theory of philosophy that was not philosophical, and no one could break out of the infernal circle: either a philosophy without science, or a science of philosophy that was still a philosophy.

What, then, are the principles on the basis of which a scientific theory becomes, not just possible, but also necessary for the class struggle of the proletariat and its allies?

Marx stated them in his rather well-known theory of historical materialism. He demonstrated that human beings living in society are determined by the class structure of the social formation in which they live and reproduce themselves (in the case of class societies, obviously). He demonstrated that every social formation is organized in accordance with a 'determinate mode of production', and that this mode of production of people's material subsistence assigns the production of material goods the function of determining, in the last instance, all the effects of the superstructure. This presupposes the joint existence, in the social formation, of a base (productive forces reproducing themselves in the course of production under the dominance of the relations of production) and a superstructure, bringing together, on the one hand, law and the state, and the different ideologies on the other.

Marx thus demonstrated that every class social formation is based on a relation of production that is a relation of exploitation, and that this relation of exploitation varies with the modes of production, but ensures, in all cases, the extortion of surplus labour from the immediate producers, who are exploited by those who possess the means of production. He demonstrated that only the capitalist mode of production has a relation of production which implies the freedom and legal equality of the immediate workers (the proletariat) as well as those who possess the means of production (the capitalists); that the proletarians sell their labour-power to the capitalists in exchange for a wage calculated to make their reproduction and that of their families possible, without ceding the value of their production to them. The surplus of this value over their wage represents the surplus-value that the capitalist class appropriates by force disguised as law. For what is involved here is not individual, intersubjective, 'human' relations, but class relations, hence class struggle. The proletarian, like the capitalist, is, as Marx says, a representative of his own species, that is, his own class, and it is on the basis of classes that we should understand the situation imposed on individuals, just as we should understand classes on the basis of class struggle.[1] The materialist thesis of the primacy of contradiction over the contraries finds an echo in the scientific concept of the determination of classes by class struggle.

But Marx did not leave it at that. He showed that if a social formation exists (a matter of fact), it is because it has survived down to the present; if it has managed to survive, it is because it has managed to reproduce part of the conditions of its production. For it is characteristic of human societies that they draw their subsistence from immediate nature, but only on condition that they work on it, that they 'cultivate' it. Increasingly, the process of producing human subsistence is becoming independent of brute nature; it bears on a nature that has already been worked on, which must be reproduced to produce. For a social formation to exist, it must be reproduced. To exist in history, for a social formation, is to have reproduced and to reproduce itself. A social formation that is for some reason (catastrophe, war and so on) incapable of securing the means of its reproduction quite simply perishes. It is on this condition that 'we civilizations know that we are mortal' (Valéry).[2]

The reproduction of the conditions of production is realized, obviously, in the course of production in the broad sense: both immediate material production and its legal, political, and ideological conditions. The reproduction of the raw materials and machines needed to replace those worn out or used up in production is secured in material production. The reproduction of labour-power is likewise secured in material production (through wages and their 'indirect' modern social forms). Yet this does not exhaust the process of reproduction. We should, moreover, slightly modify the word when we move from the base to the superstructure, and talk about perpetuation and conservation rather than reproduction. For the length of the periods involved is by no means the same in the superstructure as in the base. In the base, reproduction is realized over a very short cycle that can measure as little as one day (in the case of a daily wage) and is generally calculated on the basis of a civil year in accounting practice. In the superstructure, the reproductive cycle takes place over a longer period. In certain cases (philosophy), it is virtually indeterminate, or even experienced as 'eternal'.

The reason is that the function of the superstructure is to ensure the perpetuation of the general conditions of production, hence of exploitation, hence of class struggle, hence of the class domination of the exploiting class and the submission of the exploited classes. It is obvious that this task extends over a much longer period and is realized over a cycle very different from that of the economic infrastructure.

The state, the state apparatus, must first be in place. This supposes not just that the ascendant class must already have taken state power, but also that that class has transformed the state, the state apparatus, so as to adapt it to its exploitation and oppression, something that cannot come about without a class struggle in the economy, politics, and ideology that always takes a long time. Second, law has to be put in place or, at any rate, to have begun to function (this happens beforehand in the case of capitalism). The state has to see to it that the courts and police impose constraints so that law as well as the value of the money in circulation is recognized – with law sanctioning capitalist commercial relations and the currency sanctioning the equivalence of commercial values. The state must, further, be able to call on an army to maintain the integrity of the national market that the capitalist bourgeoisie needs in order to develop. Finally, the state has to fit itself out with state ideological apparatuses capable of ensuring the dominant class's ideological unity and its hegemony over the exploited class. History shows that, to accomplish this general task (ensuring the legal, political, and ideological conditions of reproduction and production), a new class needs centuries. The bourgeoisie took its inception in England in the late thirteenth century, and there still exist very many countries in the world, the majority, in which the bourgeois revolution has yet to be completed.[3]

I have tried to show what ideology consists of and why it is impossible to conceive of it apart from 1) the class struggle, 2) the social practices, and 3) the state apparatuses that endow it with a body [*corps*, which also evokes the various corps of civil servants and state officials] and state force, even when these 'apparatuses' are private from the legal standpoint (the churches, some schools and so on).[4]

In this connection, I have often been asked whether my views exactly coincide with those defended by Gramsci, who made remarks very similar to mine (I was unaware of them at first writing). It is not easy to make up one's mind about Gramsci, who worked under appalling conditions and took into account the pressure of the censorship brought to bear on him by the fascist regime when formulating his ideas. What is more, Gramsci thought in the terrible ideological and political conditions of the period immediately following the failure of the revolution of the Torino workers' councils, in the conditions of Mussolini's fascism, and in the conditions of the turn represented by the Stalinist deviation, and he had no direct information about what was going on in the world. It is, however, possible that I do not approach the question exactly the way Gramsci does. I put the accent, more than he does, on the state character of the ideological apparatuses, their objective connection [*rattachement*] to the dominant class, and the compact force represented, from the standpoint of that class's interests, by the block comprising the repressive state apparatus/the ideological state apparatuses.

This fine point is not insignificant when it comes to a question of current interest, that of the dictatorship of the proletariat.[5] When we picture the ideological apparatuses (Gramsci talks about hegemonic apparatuses, not by accident) as closely connected to the state and marked by the state, we accentuate the strength of the class dictatorship guaranteed by means of the state, and we necessarily arrive at a different assessment of the balance of power in the class struggle, one that does not, this time, underestimate the adversary. In contrast, if we are inclined, like Gramsci, to associate the ideological apparatuses with what he calls, after Hegel, albeit in a completely different sense, 'civil society', which is for him the sphere of the ideological and political apparatuses, we grant them an autonomy that exceeds their real force; this means that, in return, we tend to underestimate the force of the state and, therefore, the force of the domination of the class in power. The result is a strategy of the kind observable in Italy or even Spain (but it is more interesting in Spain), which consists in investing the ideological apparatuses from within. This is possible, because they are not very strong; and, once the ideological and political apparatuses have been occupied from within, the proletariat is in some sort in possession of the state, hence of state power – without having previously seized it. I say elsewhere what I think of this strategic conception: it does not correspond, in my opinion, to the current balance of power, even if, in a certain way, it reflects the weakness of the bourgeois state and its ideological apparatuses in a country such as Italy. Thus it would seem that Gramsci was swayed by the situation of real weakness of the Italian bourgeoisie, incapable of endowing itself with an organic bourgeois state, and that he drew mistaken conclusions from it, not just at the general theoretical level, but also, perhaps, at the level of Italian history. For even if a bourgeoisie is weak, it is never alone: Imperialism is there to provide it with the strength it lacks and, if need be, to intervene directly in its country in order to enable it to settle problems it cannot solve alone.

22

Let us go back to ideology; for, without a clear picture of the ideologies, it is impossible to forge a theory of philosophy. What must be well understood is 1) the universal character of ideology; 2) the practical character of ideology; 3) the political character of ideology; and 4) the recursive (after-the-fact) character of any theory of ideology.

We know that 'the soul always thinks' (Descartes).[1] Freud even showed that it thinks unconsciously. In any case, we know that human beings have always had ideas, at least from the moment they began living in society and had language at their disposal (Engels). We have, however, become increasingly aware, thanks to the work of ethnologists, that the ideas of the most primitive men we know are not, at bottom, individual or psychological ideas, pure, direct perceptions of nature or their fellow men; they are implacably structured in systems of representation that integrate all known beings, heavenly, earthly, animal, vegetable, human and other (divine) beings, in an extraordinarily orderly arrangement in which rules of circulation ensure the transition from one category of beings to another, the translation of one discourse (natural, political, familial, sexual, religious) into another, and an internal isomorphism (similarity of forms) guaranteeing all these possibilities. Thus nothing in all this is immediate or the result of empirical operations; nothing in it is psychological and subjective. We have, rather, an order of extraordinarily determinate representations that plainly plays a regulating role, similar to the role of knowledge, in a so-called primitive society's productive practice (its relationship with nature) as well as its social practice.

We must therefore give up, once and for all, the idea that *ideology is nothing but ideas* – in other words, the bourgeois conception of ideology. The ideas that we find in every ideology constitute, on the one hand, a more or less strict system (primitive societies, without classes), or a more or less loose system (class societies, in which class struggle introduces this 'play' and this flexibility, which can be extreme, into the system). On the other hand, these ideas are also practical or else stand in direct or indirect relation with practice, whatever form that practice takes: linguistic, productive, social, religious, aesthetic, moral, familial, sexual and so on.

In a primitive society, in which there are no classes, but social distinctions not based on exploitation of one segment of the population by those who possess the means of production, the relationship of these ideas to practice, albeit invested with the attributes of a vast imaginary system, is not really imaginary: everything is practised and experienced in the real, as real. In a tribe that has the beaver as its totem, all members of the tribe really are beavers and so on. The proof that all these representations are quite real is provided by their effectiveness: the effectiveness of magic, initiation rites, exogamy and so on, which ensure, in positive fashion and without fail, human beings' relationship to nature and each other, despite the great complexity of this relationship. The term 'primitive communism' has been applied to such societies. Marx and Engels used that term in affirming that communism would have nothing to do with this form of existence. It is, in fact, purchased at a high price: not only nature's overwhelming domination of 'society', but also, and above all, the sacrifices in human life required to maintain this equilibrium, whether it is a question of wars or of all the ritual murders perpetrated to ensure that equilibrium reigns. These apparently peaceful societies are among the cruellest in human history.

Of course, the emergence of classes, and thus of class struggle, completely altered ideology's forms of existence. In class societies, the division of labour, which had existed in classless societies too, where it was, however, communal, found itself subordinated to, and multiplied by, the class struggle and its effects. The result was a social division of the practices, a division that had class significance, and an apparent fragmentation of ideology that likewise had class significance. The principle that there is no practice except under the domination of an ideology and by means of an ideology (in part, the ideology of this practice) was generalized and, in the process, even as it was subordinated to the class division of ideology then under way, culminated in the constitution of distinct practices to which there corresponded distinct ideologies, which we may call *local* and *regional* practical ideologies. At the limit, every craftsman could have his own ideology, for a certain relationship to raw materials and a certain rhythm of labour and repose leave their mark on people's thinking. It was observed a very long time ago, even before Hesiod, just how profoundly 'works' determined people's thinking: that peasants' thinking was different from sailors'; sailors', from merchants'; merchants', from politicians' and so on. This ideological division at the micro-level, however, seemingly the ultimate basis for the relationship between each ideology and its practice, cannot mask the great political and class divisions of ideology. These minute ideologies would not exist without the social division of labour, which produces its own ideology in its turn, independently of these mini-ideologies, because it is elaborated above all on the basis of the division into classes, and therefore the class struggle.

Thus this double observation leads us to the recognition that ideology exists in the form of a double and even triple division: 1) the division of ideology as a function of the division of the multitude of practices, in which scientific practice will soon intervene; 2) the division of ideology into ideological regions corresponding to the practical ideologies that come into play in the class struggle to perpetuate the relation of production (the ideology of economic production, legal, moral, political, religious, aesthetic, philosophical, familial ideology and so on), ideologies that will take the form of ideological state apparatuses; and 3) the division of ideology into tendencies reflecting the tendencies of the economic and political class struggle.

These three divisions must not be imagined as simple, distinct entities, nor even as moments such that, once the first is established, the second proceeds from it and so on. This distinction is itself the result of a historical process in which, for example, each ideology of a practice affirms its identity [*se reconnaît*] by constituting itself in distinction to a different or opposed practice, under the domination of regional ideologies and their division into opposing political tendencies. Involved here is a gigantic process of division and unification that is constantly being reorganized and never attains finalized form, because the class struggle is always there to call whatever results have been achieved into question.

Yet this whole process tends to put a very precise dispositive in place, one well-suited to serving the dominant class's interests. It tends to constitute all the elements of existing ideology, in their diversity or even despite their diversity (it uses whatever means it finds to hand), as a *dominant ideology*, capable, by virtue of its contents and the positions it occupies, of serving the dominant class in the class struggle of ideas. Why does the dominant class (defined as the class that has seized state power to exercise its class dictatorship) need a dominant ideology? Not just to dominate the ideas of the dominated class, but also, and above all, to ensure its own ideological unity, indispensable to its political unity, without which it would be at the mercy of a revolt by the exploited. For the fact is that the dominant class is not unified a priori. On the contrary, it expends tremendous effort to overcome its internal divisions, because it is made up of elements of the old dominant class that have rallied to it and, at the same time, of all of its own fractions, corresponding to the different economic functions of a given mode of production (in the case of the capitalist bourgeoisie, the fractions of industrial capital, commercial capital, and financial capital, to say nothing of the middle strata that have emerged from the decomposition of the feudal mode of production: the productive urban and peasant petty bourgeoisie, intellectuals, the liberal professions, small merchants and so on). The considerable effort involved in the ideological (and political) unification of the dominant class as a unified class does not come about thanks merely to proclamations and publications, through propaganda and agitation. It comes about as the result of a protracted class struggle in which the bourgeoisie conquers its unity and identity as the dominant class against the old dominant class and, simultaneously, the new dominated class.

The struggle of the dominant ideology (that of the dominant class) against the dominated class's ideology unfolds within this long struggle, and always in the form of class struggle (in politics, ideology, and the economy). For there is an ideology of the dominated class, even if it succeeds in affirming its identity and unifying and consolidating itself only with great difficulty. This ideology of the dominated class emerges, precisely, from these concrete practices of exploited worker and peasant labour, and from the forms of exploitation and oppression that workers undergo. These practices are inseparable from elementary ideological forms, as we have seen. This spontaneous ideology is, naturally, sustained by the experience and ordeal of exploitation and oppression originating in the capitalist class struggle; it is not without reason that Marx insists on the role of ideological education played, to the benefit of proletarian ideology, by the organization and work discipline of capitalist production, which concentrates large numbers of workers in big industry and subjects them to forms of discipline that inculcate in them, besides real knowledge, the habit of organization and discipline. This is a convincing example of the dialectical theses of Marxist philosophy: it attests the identity of contraries in the very essence of the thing, inasmuch as the forms of capitalist class struggle, precisely those of organization and exploitation, contribute directly to the constitution of the ideology of the working class as a class ideology and, consequently, to the trade-union and, later, political organization of the working class as it carries this ideology into practice. Thus the bourgeoisie prepares 'its own gravediggers'.[2]

Nothing in the foregoing should cause any problem. Things become more difficult, however, when we try to account for the existence of the sciences and philosophy in this ensemble. Let us try to shed some light on this subject.

The sciences have not always existed. Practical knowledge, however, has, arriving at its results thanks to extremely ingenious empirical procedures involving simple observation of the movements of the heavenly bodies, animals, plants, seas, and winds, or the properties of various kinds of matter, among which fire and iron played a crucial role. Such practical knowledge has always been bound up with the productive forces and their development (first tools, then simple machines – for instance, machines for the elevation of water). Initially due to individual producers, this practical knowledge slowly became the prerogative of workers specialized in certain techniques: thus blacksmiths played a decisive part in primitive societies that had developed to a certain extent, as did magicians, shamans, and others who regulated the rhythms of labour and the hunt according to the relevant magic signs. Gradually, the division of labour became more pronounced in the realm of practical knowledge and the techniques for producing work tools. The same thing happened in the realm of knowledge of the biological reproduction of the species and the reproduction of the social order. But all this knowledge was confined to the empirical realm.

This remained the case until the day the first science in the world irrupted, the science of numbers and geometrical figures: arithmetic and geometry. We have said a word about how this science is likely to have originated. When it finally came into existence, there occurred something like a 'break' between it and its prehistory. The reason was that it did not bear on the same objects or apply the same techniques to produce results. It worked on an abstract object (numbers, space, figures) and proceeded by way of pure demonstrations that abstracted from all concrete determination. The results it obtained were then objectively, that is to say, universally valid, no matter which concrete objects they were brought to bear on. This was a revolution in the field of knowledge as a whole and in all the practices linked to existing knowledge.

Philosophy dates from the irruption of the first science in the world. When Plato engraved on the pediment of his academy, 'Let none who is not a geometer enter here',[1] he was taking due note of this fact, and demanding that every aspiring philosopher begin by acquiring knowledge of mathematics. Plato would undertake to teach the candidate what he was supposed to learn in familiarizing himself with it.

What does philosophy owe mathematics? Precisely the idea of objects and demonstrations that are pure: in other words, abstract, rigorous, exhaustive, and objective, or universal; furthermore, the idea that, between practical knowledge and the pure knowledge of the sciences, there exists this 'break' of which I have spoken, hence that this 'break' poses questions that philosophy should think and should answer if it wishes to 'save appearances', real appearances, and gain the ear, not just of those who are still in practical knowledge, but also of those who govern the state. All of Plato's work rests on this foundation: not only the Ideas, but also their opposition to the world of sense perception; the distinction between opinion (*doxa*) and mathematical understanding (*dianoia*); the distinction between these two orders of knowledge and philosophical knowledge, superior to all other kinds and capable of thinking this difference and surmounting it; anabasis and katabasis; participation; the theory of essence and the beyond of essence and so on.

If we content ourselves with this view of the matter, we may well come to the conclusion that philosophy emerged as an effect of the irruption of the first science. Examined a little more closely, however, things turn out to be more complicated. For the advent of mathematics was not neutral. It irrupted as the solution to a crisis in a world in crisis that was not prepared to take mathematics in its stride – indeed, a world that mathematics disrupted somewhere, at a vulnerable point in its ideological resistance. Philosophy can accordingly be regarded as a response to this threat and a safeguard against it, a means of 'patching up' this tear in the unified tissue of the dominant ideology. The most urgent things had to be attended to first: it was necessary to take possession of mathematics and gain the upper hand over it in order to put it back in its place in the order it threatened to disrupt. We can also interpret Plato along these lines, for the same author who requires that every philosopher be a mathematician subjects mathematics to a singular treatment in his philosophy: he relegates it to second place in knowledge in order to subordinate it to philosophy, which, even as it provides mathematics with guarantees, controls it, and controls it in the name of the Good, that is, of politics (the good of the polity).

But if philosophy thus 'patches up' or 'sutures' the tear produced in the dominant ideology by the subversive irruption of science, which is always directly or indirectly assoicated with atheism and materialism; if philosophy thus philosophically restores order to an ideology which, clearly dominant though it may be, suddenly feels itself threatened by a mysterious danger, the reason is that philosophy is in league with this dominant ideology, performing, even if it is not purely ideological, an undeniable ideological function, at least on this occasion.[1]

Thus philosophy seems to be endowed with an odd status. On the one hand, it gives itself all the appearances – and more than just the appearances, the theoretical arms – of science; on the other, it performs an ideological function, at least in certain very conspicuous, very important cases. Here it is precisely science that seems to constitute the danger which it, philosophy, must ward off so that ideology, which it serves in this instance, can recover its unity and serenity. But the reader will have noticed that all things are not equal in this apparent symmetry and opposition. For if philosophy is akin to science by virtue of its *form*, the abstraction of its categories, and the demonstrative character of its reasoning, which is always reasoning of a pure kind bearing on pure, because abstract 'objects', that is, objects purified of all empirical content, it is not at all by virtue of its form that philosophy is akin to ideology. It is so by virtue of its *function*, or the role that even its form starts to play when it functions in the dominant ideology's service. And if ideology's ultimate function (its function in the last instance) is to serve the class struggle – the function of the dominant ideology being to serve the dominant class's class struggle, while that of the dominated ideology, when it has been constituted, is to serve the dominated class's class struggle – if, in sum, ideology's function is ultimately political, we must not be afraid to acknowledge this for philosophy as well, and to say, with Mao, Lenin, and Gramsci: yes, philosophy is ideological and political by virtue of its function.

Under these conditions, philosophy seems to be double: political by virtue of its function, theoretical-scientific by virtue of its form, with its political function representing the essential determination of this double aspect.

This makes it possible to understand the fact that philosophy begins, and that its beginnings are marked by the theoretical-scientific form that constitutes its specificity. For the content (function) of philosophy goes back far beyond the birth of the philosophy of the philosophers. If this content is that of the dominant ideology, we encounter it from the moment a dominant ideology exists in class societies. It exists then in a form which (as we saw in connection with a religious question about Being), although it does not yet possess philosophy's rationality and demonstrative character, nevertheless testifies to a certain logic. That is why the great religious and political questions (the latter are usually disguised as religious questions) long preceded the birth of philosophy and have survived it; for philosophy, which represented new class interests, was for a long time subject to the domination of religious questions. Under these conditions, it is understandable that the advent of a science, the first, itself associated with precise social interests, should have provided the occasion for the birth of philosophy by providing it with the form of pure abstraction, rationality, and demonstration that would characterize it thereafter.

But then we can also understand why adopting this form did not impair philosophy's ideological-political function, which was, rather, reinforced by the introduction of these new forms of reasoning and demonstration. This very special situation seems to make it possible to understand the 'double position' of mathematics – in other words, of what was then science – in Plato, the first great idealist philosopher known to us. One has to be a geometer to be a philosopher, and that puts science in first place; but, as soon as the philosopher starts talking about science, it is to put it in second place, after philosophy itself. This attests to the primacy of politics over the forms of scientific rationality in philosophy itself. Philosophy acknowledges that primacy in its practice.

But if this is so, a problem inevitably arises. Of what use is it to philosophy to borrow the dominant forms of rationality and scientificity? What does the dominant ideology gain by thus appropriating the services of this rationality, given that, in any case, this appropriation changes basically nothing as far as the dominant ideology's function or its objectives and stakes are concerned? We have to resolve this problem.

We cannot, however, resolve it without going back to the dominant ideology and its relationship to the state. We have insisted on the fact that ideology exists in (ideological) state apparatuses. We have also insisted on the long process of class struggle indispensable to constituting the ascendant and, later, dominant class's ideology as the dominant ideology. We must be careful not to lapse into an idealism of the class struggle here, the belief that all these struggles, from the economy through politics to ideology, are struggles for pleasure, or prestige, or simply for victory. The fact is that these struggles have *stakes*: not just state power (the highest stakes), the state apparatus, or one of the state's (repressive or ideological) apparatuses, or even exploitation and, with it, the relation of production. In other words, these class struggles do not have as their sole stakes the relations or apparatuses which constitute the forms in which they are waged. Also at stake in them – indeed, fundamentally at stake in them – are *the practices* in which exploitation is imposed and undergone; among these practices figures the practice of the sciences and techniques. In all these struggles, it is a question, at the summit, of maintaining or capturing state power and the state apparatuses and, at the base, of controlling and orienting the different practices as a function of the class antagonism that divides society into classes.

I said earlier that there can be no practice that is not under the domination of an ideology, and I also talked about the microscopic ideologies that are occasioned by each practice and simultaneously govern it. Furthermore, I tried to show that the constitution of the dominant ideology enlisted all local and then all regional ideologies by subordinating them to itself, while, obviously, enlisting them under the unity of the grand class ideas around which this dominant ideology could, if it managed to, constitute itself. Even before the philosophy of the philosophers existed, there was a political task here, that is, a task for the class struggle in ideology, that could be perfectly well defined. It was, above all, a matter of unifying the extreme diversity of local and then regional ideologies around a few grand ideas in line with the dominant class's positions in order to constitute the unity of the dominant ideology indispensable to its double role: helping the dominant class to unify itself and subordinating the dominated class to it by taking up and neutralizing [*absorber*] the dangerous elements in its ideology. History shows that this ideological-political task was performed, before the advent of philosophy, by an important regional ideology that imposed itself on the other regional ideologies: for instance, religious ideology or political ideology. With the advent of philosophy, this task took a relatively new turn.

I do not mean to say that philosophy replaced the regional ideology that earlier unified, somehow or the other, the whole field of ideology in the dominant class's service. Quite the contrary. History shows that *it is not philosophy that has played the essential role in the unity of bourgeois ideology*, as far as its substance goes, but, rather, *legal ideology*. This, moreover, is why we were able to see that bourgeois philosophy itself had come about by basing itself on bourgeois legal ideology, borrowing from it not just the category of the subject, but also the idea of posing a question of right to all that exists: the beings and knowledge in the world, the world itself, and God. The fact remains, however, that philosophy played a very special, very precise part in this entente, and that this part refers us once again to the relationship that binds philosophy to the rationality of the existing sciences.

It seems to me that we can basically say the following, taking bourgeois philosophy as our example. In the labour of centuries that was required to constitute and, consequently, unify the dominant bourgeois ideology, *legal ideology was determinant* and *philosophy was dominant*. Legal ideology has, at least through the first fifty years of the nineteenth century, furnished the master ideas indispensable to constituting bourgeois liberal ideology, and it was around these ideas that all the work of unification was carried out. Philosophy was then able to play its own particular part by theoretically elaborating questions and answers, hence theses and categories that were, first, expressions of this legal ideology and, second, could work on the ideas of the existing ideologies in order to transform them in a way tending towards their unification. To attain this objective, it is necessary to produce abstract ideas, for, otherwise, how would it be possible to unify local and regional ideologies or to occupy the adversary's positions, which always display an extreme diversity?

It must not be supposed that the philosophy of the philosophers has enjoyed, in history, a monopoly on abstraction, *on this type of abstraction*. Before philosophy existed, the dominant regional ideology likewise produced and practised a very special type of abstraction, metaphorical most of the time, which enabled it to accomplish its mission of ideological unification. The only difference turns on the fact that philosophical abstraction is borrowed from scientific abstraction. This is a fact, and here we should perhaps again speak of the 'tear' produced by the advent of science in a cultural universe whose ideological-political equilibrium was unstable. The fact is that, since the interests at stake were doubtless too great (but there is a cruel lack of studies on this point), *the unification of the dominant ideology could not do without philosophy's services* from a certain point in history on, even when this philosophy was bent to the service of theology (a case that illustrates our previous remark: it is not necessarily and, to date, has never been philosophy which determines the dominant ideology).

25

If we are prepared to admit that the whole process of constituting the dominant ideology is simply a form of the class struggle, and if we are prepared to admit that the basic stakes of this class struggle are, behind the forms of the state, possession of the means of production and the different practices connected with them, scientific practice included, we can understand philosophy a little better.

We said that philosophy has no object, in the sense in which science has an object. We added, in the course of our exposition, that philosophy has, in contrast, objectives in the class struggle that oppose it to its philosophical adversaries in the realm of theory. We may now say that philosophy has objectives because it has stakes, like every struggle that is not an idealist struggle. But the stakes of the class struggle in theory known as philosophy are rather special: they are not in easy reach, they are remote, they are even so remote from the practice of philosophical class struggle that one wonders how philosophy can ever attain them. What are these stakes, beyond the refutation of one or another philosophical thesis? (Since philosophy is not a science, there is never any identifiable error in philosophy and, consequently, never any erroneous, untenable thesis.)

The stakes of the class struggle in theory are, precisely, the practices we mentioned a moment ago: *the stakes of philosophy are what happens in these practices.* Above all, in the practice of class struggle (economic, political, ideological), but also in all the other material practices, to which the sciences of nature are closely connected, and in the most diverse social practices as well (sexuality, the family, law, culture and so on). For the dominant class, it is a question of controlling these practices and the people who are their agents, and aligning these practices with its own class interests. Control of these practices does not come by way of possession of the means of production, exchange, and research alone, but also by way of the ideologies of which these practices are the site and the object. The full meaning of the unification of the dominant ideology is conferred on it by this demand, for it is through the unification of the ideologies and through their penetration by the dominant ideas that the dominant class's control and domination of these practices and their agents comes about. It is here that philosophy plays its part, since it works, as in a laboratory, on legal ideology's orders, to elaborate questions, theses, and categories that the dominant ideology adopts and carries to the heart of the ideological forms dominating the practices and their agents.

This clarifies, finally, a circumstance that has always been something of a mystery in the history of philosophy: the fact that philosophies take the form of *systems* – not all of them, but the great majority. Engels uttered a bit of foolishness on this subject, thereby proving that a materialist is never entirely immune to idealism, when he wrote, in *Ludwig Feuerbach*, that philosophical systems exist to 'satisfy an imperishable desire of the human mind – the desire to overcome all contradictions'.[1] What he said is true as far as *contradictions* go: but it is idealist to evoke the 'contradictions of the human *mind*'. The contradictions in question, which are very real, are the ones the dominant class encounters in constituting its dominant ideology; they are therefore, in the last instance, class contradictions, it being understood that there also exist other contradictions, in human beings' relation to nature as well as in individuals' unconscious relationship to themselves. It is perfectly true that the dominant class tends to resolve these contradictions, for they are incompatible with its class domination. And the unification of ideology as the dominant ideology is, precisely, one means of resolving class contradictions.

This is the demand to which the systematic form of most philosophies is a response, as is the 'object' that the whole idealist tradition, from Plato to Comte and Hegel, proposes to philosophy: 'thinking the whole'. When philosophy assigns itself the objective of 'thinking the whole', it freely confesses that it too plays its theoretical part, an abstract part, in the task of unifying the dominant ideology. We should, moreover, take care to avoid the trap represented by the existence of non-systematic philosophies, such as Kierkegaard's or Nietzsche's: for they are 'reactive' – dependent on the systems they criticize – and contribute, by playing devil's advocate, to representing, in the dominant ideology, oppositions that could have been very dangerous if they had remained unspoken or unknown. This remark of course has its limits, as does the role of philosophy in constituting the dominant ideology, as we have seen.

All this is well and good and, in a certain way, coherent; but, since it is class struggle which, in the last instance, motivates this resolution [of ideological contradictions], what shall we say about science? On the horizon of this naïve question, there appears the spectre of the class character of the sciences and of scientific objectivity. On this last point, I refer the reader to Dominique Lecourt's book.[2] The principle involved, however, calls for explanation. For scientific practice is a practice and, as such, it too is carried out under the domination of a determinate ideology, an ideology which, like the spontaneous ideologies of all the practices, reflects something of the truth of its practice.

Some time ago, I tried to show that we can distinguish, in the 'spontaneous philosophy of scientists', two different elements: element 1, the intrascientific element, tendentially materialist; and element 2, tendentially idealist, since it originates outside science, that is, in the last instance, in the dominant ideology, in which philosophy plays the role we have seen.[3] Thus every researcher works on a material object, concrete or abstract, under the domination of a certain ideology, which also includes philosophical categories that have become so completely a part of everyday life that they no longer even appear to be philosophical, or to be fraught with, and overdetermined by, philosophical echoes. Drawn from currently prevailing philosophy or even the philosophy of the past, these categories can either constitute obstacles to research, to researchers' theoretical practice, or can facilitate it. As a rule, scientists are unaware of this; they content themselves with solving the problems posed by the nature of their object, thanks to their experimental set-up. All this work naturally produces a materialist reduction, a materialist critique *in actu* of the idealist contents of the categories and ideas under whose domination scientists work: this reduction culminates in the production of objective knowledge, which consigns to oblivion the false or partially false ideas by which the process might have been momentarily tempted or dominated. A scientist rids himself of them without a word or a comment. For him, error does not exist: either he is in it, but does not think it, or he has eliminated it and it has disappeared from his mind. Hence his vulnerability to ideology's ready-made ideas, which present themselves to him without his being aware of it at the very moment in which he rids himself, without noticing it, of other ready-made ideas.

Why has there never been any serious attempt to struggle against this diabolical trap in which the scientist finds himself caught? It is all too obvious that bourgeois idealist ideology stands to gain from it. It manipulates the scientist unawares, taking him as far as the threshold of the knowledge that he produces, and then leads him astray again. The scientist's ideological submission matters more to the bourgeoisie than the productivity of research, all the official declarations notwithstanding. In vain does materialist philosophy warn the scientist and even enlighten him about the mechanisms of the mystification and exploitation to which he is subject; for it runs up against the redoubtable barrier of class ideological domination.[4]

The seventeenth-century and eighteenth-century philosophers wished to reform the human race's understanding, that of kings and scientists included. They came a cropper. Human understanding does not precede the decisive class struggles, it follows them. To change people's ideas, it 'is necessary to change the state' (Marx).

Yet what has just been said about philosophy and, via the dominant ideology after its conversion into the currency of local ideologies, about philosophy's role in unifying the dominant ideology, explains the proposition that we took as our starting point: *everyone is a philosopher*. Everyone is not, to be sure, a philosopher in the sense of the philosophy of the philosophers, which is not something everyone knows. Everyone is a philosopher to the extent that he too thinks in the philosophical categories which, after being elaborated in the laboratory of the philosophy of the erudite to fill the dominant ideology's order, penetrate the ideologies that dominate human practice. As a rule, people do not know that they are philosophers in this sense, although popular wisdom suspects as much, as Gramsci rightly pointed out. This characteristic is of great importance from the viewpoint of the practice of the class struggle, for it allows us to understand the need for philosophy in the class struggle, as well as the fact that activists, and also members of the broad masses, can be initiated into philosophical terminology and can, in principle, make sense of it.

Now that we have assembled enough elements for a theory of philosophy, we can answer the question as to what Marxist materialist philosophy might be. We shall do so by going back to our definition: Marxist materialist philosophy can exist only on condition that it assume, in radical fashion, the nature and mechanisms of philosophy. Since philosophy implies partisanship, Marxist philosophy takes sides in the philosophical class struggle. It is, in the last instance, class struggle in theory and, conscious of the class interests it represents, it joins the materialist camp and takes proletarian positions. Consequently, it fights: a philosopher is someone who fights in theory. Not against just anyone, just any time, just any way, but by recognizing the principal adversary of the moment, familiarizing himself with his contradictions, his strengths and weaknesses, discerning the 'weakest link' to seize for the attack, and choosing, as well, the best operational bases and the best allies (good theses, good categories), without ever losing control of them, etc.

How does the Marxist philosopher fight? He fights the way any philosopher does: by practising philosophy – but in a *new practice of philosophy*[5] that allows him to sidestep the pitfalls of idealism, especially when it has infiltrated his own ranks. He fights by formulating new theses that are so many weapons for the attack on positions that the history of the class struggle has led the adversary to occupy. These theses are composed of categories; it sometimes happens that he forges categories to respond to an unprecedented question. He knows that these categories can, if they have been properly 'adjusted', also prove useful in scientific practice and political practice – can prove useful, therefore, at a far remove from where he is, working at the distance imposed by philosophical theory – although he is also active in the Marxist-Leninist organization of class struggle. He does not lapse into the inanity of drawing distinctions between materialism and the dialectic, or into the theory of knowledge, or into ontology. Nor does he mistake the so-called human sciences, which are merely bourgeois ideology's theoretical formations, for sciences. He knows that this domain, occupied by the adversary, has to be conquered for scientific knowledge, thanks to the principles and concepts of historical materialism, the science of the laws of class struggle.

Finally, he does not succumb to one last bourgeois illusion: the belief that there exists a 'Marxist philosophy'. Yet this notion is widespread even among Marxists. There is no denying that it is based on a daring idea, because, such Marxists claim (I shared this mistaken idea for a few years),[6] Marx founded a new science and, at the same time, *a new 'philosophy'*. On closer inspection, however, this idea proves untenable. For while there are clearly 'breaks' in the history of the *sciences*, philosophy is so constituted that it does not really have a history, inasmuch as its pseudo-history is simply the recurrent manifestation, in varied forms, of one and the same function.

Marx, therefore, thought in existing philosophy; he did not found a new philosophy. He simply practised existing philosophy in a revolutionary way, by adopting theses that expressed the proletariat's revolutionary class positions. But if this is so, we are justified in saying that Marxist philosophy *does not exist* and *cannot exist* in the sense in which a philosophy, whether ancient, medieval, or bourgeois, must have a particular form of existence, that of systematicity. We have seen the reason for this systematicity: to sustain the labour of unifying the categories intended to facilitate the unification of the dominant ideology. Ultimately, then, a class reason comes into play here – a reason, consequently, specific to class societies.

Very strikingly, Marx said practically nothing about philosophy. In principle, he was right. Priority had to be given to utterly different forms of class struggle. Marx practised philosophy in his scientific and political work alone, and Lenin basically followed suit: they practised it silently, but concretely and effectively. I think, however, that more was involved. If the constitution of the dominant ideology is linked, as goes without saying, to the state and state power, there exists *a close relationship*, to which the whole history of philosophy bears witness, *between the state and philosophy*, between the state and the unified dominant ideology, hence between the state and the systematicity of the exploiting classes' philosophy.

As is clearly shown by Engels's unhappy attempt with regard to matter in motion, and by other examples of a sort that keeps recurring, this form of systematicity can be said to represent another ideological trap for the dominated class. If the proletariat's philosophy had to imitate bourgeois philosophy to the point of borrowing the form of the system from it, it would be in danger – and, as a matter of fact, it *is* in danger. For the conditions for unifying the proletariat's ideology have not yet been realized, except in caricatural form; and, even if they were realized, the historical task before the proletariat, once it is in power, will be to smash the bourgeois state and its apparatuses, and then conduct the state to its demise. In the latter perspective, it would be inappropriate to practice a systematic philosophy that could only – at its level, of course – reinforce the state. That is why it seems to me correct to say that *there can exist no Marxist philosophy in the classic sense of the word philosophy*, and that the revolution that Marx brought to philosophy consisted in practising it in a new way: in accordance with its true nature, of which historical materialism produces the knowledge; and, at the same time, in practising it on the basis of the proletariat's class positions.

We must, however, add one important point to make this whole analysis more precise.

If, because the class struggle for the constitution of the dominant ideology enlists philosophy in that struggle's opposing ranks, it is characteristic of all philosophy that it helps to unify the dominant ideology by adjusting categories and theses – if it is therefore characteristic of all philosophy that it is determined in this function by an ideological region essential to the ascendant or the dominant class – the fact remains that this determination is marked by class limits.

However we approach the matter, we cannot help but think that a philosophy such as bourgeois philosophy, developed on the basis of bourgeois legal ideology and under its determination, is defined 'in the last instance' by its role in the class struggle, and that it cannot, consequently, escape a *subjective* class determination.

If we now turn to the philosophy or the new practice of philosophy that the working class needs to unify the ideology of its class struggle, we will find ourselves confronted with the same determination, assuming that our definitions are correct. The new 'practice of philosophy' will be, willy-nilly, and even if the formula is offensive, a new avatar of the 'handmaiden of politics' – of proletarian politics. It is well known how the young Lukács dealt with this problem: by endowing the proletariat with a 'universal' essence that brought about the desired coincidence between, on the one hand, the proletariat's *subjectivity* and, on the other, the *universality* of this subjectivity, become *objective* as a result. Marxism, however, cannot endorse that sort of idealist solution.[1]

The fact is that Marxism has the principle of a materialist solution to hand, a solution in conformity with the science, founded by Marx, of the conditions and forms of class struggle. For what was the novelty that Marx introduced here? It was a theory of the dialectic connecting the different levels of the class struggle, a theory which, consequently, made it possible to think the necessity and the objective laws of what happens in and between the different levels of the class struggle: economic, political, ideological, theoretical. Marx gave us, among other things, the wherewithal to outline a theory of philosophy's role in the theoretical class struggle, and of its effects and repercussions in the ideological class struggle, in regional and local ideologies and, through them, in the different practices. Finally, he allowed us to see that the philosophy charged with the role of theoretical elaboration of the unification of existing ideologies as a dominant ideology did not itself determine this role, but that its forms were 'commanded' from without by an ideology determinant of the dominant class's practice and class struggle.

Before Marx, philosophy may be said to have played its role without being aware of the conditions determining it: to have played its role blindly. Since it had no idea of the laws governing it 'behind its back', it thought it had no 'back', and identified its own nature with the only consciousness of itself that it had, of what it considered to be its 'object' and vocation: unveiling the Truth, Meaning, the Origin, and the End. And it conceived of its own history as the history of the forms of this unveiling, which, paradoxically, had always been attained and had always to be undertaken anew.

By providing the militants of the workers' class struggle with what neither the philosophers nor the politicians of any class society could know, Marx gave them, for the first time in history, a critical purchase on philosophy that was not philosophical, but scientific. By acquainting them with what philosophy is in the last instance, namely class struggle in theory disguised as a search after the truth or an unveiling of the truth, Marx gave them the means of knowing, scientifically, both philosophy's role and the conditions of the determination, by the proletariat's political ideology, of Marxist practice in philosophy. With that, he also gave them the means of rectifying this determination and adjusting it to the strategic objectives of the workers' class struggle.

Knowledge of philosophy's conditions of existence and role by no means leads to replacing philosophy with the science of its conditions of existence, no more than knowledge of the laws of gravity leads to the disappearance of gravity. However, just as knowledge of the laws of falling bodies has allowed us to act on the effects of gravity and discover the means of annulling them, so knowledge of the laws of the determination of the philosophical practice of Marxism by proletarian political ideology allows us, in principle, to criticize the effects of that determination and inflect those laws, so as to avoid the blind automatism of a subjective class determination.

Philosophy does not thereby become an objective science. It can, however, withstand the temptation of a withdrawal into itself to which subjective class politics is exposed in all great political crises [*épreuves*], and serve, ever more effectively, the liberation of the social practices.

All this shows why it is impossible, in a historical period marked by the crisis of Marxism, to restore Marxist practice in philosophy without simultaneously restoring the science of the laws of the class struggle. For, without the help of the results of this revolutionary science, Marxist philosophy can no longer control its political determination; it lapses into a class subjectivism that is always, when the situation is dominated, as it is, by the bourgeois class, a *form* of bourgeois class subjectivism, despite the Marxist terminology that lingers on as a façade (consider Stalin). It is enough, today, to ask: What is the current situation of Marxism in philosophy? in order to state the answer: We have, on the one hand, the Soviet philosophers' ontology and gnoseology and, on the other, the far-leftism of this or that petty bourgeois. But what is proletarian about all that? Nothing but the proclamations.

You who have just read these pages should be aware that you will find the dialectical-materialist practice of Marxist philosophy that I have just discussed in Marx's and Lenin's theoretical and political works. You will also find it in the courageous, difficult struggles waged by the working class on the basis of correct positions that are themselves difficult to develop and defend. At all events, this philosophy, available in living form in these books and these struggles, has been handed down to us by the tradition of these combats, and we are not alone in the world.

But you should also know that if you look for this tradition in the official declarations of most of the leaders of the communist parties, in the commentaries of the 'Marxist philosophers' recognized by these parties or, a fortiori, in courses or books by 'professors of Marxism-Leninism' in the USSR and the socialist countries, you will find nothing but a caricature of it. I do not mean to cast the first stone at anyone. But, as a result of the titanic class struggles of the period dominated by imperialism, socialism has lurched into the Stalinist deviation, and the Workers' and the International Communist Movement has emerged from this unprecedented crisis, after the victory over fascism, only at the price of a bizarre theoretical and philosophical retreat that can be regarded as a defeat in the proper sense of the word.

You must, however, also know that the defeats of the workers' movement are not like military defeats: for, even in defeat, the workers' class struggle does not cease. That struggle assumes and invents new forms; it abruptly reappears in places where no one was expecting it; it is pursued even in countries where it seems to have been completely extinguished. Witness what is going on today. Although Marxism has been overwhelmed by bourgeois ideology, although Marxist theory has literally 'disappeared', look and you will see that it is being reborn in the class struggles that imperialism has precipitated in the big metropolitan countries no less than in those of the 'Third World'. You will see that it is being gradually restored by new generations of fighters, workers and intellectuals, who are assimilating it because they need it; who have, in order to assimilate it, set about rediscovering Marxist theory and working on Marxist theory, and drawing from it the new knowledge and new theses capable of guiding their political and theoretical practice.

To all those who, today, have doubts about philosophy, all those who doubt that Marxism is capable of intervening in philosophy in a way that is not arbitrary or subjective, but correct and effective, I say: Just look at what is going on around you! Look how fast things are moving! Look at the struggles into which young people are throwing themselves side-by-side with the old, look at the combats from which Marxist theory is emerging rejuvenated and reinforced! Look how the errors of the past are being corrected! Look at the perspectives that are opening up before us! Look how close the future is!

You are fighting in the workers' and the people's class struggle? Remember that the class struggle needs philosophy, 'class struggle in theory'.

You want to be a philosopher? Remember that a philosopher is someone who fights in theory – someone who, when he has understood the reasons for this necessary combat, joins the ranks of the workers' and the people's class struggle.

Remember Marx, in 1845, scribbling a few lines on a sheet of paper. 1848 had not yet appeared on the horizon. The darkest oppression reigned. Marxist theory had yet to be firmly established on its foundations. But Marx had at least understood that he could do no scientific work in history unless he 'shifted terrain', unless he abandoned bourgeois class philosophical positions and went over to proletarian class theoretical positions. The result was the 'Theses on Feuerbach', and this short sentence, which we continue to live by: 'The philosophers have only interpreted the world in various ways; the point is to change it.'[2]

July 1976

APPENDIX: CAN EVERYONE BE A PHILOSOPHER?[1]

In spring 1957, René Julliard's Paris publishing house released Jean-François Revel's polemical *Pourquoi des philosophes?* (Why philosophers?). Its main thesis was that philosophy had seen its day and should now efface itself in favour of the sciences and psychoanalysis, which had taken over the role that philosophy had played as well as it could before their appearance on the scene. Revel saw proof of what he said in the distressing poverty, masked by affectation and deliberate obscurity, of the philosophical thought – or the thought that, at any rate, purported to be philosophical – of Heidegger, Lacan, Lévi-Strauss, Merleau-Ponty, Sartre and other illustrious names. His broadside stirred up something of a brouhaha. Lacan, whose 'two-bit Mallarmeism' offered Revel one of his favourite targets, is supposed to have trampled *Why Philosophers?* underfoot (in the literal sense) in the middle of his seminar. Merlau-Ponty took advantage of a February 1958 interview that he gave Madeleine Chapsal to excoriate the book almost as elegantly as Lacan ('this book recalls the Stalinist denunciations of the finest hour'). Sartre attacked (in a lecture he may never have delivered) an unnamed philistine 'non-philosopher' who was supposed to have concluded that 'philosophers were only fit to be thrown to the dogs'. And Lévi-Strauss, striking his best schoolmaster's pose, devoted several pages of *Structural Anthropology* to why 'Monsieur Revel should refrain from discussing me'.[2]

Althusser saw things differently. 'I find impertinence of this sort enchanting', he wrote to a friend in 1957. The *caïman* or head tutor of philosophy at Paris's École normale supérieure had an unmistakable taste for such provocations. What is more, Revel was, at the time, a close friend of his with whom he was planning to launch a series of critical books in the humanities. But Revel's polemic, which, he admitted in the same letter, was 'rather weak', interested him for a deeper reason. In his way, he shared its anti-philosophical inspiration.

In what way, exactly? The reader may judge for himself. On 8 October 1957, there took place in Paris, in a hall at 44 rue de Rennes, in the framework of a series of lecture-debates called *Cercle ouvert* (Open circle) that was chaired, at the time, by Jacques Nantet, a discussion around *Why Philosophers?* The participants in this event, which bore the title 'Can everyone be a philosopher?', included François Châtelet, Maurice de Gandillac, Lucien Goldmann, Robert Misrahi, and Jean Wahl. Althusser's intervention in the discussion that followed the debate proper – a 'triumph', according to a letter he wrote the next day – was published two months later in the little review *Cercle ouvert*. It is here reproduced unabridged.

* * *

I wonder whether the question, posed the way it's been posed, deserves to be examined at such length. Can everyone be a philosopher? I think Misrahi is clearly right to say that, however we define philosophy, it's obvious that no one can philosophize without training. It's as hard to learn to philosophize as it is to learn to walk. I think, however, that, in the presentations we've heard here, a number of important problems have been identified and broached.

The first one is that of the language of philosophy, or of what has been called, to cite Marx's phrase, 'philosophical jargon'. This is an important problem, but it's a screen-problem and, relatively, a false problem. For we always imagine we have to show that philosophy has a right to a technical terminology. The problem is whether philosophy has a right to consider itself a specialized discipline. Consequently, it seems to me that the problem of philosophical jargon can't be considered by itself, but has to be immediately related to what comprises its justification, its legitimization: namely philosophy's right to exist as such. There we have the fundamental problem that seems to have emerged from this discussion.

Whatever reservations I may have about Revel's book – and I could endorse many of those I've heard this evening – I share, at bottom, its essential inspiration. I believe that Revel has taken on, in a way all his own, with his personal talent and from one particular angle, a problem at the heart of contemporary preoccupations, even if it doesn't date from today. It dates, in fact, as Châtelet and Goldmann have said, from the eighteenth century.

Basically, this problem is whether we have to get rid of philosophy, at least of philosophy in its fundamental essence – with respect to what it claims to be and what differentiates it from other disciplines, other activities, other spiritual and intellectual attitudes – the same way we have to get rid of religion.

There exists in the world a whole series of different spiritual attitudes that claim to be justified, yet aren't exempt for all that from criticism or examination of their titles to existence. When we ask whether philosophy can exist, if it exists, if it has a right to exist, we ask a question similar to those which, in the nineteenth century, were often asked about religion. Does it have a right to exist? What are the titles that justify, not just its existence in the present, but its ambitions to continue to exist in future?

I think it's pretty much impossible to pose this problem today in anything but a historical perspective. A simple glance at history shows that the titles that philosophy can invoke and the relations that it maintains with different disciplines vary with the period. Yet what seems essential about philosophy is that it justifies itself with one basic claim.

What I would propose is an effort to bring out what philosophy can be, the titles it confers on itself. It is certain that Revel can contribute to this critique by showing that philosophy seizes on problems that originate outside it – that philosophy is simply the knowledge [*la science*] of solved problems. Thus when philosophy has eliminated everything that has heterogeneous origins, when it is face-to-face with itself, how can it legitimate and define itself, and what titles does it present in its own defence?

There are two ways of broaching the problem: by trying to make the philosopher speak, or by trying to see how the philosopher's discourse actually appears. If, when we make the philosopher speak, we ask him for the titles that ultimately justify his pretensions, he will say – and this is a grand tradition, found in Plato, Descartes, Kant, Hegel, Husserl, and Heidegger alike – the philosopher will say, above all, that he is the one who asks himself what the originary meaning of things is. The philosopher always knows, more or less, what the radical origin of things is. He is the one who has in his possession – thanks to a reflection that aims at what is prior to [*en deçà de*] all existing meanings – the origin of all possible meanings, all existing meanings. At bottom, he is the one who knows what others don't, and who also knows what the true meaning of what others know is, what the meaning of the meanings that others possess is, what the meaning of the gestures that men accomplish is, as well as the meaning of the acts in which they are engaged. The philosopher is someone who, in a certain way, claims to possess, from the very beginning, the truth's birth certificate. Whether he is a Platonist, becomes one of the encyclopedists of whom history offers us several examples, or isn't particularly sensitive to the need to totalize human experience, he is always someone who tries to discover the essential meaning of everything that has a meaning. Such would be the defence of philosophy that the philosopher would make.

I'd now like to put the question differently, by asking how this self-justification of the philosopher's actually appears. I would like to pose this question in a more historical perspective. I'm going to say some very general things here that need to be justified in detail. I hope I won't offend my audience's sensibilities.

Whether it is a question of Plato, Descartes, Kant, Hegel, Husserl, or Heidegger, it seems to me that the philosopher actually finds himself, when he defines himself in terms of this claim, in an ambiguous, contradictory position. Monsieur Jean Wahl said a moment ago that, according to Malraux, the artist defines himself as a function of other artists, the poet as a function of other poets. Now what is striking about philosophers, at least the great philosophers, is that they define themselves in fact – and they are, to an extent, aware of this – as a function of the philosophies they reject. In other words, the effort we are engaged in making now, to the extent that we are making it in order to try to get rid of philosophy, is an effort that that all the great philosophers in history have made. We see Plato trying to liquidate a philosophy that seems threatening to him, that of the Sophists, the subjectivists of his day; we see Descartes trying to get rid of what he calls false metaphysics, the metaphysics of the Scholastics; we see Kant developing an elaborate critique of metaphysics and so on. In that respect, we're simply their heirs: we're pursuing and extending one and the same inspiration.

Why do philosophers feel the need to get rid of existing philosophies? Because they consider them to be threatening in certain respects, to be compromising certain causes in question, certain historically important causes. Whether it's a matter, in Plato's day, of constituting an objective reflection; whether it's a matter, with Kant, of defending Newtonian physics or constituting a field of objectivity in which the natural sciences can develop; whether it's a matter, with Husserl, of struggling against the subjectivism which, in the late nineteenth century (shortly after the crisis in physics), threatened all of the natural and human sciences, we see philosophers tempted by the idea of ridding themselves of the philosophies that seem to them to put the future of humanity in jeopardy.

Here, then, is where the basic drama of the problem of philosophy is played out: in the very moment in which the great philosopher tries to get rid of philosophy, in order to get rid of it (that is, in order to remain true to the goal preoccupying us), he founds a philosophy. Take the example of Kant or Husserl. As far is Kant goes, his effort to free himself of the trammels of a relativistic empiricism culminates, in fact, in a struggle against a form of ideology that seems threatening to him; but he can take up this struggle only on condition that he found a philosophy, in other words, on condition that he go back to what is, in his opinion, at the origin of all meaning and all objectivity.

The great philosopher's effort to rid himself of philosophy seems to me to have, as its necessary counterpart, a recourse to what we call philosophy. In this combat, the philosopher who wishes to destroy philosophy takes refuge, in some sense, in what must clearly be called a philosophical hinter world [*arrière-monde*]. That is, the philosopher leaves our world, which is an egg. He is someone who sees this egg from the outside: he emerges from it in order to declare that it is an egg, that the meaning of this egg he has emerged from is such-and-such; and he goes on to spell out that meaning. It seems to me that this distance the philosopher takes from the meanings that he wants to found is, emphatically, constitutive of the very essence of philosophy.

Since I have used the word foundation: I believe that the philosopher lives with the feeling that, to justify a cause he wants to defend, he has to leave the field, precisely, in which this cause appears; that is, he has to leave the world in which this cause is defended and attacked. It seems to him necessary to take a sort of originary distance from this world. That is why we see a double combat playing itself out in the great philosophers: a destructive combat and, at the same time, a foundational combat.

The problem that arises for us is the following: Is it possible to return to the grand philosophical tradition, a critical tradition destructive of the ideologies of the present, without once again founding a philosophy – and 'philosophy' has a very precise meaning this time – without taking refuge in this kind of point removed from both time and space that will be, for the philosopher, the origin of everything that it will be possible to state and the foundation of everything it will be possible to affirm? Is it possible, for us, to reject philosophy without founding a philosophy?

On this point, the opinion that seems to have crystallized is that, as far as the natural sciences go, philosophy has played its role and the natural sciences have extricated themselves from philosophy. The situation isn't the same for the human sciences. Goldmann has rightly said that the existing mode of social relations[3] doesn't make it possible to display a state of mind that would make the confrontation superfluous.

I would like to cite as an example here, without pretending to resolve the problem, that of Marx, who tried, precisely, to destroy philosophy in the very field in which it seemed to be the most vital, that of the human sciences. Marx's texts on the end of philosophy are famous. Marx proclaimed the necessity of putting an end to philosophy in the field of history, precisely, the fundamental field of the human sciences. What seems important to me is not so much this affirmation, but, basically, the path Marx followed to arrive at it. We are familiar with this path: it is that constituted by the works of his youth, in which he frees himself from Hegel's and Feuerbach's influence and arrives at the maturity of his thought.

As far as the human sciences are concerned, Marx realized that the word 'philosophy', that is, this pretension of discovering the meaning of history – for what is in question here is history – ultimately came down, in the work of a philosopher, to coinciding with an epoch's illusions about itself, that is to say, with a dominant ideology. And, in a way that is very precise in Marx, putting an end to philosophy in the field of history consisted in carrying out a critique of existing ideologies, of their relations with the whole historical corpus under consideration, a critique that was possible only after a scientific theory of history had been constituted. Marx made this attempt, which Goldmann has also undertaken in one particular field, with respect to Hegel. He produced a critique of the philosophy in which he had grown up and from which he had freed himself. For him, the slogan 'put an end to philosophy' had a very precise, very concrete goal: its sole meaning was to coincide with a historical discipline that allowed him to forge a theory of philosophy.

I believe that if we ask: What will become of philosophy? we can in any case assign it the task of becoming the history of philosophy, not in the sense this had for classical philosophers, but in the Marxist sense, in which the task consists in asking from which point on a philosophy is born, flourishes, and dies.

NOTES

Introduction

1 L. Althusser, *Sur la philosophie* (Paris: Gallimard/NRF, 1994), p. 93.

2 F. Navarro, Présentation, in *Sur la philosophie*, p. 22.

3 Published in English as 'The Underground Current of the Materialism of the Encounter', in Althusser, *Philosophy of the Encounter: Later Writings, 1978–1987*, eds. O. Corpet and F. Matheron, trans. G.M. Goshgarian (London: Verso, 2006), pp. 163–207.

4 A. Negri, 'Notes on the Evolution of the Thought of the Later Althusser', trans. O. Vasile, in A. Callari and D.F. Ruccio, eds., *Postmodern Materialism and the Future of Marxist Theory: Essays in the Althusserian Tradition* (Hanover and London: Wesleyan University Press, 1996), p. 58.

5 L. Althusser and É. Balibar, *Reading Capital*, trans. B. Brewster (London: Verso, 1970), pp. 45, 281, 82.

6 L. Althusser, 'Three Notes on the Theory of Discourses', in Althusser, *The Humanist Controversy and Other Writings*, ed. F. Matheron, trans. G.M. Goshgarian (London: Verso, 2003), p. 59, translation modified.

7 See, for example, Althusser's unpublished 1966 notes on Pierre Macherey's *A Theory of Literary Production*, cited in G.M. Goshgarian, 'The Very Essence of the Object, the Soul of Marxism, and Other Singular Things', *Encountering Althusser: Politics and Materialism in Contemporary Radical Thought*, eds. K. Diefenbach *et al.* (New York: Continuum, 2012), p. 107; L. Althusser, 'Philosophy and the Spontaneous Philosophy of the Scientists (1967)', trans. W. Montag, in Althusser, *Philosophy and the Spontaneous Philosophy of the Scientists and Other Essays*, ed. G. Elliott (London: Verso, 1990), p. 154 ('since Epicurus ... [chance] has played a positive materialist role in combating teleological exploitations of biology'); and Althusser's 1972 (?) letter to F. Markovits-Pessel, cited in Markovits-Pessel, 'Althusser et Montesquieu: L'histoire comme philosophie expérimentale', in *Althusser philosophe*, ed. P. Raymond (Paris: Presses Universitaires de France, 1997), p. 31: 'I have always suspected, on the basis of hints we can make out in *Capital*, that the contact between Marx and Epicurus was not without reason and had major repercussions.'

8 L. Althusser, Letter of 15 March 1969 to M.A. Macciocchi, in Macciocchi, *Letters from inside the Italian Communist Party to Louis Althusser*, trans. S.M. Hellman (London: New Left Books, 1973), p. 306; Letter of 25 March 1969 to Macciocchi, in Althusser, *Lettres à Hélène, 1947–1980*, ed. O. Corpet (Paris: Grasset/Imec, 2011), p. 539.

9 L. Althusser, 'Is it Simple to Be a Marxist in Philosophy?' trans. G. Locke, in *Philosophy and Spontaneous Philosophy*, pp. 216–217; Althusser, 'The Transformation of Philosophy', trans. T.E. Lewis, in *ibid.*, p. 261.

10 L. Althusser, *Cours sur Rousseau*, ed. Y. Vargas (Paris: Le Temps des Cerises, 2012), p. 105. The reference is to the transformative role of accident in Rousseau, the main champion of the swerve in Althusser's work before his (re)discovery of Epicurus in the 1970s.

11 L. Althusser, *How to Be a Marxist in Philosophy*, p. 101.

12 L. Althusser, *Les vaches noires: Interview imaginaire (Le malaise du XXIIe Congrès)*, ed. G.M. Goshgarian (Paris: Presses Universitaires de France, 2016, English translation forthcoming from Bloomsbury).

13 On the speakers' platform were François Châtelet, Maurice de Gandillac, Lucien Goldmann, Robert Misrahi, and Jean Wahl. Revel was not present.

14 L. Althusser, 'Can Everyone be a Philosopher?' pp. 148–149 below.

15 L. Althusser, *For Marx*, trans. B. Brewster (London: Verso, 1969), p. 169.

16 L. Althusser, 'Reply to John Lewis', in Althusser, *Essays in Self-Criticism*, trans. G. Lock (London: New Left Books, 1976), pp. 67–72; Althusser, 'Elements of Self-Criticism', in ibid., pp. 101–150.

17 L. Althusser, 'Note sur la conjoncture politico-théorique, 4 mai 1967', Imec, Fonds Althusser, Alt2.A11-03.02, p. 2 verso.

18 L. Althusser, 'Livre sur le communisme', Imec, Fonds Althusser, Alt2. A19–02.02.

19 P. Macherey, 'Althusser and the Concept of the Spontaneous Philosophy of the Scientists', trans. R. Mackay, *Parrhesia*, 6 (2009), p. 14.

20 L. Althusser, 'Philosophy and the Spontaneous Philosophy of the Scientists', in *Philosophy and Spontaneous Philosophy*, pp. 71–165 (the first four lectures); 'Du côté de la philosophie', in Althusser, *Écrits philosophiques et politiques*, ed. F. Matheron, vol. 2, pp. 255–298 (the fifth lecture).

21 L. Althusser, 'The Historical Task of Marxist Philosophy', in *The Humanist Controversy*, pp. 207–218.

22 L. Althusser, 'Lenin and Philosophy', trans. B. Brewster, in *Philosophy and Spontaneous Philosophy*, pp. 167–202.

23 L. Althusser, 'Philosophy and Spontaneous Philosophy', pp. 130–131; Althusser, 'Lenin and Philosophy', pp. 198, 200, translation modified.

24 L. Althusser, 'Lenin and Philosophy', 199–200, translation modified.

25 L. Althusser, 'Du côté de la philosophie', p. 265.

26 L. Althusser, 'Lenin and Philosophy', pp. 177, 199–200.

27 L. Althusser, 'Can Everyone be a Philosopher?', p. 149 below.

28 Ibid., p. 147 below.

29 L. Althusser, 'Philosophy and Spontaneous Philosophy', pp. 101–102.

30 L. Althusser, 'Lenin and Philosophy', p. 201.

31 Ibid., p. 197.

32 Ibid., p. 196; translation modified. *Ligne de démarcation* is the standard French translation of the unspectacular, but now famous metaphor Lenin uses in *Materialism and Empirio-Criticism*, chap. 2, sec. 5, chap. 5, sec. 2, and elsewhere. The most common English translation is 'boundary'. One finds 'draw a dividing-line between' or 'dissociate ourselves from' as equivalents of '*tracer une ligne de démarcation entre*' in published translations of Althusser.

33 L. Althusser, 'Lenin and Philosophy', p. 197.

34 L. Althusser, 'Rousseau: The Social Contract (The Discrepancies)', in Althusser, *Politics and History: Montesquieu, Rousseau, Marx*, trans. B. Brewster (London: Verso, 1972), p. 113.

35 L. Althusser, *For Marx*, pp. 29–30, translation modified.

36 L. Althusser, 'The Humanist Controversy', p. 270; Althusser, 'Lenin and Philosophy', p. 181 (where *coupure continuée* is translated as 'sustained break').

37 L. Althusser, 'Lenin and Philosophy', pp. 199, 201.

38 L. Althusser to L. Sève, 27 April 1972. Imec, Fonds Althusser, Alt2.C6-02.

39 L. Althusser, 'On the Reproduction of Capitalism', trans. G.M. Goshgarian, in *On the Reproduction of Capitalism: Ideology and Ideological State Apparatuses*, ed. J. Bidet, trans. Goshgarian and B. Brewster. This book includes a slightly revised version of Brewster's translation of 'Ideology and Ideological State Apparatuses' (originally published in Althusser, *Lenin and Philosophy and Other Essays*, pp. 127–186).

40 Althusser, 'Can Everyone be a Philosopher?', p. 145 below.

41 L. Althusser, *The Facts*, in *'The Future Lasts a Long Time' and 'The Facts'*, eds. O. Corpet and Y.M. Boutang, trans. R. Veasey (London: Chatto and Windus, 1993), p. 360.

42 This summary of the response developed at length in *How to Be a Marxist in Philosophy*, pp. 129ff., is drawn from 'The Facts', pp. 359–360. On the importance of the facts, see *How to Be a Marxist in Philosophy*, pp. 99–100.

43 L. Althusser, *On the Reproduction of Capitalism*, pp. 17, 16.

44 Ibid., pp. 17, 7, 2.

45 L. Althusser, 'Du côté de la philosophie', p. 265; *On the Reproduction of Capitalism*, p. 256.

46 L. Althusser, *On the Reproduction of Capitalism*, p. 194 (cf. p. 266).

47 Ibid., p. 196; Althusser, 'Du côté de la philosophie', p. 282.

48 L. Althusser, *On the Reproduction of Capitalism*, pp. 145, 93.

49 Ibid., pp. 15–16.

50 The posthumously published version of the course is based on these corrected proofs.

51 L. Althusser, 'Lenin and Philosophy', pp. 195, 199.

52 Ibid., pp. 181–182.

53 L. Althusser, 'Notes sur la philosophie', in *Écrits philosophique et politiques*, ed. F. Matheron, vol. 2, pp. 318–322.

54 L. Althusser, 'On the Evolution of the Young Marx', in *Essays in Self-Criticism*, pp. 158–161. This essay first saw the light in January 1973, in English translation. The original French version was published in 1974.

55 Althusser, 'Reply to John Lewis', pp. 69, 58, note 17; translation modified, here and in subsequent citations. It is by no means certain that Lewis intended to make the vaguely Maoist point Althusser grants him, or even that Althusser ever thought he did. The passage Althusser no doubt has in mind is a characterization of his own Marxism as 'a "knowledge" reserved for the elite, completely separated from the masses by the "break" between involvement and conscious search ... and the level of a detached system of organized abstraction' (Lewis, 'The Althusser Case [Part 2]', *Marxism Today*, 16, no. 2 (1972), p. 46).

56 L. Althusser, 'Reply to John Lewis', p. 58.

57 Ibid., p. 49.

58 L. Althusser, 'Lenin and Philosophy', p. 193.

59 L. Althusser, 'Rousseau: The Social Contract', p. 120.

60 L. Althusser, 'The Humanist Controversy', p. 238.

61 L. Althusser, 'Elements of Self-Criticism', pp. 143–144.

62 L. Althusser, 'Socialisme idéologique et socialisme scientifique', Imec, Fonds Althusser, Alt2.A8-02.02, p. 17.

63 '*Exister c'est se reproduire.*' L. Althusser, *On the Reproduction of Capitalism*, p. 219.

64 L. Althusser, 'Note on the ISAs', trans. G.M. Goshgarian, in *On the Reproduction of Capitalism*, p. 226.

65 F. Engels to A. Bebel 18–25 March 1875, in *Marx and Engels Collected Works*, Volume 24 (London: Lawrence and Wishart, 2010), p. 71; V.I. Lenin, *Marxism and the State: Preparatory Materials for the Book State and Revolution* (Moscow: Progress Publishers, 1972), marginal annotation of Engels' Letter to Bebel of 18–25 March 1875.

66 L. Althusser, 'Lenin and Philosophy', pp. 182–184.

67 The same November 1967 Note that anticipates Althusser's post-1968 position on the determinant role of politics in the Marxian theoretical revolution also anticipates his mid-1970s abandonment of the idea that the task of Marxist philosophy is to develop what he calls, in the Note, a materialist-philosophical 'counter-system'. See 'Notes sur la philosophie', pp. 320–321.

68 Althusser and his collaborators had since late 1966 been planning to produce a systematic work on dialectical materialism – 'a true work of philosophy that can stand as our Ethics', Althusser wrote in a letter to Étienne Balibar (14 October 1966, IMEC archives, Alt2.C1bis-01). The idea was still alive when Althusser delivered the lecture 'Lenin and Philosophy', but probably not when he published it in 1969.

69 F. Engels to A. Bebel, 18–28 March 1875, cited in Althusser, 'The Transformation of Philosophy', p. 263.

70 Ibid., p. 261; *The Facts*, p. 361.

71 L. Althusser, 'The Transformation of Philosophy', pp. 264–265, translation modified.

72 L. Althusser, 'Une conversation philosophique', *Digraphe*, 66, December 1993, pp. 55–62.

Chapter 1

1 Note on the text: Capitalization, erratic in the original French text, has been standardized in the present translation.

2 M. Descartes, 'Letter to Mersenne 24th December 1640', in *The Philosophical Writings of Descartes*, Volume 3: *The Correspondence*, trans. J. Cottingham, R. Stoothoff, D. Murdoch and A. Kenny (Cambridge: Cambridge University Press, 1997), p. 163: 'It should be noted that throughout the work the order I follow is not the order of the subject-matter, but the order of the reasoning.'

3 I. Kant, *Groundwork for the Metaphysics of Morals*, ed. and trans. A.W. Wood (New Haven: Yale University Press, 2002), p. 26: 'This condescension to popular concepts is to be sure very laudable when the elevation to principles of pure reason has already been achieved to full satisfaction, and that would mean first *grounding* the doctrine of morals on metaphysics, but procuring *entry* for it by means of popularity, once it stands firm. But it is quite absurd to want to humor popularity in the first investigation, upon which depends the correctness of principles ... there is no art in being commonly understandable if one relinquishes all well-grounded insight; this produces only a disgusting mish-mash of patched-together observations and half-reasoned principles, in which superficial minds revel, because there is always something serviceable for everyday chitchat, but which insightful people disregard, feeling confused ...'

4   A. Gramsci, 'Notes for an Introduction and an Approach to the Study of Philosophy and the History of Culture', in *The Gramsci Reader: Selected Writings 1916–1935*, ed. D. Forgacs (New York: New York University Press, 2000), p. 325. Cf. 'Intellectuals and Non-Intellectuals', in *The Gramsci Reader*, ibid., p. 321: 'Each man ... is a "philosopher", an artist, a man of taste, he participates in a particular conception of the world, has a conscious line of moral conduct, and therefore contributes to sustain a conception of the world or to modify it, that is, to bring into being new modes of thought.'

5   Crossed out in the manuscript: 'hence the present attempt at an initiation into philosophy as well'.

Chapter 2

1   Descartes, *Meditations on First Philosophy with Selections from the Objections and Replies*, ed. J. Cottingham (Cambridge: Cambridge University Press, 1996), pp. 14ff.

2   Plato, *The Republic*, V, 476d ff.; *Meno*, 85cd.

3   B. Spinoza, 'On the Improvement of the Understanding', trans. R.H.M. Elwes, in *Ethics,* preceded by 'On the Improvement of the Understanding', ed. J. Gutmann (New York: Hafner, The Hafner Library of Classics, 1963), p. 7; *Ethics*, trans. W.H. White, trans. revised by A.H. Stirling, in ibid., Book II, Proposition XL, Note 2, p. 112.

4   Descartes, 'Fifth Meditation' in *Meditations on First Philosophy with Selections from the Objections and Replies*, ed. J. Cottingham (Cambridge: Cambridge University Press, 1996), p. 44. See also 'On Meditation Two', ibid., p. 68, and 'On Meditation Six', ibid., p. 107.

5   P. Gassendi, *Disquisitio metaphysica / Recherches Métaphysiques, ou doutes et instances contre la métaphysique de R. Descartes et ses réponses*, bilingual edition, ed. and trans. B. Rochot (Paris: Vrin, 1962), p. 80: 'When I reached this passage on my first reading of your meditations, in which I had hoped to find some truth unheard of to this day ... I exclaimed: My God, the novelty that one had to look for with such a big apparatus and with so much effort is – that *you exist*!'

Chapter 3

1 G.W.F. Hegel, *Science of Logic*, ed. H.D. Lewis, trans. A.V. Miller (Atlantic Highlands, New Jersey: Humanities Paperback Library, 1969), p. 82.

2 G.W.F. Hegel, *Phenomenology of Spirit*, trans. A.V. Miller (Oxford: Oxford University Press, 1977), pp. 58–79.

3 V.I. Lenin, *Philosophical Notebooks*, *Collected Works*, Volume 38 (Moscow: Progress Publishers, 1976), p. 318: 'The beginning – the most simple, ordinary, mass, immediate "Being": the single commodity ("Sein" in political economy). The analysis of it as a social relation. A double analysis, deductive and inductive – logical and historical (forms of value).'

4 K. Marx, *Capital Volume One*, trans. B. Howkes (London: Penguin Classics, 1990), p. 90.

5 K. Marx, Preface to the first German edition, *Capital* Volume One, in *Marx and Engels Collected Works*, Volume 35 (London: Lawrence and Wishart, 2010), p. 7; L. Althusser, 'Preface to *Capital* Volume One', in Althusser, *Lenin and Philosophy and Other Essays*, trans. B. Brewster (New York: Monthly Review Press, 1971), p. 90: 'Marx then thought that the principle that "every beginning is difficult ... holds in all sciences". In fact, Volume One Part I follows a method of presentation whose difficulty largely derives from this Hegelian prejudice.'

6 L. Althusser, 'The Humanist Controversy', in *The Humanist Controversy and Other Writings (1966–67)*, ed. F. Matheron, trans. G.M. Goshgarian (London: Verso, 2006), p. 238: 'Marx owes Hegel this decisive philosophical category: process. He owes him even more ... the concept of a *process without a subject*.' Cf. Althusser, 'Preface to *Capital* Volume One', p. 94.

7 Saint Augustine, *On the Trinity: Books 8–15*, ed. G.B. Matthews, trans. S. McKenna (Cambridge: Cambridge University Press, 2002), Book 10/x, §14–16, pp. 55–57.

Chapter 4

1 G.W.F. Hegel, *The Philosophy of History*, trans. J. Sibree, ed. C.J. Friedrich (New York: Dover, 1956), p. 56.

2 J.-B. Bossuet, *Discours sur l'Histoire Universelle*, in *Oeuvres*, eds. B. Velat and Y. Champailler (Paris: Gallimard, 1961), Chapter 8: 'Conclusion de tout discours précédent, où l'on montre qu'il faut tout rapporter à une providence' (Conclusion to the whole of the preceding discourse, in which it is shown that everything must be referred to a Providence), pp. 1024–1027.

3 K. Marx and F. Engels, 'The German Ideology', in *The German Ideology, including Theses on Feuerbach and Introduction to the Critique of Political*

Economy (Amherst, New York: Prometheus Books, Great Books in Philosophy, 1998), pp. 253–254: 'One has to "leave philosophy aside"... and devote oneself like an ordinary man to the study of actuality ... philosophy and the study of the actual world have the same relation to one another as onanism and sexual love.'

Chapter 5

1   Althusser himself grasped this point only after defending, throughout the first half of the 1960s (see Chapter 25, n. 5), the thesis that Marxist philosophy was 'scientific'. He began to modify this thesis in a 26 June 1966 lecture in which he characterized Marxist philosophy as 'a philosophy and not a science in the strict sense, albeit a philosophy of a scientific character' ('The Philosophical Conjuncture and Marxist Theoretical Research', in *The Humanist Controversy*, p. 11), and abandoned it in the 'Conclusion' to the May 1967 'The Historical Task of Marxist Philosophy', *The Humanist Controversy*, p. 209, translation modified: 'What radically distinguishes philosophy from the sciences ... is the internal, intimate, organic relationship that philosophy maintains with politics.'

2   Althusser introduced the theses that he takes up and develops in what follows in various 1967 texts and lectures, notably 'Philosophy and the Spontaneous Philosophy of the Scientists (1967)', trans. W. Montag, in *Philosophy and the Spontaneous Philosophy of the Scientists and Other Essays,* ed. G. Elliott (London: Verso, 1990), pp. 77ff. See also Chapter 10, n. 1.

3   Althusser probably has his 24 February 1968 lecture 'Lenin and Philosophy' in mind (in *Lenin and Philosophy and Other Essays*, p. 39), in which, however, he stops short of declaring that Freud founded a new science. Even in the 1963–64 lectures collected in *Psychoanalysis and the Human Sciences*, trans. S. Rendall (New York: Columbia University Press, 2016) and the 1964 essay based on them ('Freud et Lacan', in Althusser, *Writings on Psychoanalysis: Freud and Lacan*, trans. J. Mehlman (New York: Columbia University Press, 1996), pp. 147–173), reprinted in the 1976 collection *Positions*, he hesitates unambiguously to affirm the scientific character of psychoanalysis (and makes no mention of 'continents').

4   Crossed out in the manuscript: 'Nor can it be said that psychoanalysis has succeeded in establishing a connection to either the neuro-chemical biology of the brain, on which it nevertheless very obviously depends, or historical materialism's theory of ideological state apparatuses, which is nevertheless located in the "neighbourhood" of psychoanalysis. Indeed, one must go so far as to say that psychoanalysis has been left hanging as a result of its inability to attach itself to another scientific continent. It resembles a field that has undoubtedly been cultivated, but in a way that seems to many more artisanal than scientific. We know, after all, that our grandfathers' gardening techniques are quite capable of producing carrots, tomatoes, and chervil.'

5   Galileo, 'The Assayer (1623)', in *The Essential Galileo*, ed. and trans. M.A. Finocchiaro (Indianapolis and Cambridge: Hackett, 2008), p. 183: 'this all-encompassing book that is constantly open before our eyes, that is the universe ... is written in mathematical language, and its characters are triangles, circles, and other geometrical figures.'

6   R. Descartes, *Discourse on Method and Meditations on First Philosophy*, trans. D.A. Cress (Indianapolis and Cambridge: Hackett, 1998), p. 31: 'if there were such machines having the organs and the shape of a monkey or of some other animal that lacked reason, we would have no way of recognizing that they were not entirely of the same nature as these animals ...'

7   Undated letter (1679?) to an unidentified correspondent (Duc Jean-Frédéric de Brunswick-Calenberg?) in G.W. Leibniz, *Sämtliche Schriften und Briefe*, Second series, Volume 1, 2nd ed. (Berlin: Deutsche Akademie der Wissenschaften, 2006), p. 782: 'We will soon forget the beautiful novel on physics that he has given us.' Leibniz, *Theodicy: Essays on the Goodness of God, the Freedom of Man and the Origin of Evil*, ed. A. Farrer, trans. E.M. Huggard (Oregon: Wipf and Stock, 2001), §403, p. 369.

8   J. Stalin, *On Linguistics* (Peking: Foreign Language Press, 1972), pp. 30–31.

9   L. Houllevigue, *L'évolution des sciences* (Paris: Armand Collin, 1908), cited in V.I. Lenin, *Materialism and Empirio-criticism: Critical Comments on a Reactionary Philosophy* (Moscow: Progress Publishers, 1970), p. 246.

10   Maurice Clavel (1920–1979), a Christian philosopher and novelist, author of *Ce que je crois* (1975) and *Dieu est Dieu, nom de Dieu!* (1976).

11   Pierre Boutang (1916–1988), a Christian royalist author, translator, and philosopher, author of *Reprendre le pouvoir* (Paris: Sagittaire, 1977): 'Marxism is nothing but an aberration of true thought, a negation of legitimacy: It has created nothing, it has only destroyed.'

12   Spinoza, 'On the Improvement of the Understanding', §95, p. 32: 'A definition, if it is to be called perfect, must explain the inmost essence of a thing [*intimam essentiam rei explicare*].'

13   Among them the biochemist and philosopher Jacques Monod, who discovered messenger RNA together with François Jacob and others. Monod sings Popper's praises in his preface to the French translation of *The Logic of Scientific Discovery* (*Logique de la découverte scientifique*, trans. N. Thyssen-Rutten and P.F. Devaux (Paris: Payout, 1973)), citing Marxism and psychoanalysis as examples of 'non-refutable' theories.

Althusser analyses Monod's 'spontaneous philosophy' in 'Philosophy and the Spontaneous Philosophy of the Scientists', pp. 145–165.

14 K. Popper, *Conjectures and Refutations: The Growth of Scientific Knowledge* (New York and London: Basic Books, 1962), pp. 37–42, 52.

15 K. Popper, *The Open Society and Its Enemies: The High Tide of Prophecy – Hegel, Marx, and the Aftermath*, Volume 2 (London: George Routledge & Sons, 1947), pp. 253–355.

16 P. Raymond, *L'Histoire et les sciences* (Paris: François Maspero, 1975), pp. 61ff.

17 I. Kant, *Critique of Pure Reason*, trans. and ed. P. Guyer and A.W. Wood (Cambridge: Cambridge University Press, 1998), Preface to the Second Edition, p. 111 and n., p. 112 n. (BXXI): 'This experiment of pure reason has much in common with what the chemists sometimes call the experiment of reduction, or more generally the synthetic procedure.'

18 Crossed out in the manuscript: 'idealist'.

19 N. Malebranche, *The Search after Truth* with *Elucidations of The Search after Truth*, trans. and ed. T.M. Lennon and P.J. Olscamp (Cambridge: Cambridge University Press, 1997), pp. 480ff., 733.

Chapter 6

1 Acts 17, 28: 'For in him [God] we live and move, in him we exist.'

2 J. Derrida, *Glas*, trans. J.P. Leavey, Jr. and R. Rand (Lincoln, Nebraska and London: University of Nebraska Press, 1986).

3 G.W. Leibniz, *Theodicy: Essays on the Goodness of God, the Freedom of Man and the Origin of Evil*, trans. E.M. Huggard (Oregon: Wipf and Stock, 2001), §7–8, pp. 127–128.

4 Plato, *Sophist*, 291d ff.

5 Aristotle, *Metaphysics*, Book Γ, 2 (1003 a 33–34); Book Z 1 ff. (1028 a 10 ff.).

6 G.W. Leibniz, *New Essays on Human Understanding*, trans. P. Remnant and J. Bennet (Cambridge: Cambridge University Press, 1996) p. 399: 'And we could introduce a Universal Symbolism . . . if in place of words we used little diagrams which represented visible things pictorially . . . This would at once enable us to communicate easily with remote peoples; but if we adopted it among ourselves (though without abandoning ordinary writing), the use of this way of writing would be of great service in enriching our imaginations and giving us thoughts which were less blind and less verbal than our present ones are.'

7 C. Levi-Strauss, *Structural Anthropology*, trans. C. Jacobson and B.G. Schoepf (New York: Basic Books, 1963), p. 333: 'The order of orders ... is the most abstract expression of the interrelationship between the levels to which structural analysis can be applied, general enough to account for the fact that the models must sometimes be the same for societies which are historically and geographically disparate.'

8 A. Badiou, *Théorie de la contradiction* (Paris: Maspero, 1975), pp. 54–60, 100–110; Badiou, seminar dated 15 December 1975, *Theory of the Subject*, trans. B. Steels (London: Bloomsbury, 2013), p. 54. 'The structural dialectic has a tendency (this is its idealist side), first, to make the structural aspect of the dialectic prevail over its historical aspect, that is, place over force.'

9 Crossed out in the manuscript: 'whose sole strength is the logic of its good will and expectations.'

Chapter 7

1 See 'Philosophy and the Spontaneous Philosophy of the Scientists', pp. 101–103.

2 Althusser first discusses this distinction at length in the concluding chapter of 'The Historical Task of Marxist Philosophy', p. 213.

3 J. Lacan, 'Science and Truth', in *Écrits*, trans. B. Fink (New York and London: W. W. Norton & Company, 2006), p. 734.

4 In a 30 April 1976 television interview, Marchais, Secretary General of the French Communist Party, said that when his conscience was clear, he did not dream at night.

5 Crossed out in the manuscript: 'the way a dog poses a turd on the pavement'.

6 T. Hobbes, *Leviathan* (Oxford: Oxford University Press, 1996), p. 131. Cf. 'Is it Simple to be a Marxist in Philosophy?', trans. G. Lock, in *Philosophy and the Spontaneous Philosophy of the Scientists*, p. 206. 'As Hobbes says, speaking perhaps to empty benches, and with reference as much to philosophy as to the society of men, war is a generalized state [and] essentially *preventive*.'

7 Crossed out in the manuscript: 'and has its Maurice Thorezes, who say that "one has to know how to end a strike"'.

8 I. Kant, *To Perpetual Peace: A Philosophical Sketch*, trans. T. Humphrey (Indianapolis and Cambridge: Hackett, 2003).

9 J.-P. Sartre, *No Exit and Three Other Plays* (New York: Vintage International, 1989), p. 45: 'Hell is – other people!'.

10 Aristotle, *The History of Animals*, Book IV, 3 (767 b 1–767 *b* 17); Book IV, 3–4 (769 b 10 – 773 a 30). See also Aristotle, *Physics*, Book II, 8 (199 a 33 – 199 b 15).

11 First draft: 'or those by means of which Lacan has constructed his ideology on the basis of Freud's work.'

12 F. Nietzsche, *On the Genealogy of Morals: A Polemic*, trans. M.A. Scarpitti (London: Penguin Classics, 2013), First Essay, §10, p. 25: 'an external and objective world, to employ physiological terminology, is vital to slave-morality; it requires objective stimuli to be capable of action at all – its action is fundamentally a reaction.'

Chapter 8

1 See Chapter 11, n. 15.

2 King Henry IV of France is supposed to have told his troops before the Battle of Évry in 1590 that, if they lost sight of their own standards, they should rally round his white panache.

3 The son of King John the Good is supposed to have shouted this to his father in the heat of the Battle of Poitiers in 1356.

4 I. Kant, *Critique of Pure Reason*, trans. and ed. P. Guyer and A.W. Wood (Cambridge: Cambridge University Press, 2000), Preface to the First Edition, p. 99 (A VIII): 'The battlefield of these endless controversies is called metaphysics.' Cf. ibid., Preface to the Second Edition, p. 106 (B XV).

5 P. Verlaine, 'Above the roof the sky is fair . . .', in *One Hundred and One Poems*, trans. N.R. Shapiro (Chicago: University of Chicago Press, 1999), p. 111.

6 I. Kant, *Critique of Practical Reason*, trans. W.S. Pluhar (Indianapolis and Cambridge: Hackett, 2002), p. 203: 'Two things fill the mind with ever new and increasing admiration and reverence, the more frequently and persistently one's meditation deals with them: *the starry sky above me and the moral law within me.*'

7 Invited to comment on the fact that the Socialist leader François Mitterrand had been nicknamed *Tonton* (uncle), the French Communist labour leader Henri Krasucki replied that if his aunt had two wheels, people would probably call her a bicycle.

Chapter 9

1 'Philosophy and the Spontaneous Philosophy of the Scientists', pp. 103ff.

2 The adjective *juste* means both 'just' and 'correct'; the corresponding negative adjective, *injuste*, means 'unjust', but not 'incorrect'. The noun corresponding to *juste* in the sense of 'just' is *justice*; that corresponding to *juste* in the sense of 'correct' is *justesse*. In the French version of the present chapter, there is constant play, obliquely announced at the end of the previous chapter, on the similarity between the sounds of the words *justice* and *justesse*.

3 Aristotle, *Nicomachean Ethics*, Book II, 7–9 (1107 a 26 – 1109 b 26).

4 Saint Thomas Aquinas, *Summa Theologica*, II/ii, Question 40, Article I.

5 'Philosophy and the Spontaneous Philosophy of the Scientists', pp. 141–144.

6 Here Althusser inserted a paragraph that he left unfinished: 'One last misunderstanding should be cleared up. If theses are *active* propositions that philosophy *adjusts* to the existing conflictual situation (depending on the position that a given philosophy takes in the philosophical struggle, which is commanded by the exigencies of the class struggle), nothing could be further from the truth than to project an idealist image of their *position* and to believe that this position, which is always opposition, goes on somewhere up in the air, with no relation to the materiality of the practices. It will have been understood that it is the reality of the social practices and their orientation which comprises the stakes of philosophical struggle (we shall see how). The stakes of philosophical struggle are thus perfectly real and material. For it is not the idea of the practices, but the *state* of the current practices which comprises the stakes of philosophical struggle. From this we can see that theses, while they are 'posed' in categorical propositions, are *anything but arbitrary*, because they are determined not just by the fact of struggle, but also by its material stakes. We must, however, go further to say that these theses are not arbitrary in a second sense as well: for the categories making them up do not fall from the sky, but are the result of the history of philosophy, which has inscribed in them not only all the ideological notions imposed by the balance of power, *but also concrete knowledge*, transformed into categories and presented in theses. The role of the knowledge thus incorporated with respect to ideological notions' (The paragraph breaks off here.)

Chapter 10

1 Chapters 10 and 11 contain a version of Althusser's fifth and last lecture in a 'philosophy course for scientists' that he and five of his collaborators gave at the Paris École normale supérieure in 1967–68. Unlike the four preceding courses, the fifth was not included in *Philosophy and the Spontaneous Philosophy of the Scientists*, the French version of which was published in 1974. It appeared posthumously under the title 'Du côté de la philosophie' in *Écrits philosophiques et politiques*, Volume 2, pp. 255–292.

2 Spinoza, 'On the Improvement of the Understanding', p. 11. See 'Is it Simple to Be a Marxist in Philosophy?', p. 224.

3 Spinoza, *Ethics*, pp. 113–115, Book II, Proposition XLIII and note: 'Truth is a standard both of itself and of falsity (*veritas norma sui et falsi est*).' Cf. Spinoza, 'On the Improvement of the Understanding', pp. 13ff., 23ff., and Spinoza, Letter 76 to Albert Burgh, in *Opera*, ed. C. Gebhardt (Heidelberg: Carl Winter, 1925), Volume 4, p. 320: '*index veram sui et falsi*'. Spinoza uses the word *veritas*/truth infrequently.

4 Saint Thomas Aquinas, *Summa Theologica*, I, Question 16, Article 2, ad 2. Saint Thomas attributes the formula to Isaac Israeli.

5 N. Malebranche, *Treatise on Nature and Grace*, trans. P. Riley (Oxford: Oxford University Press, 1992), p. 117. See also Malebranche, *Dialogues on Metaphysics and on Religion*, ed. N. Jolley, trans. D. Scott (Cambridge: Cambridge University Press, 1997), pp. 166–170.

6 J.-P. Sartre, *Being and Nothingness: An Essay on Phenomenological Ontology* (New York: Washington Square Press, 1984), pp. 59–60.

7 A. Leroi-Gourhan, *Gesture and Speech*, trans. A.B. Berger (Cambridge, Massachusetts: Massachusetts Institute of Technology, 1993), p. 75: 'Monkeys – all monkeys – are characterized by mixed quadrupedal and seated posture and by the adaptation of their feet to the conditions of life resulting therefrom; anthropoids, on the other hand, have the fundamental characteristic of mixed bipedal and seated posture, to which their foot in turn is closely adapted.' See L. Althusser, 'The Humanist Controversy', in *The Humanist Controversy and Other Writings (1966–67)*, ed. F. Matheron, trans. G.M. Goshgarian (London: Verso, 2003), p. 287.

8 Althusser is probably thinking of S. Freud, 'Civilization and its Discontents' in Freud, eds. J. Strachey and A. Freud, *The Standard Edition of the Complete Psychological Works of Sigmund Freud,* Volume 21 (London: Hogarth Press, 1957), p. 90, n. 1.

9 G.W. Leibniz, 'On the Ultimate Origination of Things', in *Philosophical Essays*, trans. R. Ariew and D. Garber (Indianapolis and Cambridge: Hackett, 1989), p. 149.

10 M. Heidegger, 'Letter on Humanism', in *Basic Writings*, ed. D.F. Krell (New York: HarperCollins, 1993), pp. 226ff., 258ff., 264.

11 B. Russell, *Introduction to Mathematical Philosophy* (London: George Allen & Unwin, 1920), pp. 159ff.

12 M. Heidegger, *Being and Time*, trans J. Macquarrie and E. Robinson (New York and London: Harper & Row, 2008), §32, pp. 188–195, §63, pp. 358–364. Cf. 'Philosophy and the Spontaneous Philosophy of the Scientists', pp. 101–102.

13 J. Derrida, *Margins of Philosophy*, trans. A. Bass (Sussex: Harvester Press, 1982 (1972)), pp. 119–127, 131 136.

Chapter 11

1 M. Caveing formulated this hypothesis around 1950 [author's note]. Althusser is mistaken, unless he is referring to an oral remark that Caveing never published. On Thales (c. 624–c. 547), Pythagoras (c. 570–c. 510), and the origins of Greek mathematics, see Proclus, 'The Commentary', in *A Commentary on the First Book of Euclid's Elements*, trans. G.R. Morrow (Princeton, New Jersey: Princeton University Press, 1992), pp. 70ff. 'Thales' was, according to Althusser, the name of 'a perhaps mythical figure' (see p. 24 above) supposed to have lived 'around the sixth century' (Althusser, *Philosophy for Non-Philosophers*, ed. and trans. G.M. Goshgarian (London, Bloomsbury, 2017), p. 40).

2 See Chapter 10, nn. 2 and 3.

3 The manuscript reads 'idealist'.

4 Crossed out in the manuscript: 'who had not quite understood Marx's positions on this point.'

5 F. Engels, *Ludwig Feuerbach and the End of Classical German Philosophy*, in *Marx and Engels Collected Works*, Volume 26 (London: Lawrence and Wishart, 2010), p. 365.

6 See L. Althusser, 'Elements of Self-Criticism', in *Essays in Self-Criticism*, trans. G. Lock (London: New Left Books, 1976), pp. 144–145.

7 L. Althusser, 'Reply to John Lewis', in *Essays in Self-Criticism*, pp. 79ff. Cf. Aristotle, *Politics*, Book III, Chapter 7, §5 (1279 b 3).

8 The French original reads 'accentuation'.

9 Althusser outlines this thesis in *On the Reproduction of Capitalism: Ideology and Ideological State Apparatuses*, ed. J. Bidet, trans. B. Brewster and G.M. Goshgarian (London: Verso, 2014), pp. 66–69, 166–170.

10 J.-J. Rousseau, 'Of The Social Contract', in *Of the Social Contract and Other Political Writings*, trans. Q. Hoare (London: Penguin Classics, 2012), p. 13: 'Let us agree then that strength does not make right, and that you are obliged to obey only legitimate powers.'

11 This phrase recurs throughout Kant's work. See, for example, *Critique of Pure Reason,* trans. and ed. P. Guyer and A.W. Wood (Cambridge: Cambridge University Press, 2000), Preface to the First Edition, p. 101 (A XII): 'and this court is none other than the critique of pure reason itself.' Cf. ibid., p. 649 A 751/B 779 ('*Gerichtshof der Vernunft*').

12 E. Husserl, *The Crisis of European Sciences and Transcendental Phenomenology*, trans. D. Carr (Evanston, Illinois: Northwestern University Press, 1970).

13 A. Comte, *The Positive Philosophy of Auguste Comte*, Volume 3, trans. H. Martineau (Kitchener, Ontario: Batoche Books, 2000), p. 263: 'In the present stage, the philosophical contemplation and labour are more important than political action, in regard to social regeneration . . . what the philosophers have to expect from wise governments is that they will not interfere with the task while in progress, nor hereafter with the gradual application of its results.'

14 In this city in southwestern France, isolated German forces held out until 17 April 1945, well after almost all the rest of France had been liberated.

15 L. Sève, *Introduction à la philosophie marxiste* (Paris: Éditions sociales, 1980), p. 281: 'Marxist philosophy (mobilizes) concepts whose signification is not purely ontological, relating solely to being, nor purely logical, relating solely to the subjective form of knowledge and science, but gnoseological. . . relating to the study of being as reflected in thought.'

Chapter 12

1 Lenin, *Materialism and Empirio-criticism*, pp. 123–130. D. Lecourt develops a conception of reflection similar to the one that Althusser summarizes here in *Une crise et son enjeu (Essai sur la position de Lénine en philosophie)* (Paris: Maspero, 1973), pp. 42ff.

2 Spinoza, *Ethics*, p. 83, Book II, Proposition VII: 'The order and connection of ideas is the same as the order and connection of things' (*Ordo, et connexio idearum idem est, ac ordo, et connexio rerum*).

3 Ibid., pp. 110–113, Book II, Proposition XL, Note 2 – Proposition XLII; pp. 269–273, Book V, Proposition XXV–Proposition XXXIII.

4 G.W.F. Hegel, 'Benedict Spinoza', in *Lectures on the History of Philosophy (1825–1826), Volume 3: Medieval and Modern Philosophy*, ed. R.F. Brown, trans. R.F. Brown and J.M. Stewart (Berkeley and Los Angeles: University of California Press, 1990), pp. 151–164. Althusser's remark is an extrapolation, not a quotation.

5 Hegel, *Phenomenology of Spirit*, Preface, p. 10.

6 N. Malebranche, *The Search after Truth* with *Elucidations of The Search after Truth*, trans. and ed. T.M. Lennon and P.J. Olscamp (Cambridge: Cambridge University Press, 1997), pp. 590–596.

7 K. Marx, *Grundrisse: Foundations of the Critique of Political Economy*, trans. M. Nicolaus (Harmondsworth, Great Britain: Penguin, 1973), pp. 81–111.

8 Spinoza, *Ethics*, p. 80, Book II, Axiom 2. See also Chapter 10, n. 2.

9 Descartes, *Discourse on Method*, p. 21; Descartes, *Metaphysical Meditations*, p. 81. See also Descartes' Letter to Reneri (for Pollot) of April or May 1638, in Rene Descartes, *The Philosophical Writings*, Volume 3 (Cambridge: Cambridge University Press, 1997), p. 98.

10 I. Kant, *Critique of Practical Reason*, trans. W.S. Pluhar (Indianapolis and Cambridge: Hackett, 2002), Book 1, chapter 1, §7, pp. 45–46 (*Faktum der Vernunft*).

11 Lenin, *Materialism and Empirio-criticism*, pp. 116–117.

12 K. Marx, 'Theses on Feuerbach', in *The German Ideology*, p. 571, Thesis 5: 'Feuerbach ... does not conceive sensuousness as practical, human-sensuous activity.'

13 I. Kant, *Critique of Pure Reason*, trans. and ed. P. Guyer and A.W. Wood (Cambridge: Cambridge University Press, 1998), Preface to the Second Edition, p. 109 (B XIII)): 'Reason, in order to be taught by nature, must approach nature ... yet in order to be instructed by nature not like a pupil, who has recited to him whatever the teacher wants to say, but like an appointed judge who compels witnesses to answer the questions he puts to them.'

14 R. Descartes, Letter to M. Mersenne, 11 October 1638, cited in J.R. Vrooman, *Rene Descartes: A Biography* (New York: G. P. Putnam's Sons, 1970), p. 115: 'he is continually digressing and never stops to explain one topic completely, which demonstrates that he has not examined them in an orderly fashion and that, without having considered nature's first causes, he has sought only the reasons for a few particular effects, and thus he has built without foundations.' See also Chapter 5, n. 7.

15 I. Kant, *Critique of Pure Reason*, Preface to the Second Edition, pp. 108–109 (B XII): 'When Galileo rolled balls of a weight chosen by himself down an inclined plane ... a light dawned on all those who study nature.'

16 Marx, *Grundrisse*, p. 101: 'The real subject retains its autonomous existence outside the head just as before; namely as long as the head's conduct is merely speculative, theoretical.'

17 L. Althusser, *For Marx*, trans. B. Brewster (London: New Left Books, 1977), pp. 183ff.

18 'Exzerpte aus Benedictus de Spinoza, *Opera*, ed. Paulus', in *Marx-Engels Gesamtausgabe*, Part IV, Volume 1: *Exzerpte und Notizen bis 1842* (Berlin: Dietz, 1976), pp. 233–276 (in Latin); 'Spinoza's Theologisch-politischer Tractat' and 'Spinozas Briefe'; ibid., *Apparat*, Part IV, Volume I, pp. 777–818 (German translation).

19 'The concept of a dog does not bark' is an Althusserian variation on a Spinozist theme. See Spinoza, 'On the Improvement of the Understanding', p. 11: 'a true idea ... is something different from its correlate' and Spinoza, *Ethics*, p. 58, Book I, Proposition XVII, Note: 'There could be no further likeness [between the human will and God's 'will'] than that between the celestial constellation of the Dog and the animal which barks.'

20 V.I. Lenin, 'Preface to the Collection *Twelve Years*' (1907), in Lenin, *Collected Works*, Volume 13 (Moscow: Progress Publishers, 1978), p. 94. Cf. 'Is it Simple to Be a Marxist in Philosophy?', pp. 210–211, and R. Descartes,

'Fifth Set of Replies', in *The Philosophical Writings of Descartes*, Volume 2, trans. J. Cottingham, R. Stoothoff and D. Murdoch (Cambridge: Cambridge University Press, 1995), p. 252.

21 See note 13 above.

22 Marx, 'Theses on Feuerbach', p. 573, Thesis 3: 'The coincidence of the changing of circumstances and of human activity can be conceived and rationally understood only as revolutionary practice.'

23 K. Marx, *Capital*, Volume 1, in *Marx and Engels Collected Works*, Volume 35 (London: Lawrence and Wishart, 2010), pp. 97–98; Marx, *Capital*, Volume 3, in ibid., Volume 37, p. 176. Cf. F. Engels, 'Supplement to *Capital*, Volume 3', in ibid., p. 887, and L. Althusser and É. Balibar, *Reading Capital*, trans. Ben Brewster (London: Verso, 1970), p. 82.

24 R. Descartes, 'Sixth Set of Replies', in *The Philosophical Writings of Descartes*, Volume 2, trans. J. Cottingham, R. Stoothoff and D. Murdoch (Cambridge: Cambridge University Press, 1995), p. 291.

25 Spinoza, *Ethics*, pp. 268–269, Book V, Proposition XXIII, Note: 'we feel and know by experience that we are eternal' (*sentimus, experimurque, nos aternos esse*).

Chapter 13

1 R. Descartes, 'Fourth Set of Replies', in *The Philosophical Writings of Descartes*, Volume 2, trans. J. Cottingham, R. Stoothoff and D. Murdoch (Cambridge: Cambridge University Press, 1995), pp. 174–175. See also Descartes, 'Letter to M. Mersenne, 28 January 1641', in *The Philosophical Writings of Descartes*, Volume 3, trans. J. Cottingham, R. Stoothoff, D. Murdoch and A. Kenny (Cambridge: Cambridge University Press, 1997), p. 171.

2 Spinoza, *Theological-Political Treatise*, trans. M. Silverthrone and J. Israel (Cambridge: Cambridge University Press, 2007), p. 195.

3 See Chapter 6, n. 5. Cf. 'Ideology and State Ideological Apparatuses (Notes towards an Investigation)', in *On the Reproduction of Capitalism*, p. 184.

4 Denys the Areopagite (The Pseudo-Dionysius), 'The Divine Names' in *The Complete Works*, trans. C. Luibheid and P. Rorem (New York: Paulist Press, 1987), pp. 54–58.

5 Plato, *Timaeus*, 28a–28b, 48e–49b, 50b–51b, 52a–53a.

6 First draft: 'most'.

7 First draft: 'although it is not yet a classic capitalist state'.

8 D. Hume, 'An Enquiry concerning Human Understanding', in *An Enquiry Concerning Human Understanding and Other Essays*, ed. E.C. Mossner (New York: Washington Square Press, 1963), p. 36.

9 R. Descartes, *Discourse on the Method* (New Haven and London: Yale University Press, 1996), p. 17.

10 I. Kant, *Metaphysics of Morals*, trans. M. Gregor (New York: Cambridge University Press, 2001), §13, pp. 83–84.

11 I. Kant, *Critique of Judgment*, trans. W.S. Pluhar (Indianapolis and Cambridge: Hackett, 1987), §56, pp. 210–211 and §59, pp. 225–230.

12 M. Heidegger, *Kant and the Problem of Metaphysics*, trans. R. Taft (Bloomington and Indianapolis: Indiana University Press, 1997), §31, pp. 112–120.

13 J.-J. Rousseau, *Discourse on the Origin and Foundations of Inequality among Men*, ed. P. Colemen, trans. F. Philip (Oxford: Oxford University Press, 2009), pp. 27ff.

14 J.-J. Rousseau, 'Considérations sur l'influence des climats relativement à la civilization', ed. S. Goyard-Fabre, in *Oeuvres complètes*, ed. R. Trousson and F. Eigeldinger (Genève: Slatkine, 2012), Volume 5, Part 2, pp. 643–644: 'If the ecliptic had been confused with the equator, perhaps there never would have been the emigration of people, and each man, not being able to support a climate other than his native one, would never have left it. To tip the axis of the world with a finger or to say to man: Cover the world and be sociable, was the same thing for Him who needed neither hand to move not voice to speak.' Cited in J. Derrida, *Of Grammatology*, trans. G.C. Spivak (Baltimore, Maryland: Johns Hopkins University Press, 2016), p. 281.

15 I. Kant, 'Idea for a Universal History with a Cosmopolitan Aim', in *Kant's Idea for a Universal History with A Cosmopolitan Aim*, eds. A.O. Rorty and J. Schmidt (Cambridge: Cambridge University Press, 2009), Fourth Proposition, p. 13: 'The means nature employs in order to bring about the development of all their predispositions is their antagonism in society, insofar as the latter is in the end the cause of their lawful order. Here I understand by 'antagonism' the unsociable sociability of human beings.'

16 G.W.F. Hegel, *Elements of the Philosophy of Right*, trans. N.B. Nibet (Cambridge: Cambridge University Press, 1991), preface, pp. 9–24.

17 'It's a verbal word' means something like 'it's just semantics'. The *Canard enchaîné* is a satirical political newspaper with a penchant for wordplay.

18 Rousseau, *Discourse on the Origin and Foundations of Inequality among Men*, p. 59. Cf. L. Althusser, *Cours sur Rousseau*, ed. Y. Vargas (Paris: Le Temps des cerises, 2015), p. 123.

19 'The drop that made the vase overflow' is the French equivalent of the 'straw that broke the camel's back'.

20 First draft: 'my comrade and friend Jacques Derrida'.

21 See Chapter 10, n. 13.

22 G. Canguilhem, *The Normal and the Pathological*, trans. C.R. Fawcett (New York: Zone Books, 1991). See Louis Althusser, 'Cours de 1958–1959', in *Althusser et quelques autres: Notes de cours, 1958–1959*, ed. É. Jalley (Paris: L'Harmattan, 2014), pp. 40–41, and Althusser, 'Présentation de Pierre Macherey, "La philosophie de la science de Georges Canguilhem: Épistémologie et histoire des sciences"', *La Pensée*, no. 113, February 1964, pp. 50–54.

23 Crossed out in the manuscript: 'Lacan will be hard at it with his objet petit a'.

24 First draft: 'especially – you don't believe it? – in the USSR.'

25 First draft: '(between us, Mao is a remarkable writer; his formulas are not always very accurate, but he has a sort of genius for coining inimitable formulas. Derrida has, moreover, worked out a whole theory of writing, as Marx had worked out a whole theory of the dictatorship of the proletariat, which our leaders have unfortunately failed to understand.)'

26 First draft: 'by putting, in very Maoist fashion, the question of the margin in the command post.'

27 First draft: 'to the theory of the dictatorship of the proletariat.'

28 J. Lacan, *Anxiety: The Seminar of Jacques Lacan*, Book X, ed. J.-A. Miller, trans. A.R. Price (Cambridge: Polity, 2014), pp. 94, 135, 204ff.

29 Sartre, *Being and Nothingness*, pp. 610ff.

Chapter 14

1 É. Benveniste, 'The Nature of Pronouns', in *Problems in General Linguistics*, trans. M.E. Meek (Miami: University of Miami Press, 1971), p. 217.

2 S. Freud, 'Three Essays on the Theory of Sexuality' (1905), in Freud, eds. J. Strachey and A. Freud, *The Standard Edition of the Complete Psychological Works of Sigmund Freud,* Volume 7 (London: Hogarth Press, 1957), pp. 133–172; M. Klein, 'Contribution to the Psychogenesis of Manic-Depressive States', in *Love, Guilt, Reparation, and Other Works, 1931–1945* (New York: The Free Press, 1975), pp. 306–438.

3 Plato, *Parmenides*, 129a–133c; *Phaedo*, 100c-e.

4 Plato, *Sophist*, 249d ff. Cf. *Philebus*, 14d ff.

5 Aristotle, *Metaphysics*, A, 9 (992b 18–24, 993a 7–10); Z, 12–16 (1037 b 8 – 1041 a 5).

6 I. Kant, *Critique of Pure Reason*, trans. and ed. P. Guyer and A.W. Wood (Cambridge: Cambridge University Press, 1998), pp. 210–218 (B 102–116/A 76–84); Kant, *Critique of Practical Reason,* trans. S. Engstrom

(Indianapolis and Cambridge: Hackett, 2002), Book I, Chapter 2, pp. 87–89.

7 Aristotle, *Organon*, I: *Categories*, 4 (1 b 25 – 2 a 4). Aristotle names ten categories: substance, action, passion, time, place, position, quantity, quality, relation, state. Cf. *Metaphysics*, E, 2 (1026 a 35 – 1026 b 2).

8 Aristotle, *Metaphysics*, B, 6 (1003 a 12–17); M, 10 (1086 b 33).

9 Aristotle, *Metaphysics*, Z, 3 (1028 b 34 – 1029 b 12ff).

10 K. Marx, *Capital* Volume One, *Preface to the First Edition* (London: Penguin Classics, 1976), p. 92. 'I do not by any means depict the capitalist and the landowner in rosy colours. But individuals are dealt with here only in so far as they are the personifications of economic categories, the bearers [*Träger*] of particular class-relations and interests'.

11 Aristotle, *Metaphysics*, Δ, 8 (1017 b 10–26); Z, 4 (1029b 12 ff.).

12 Aristotle, *Metaphysics*, Z, 4–6 (1029b 13 – 1032 a 10); Z, 10–13 (1034 b 20 – 1038 b 34). For a summary, see H, 1 (1042 a 5–33).

13 Louis Jouvet (1887–1951) was a French actor; Alain-René Lesage (1648–1747) published the novel *Le Diable boiteux* (*The Devil upon Two Sticks*) in 1707; Mikhail Kutuzov (1745–1813) was a Russian field marshal who had a hand in driving Napoleon's armies out of Russia and a talent for falling asleep to avoid compromising situations.

14 Alfred de Vigny, 'La Maison du berger (III)', in *Poésies complètes*, ed. A. Vouvet (Paris: Cluny, 1937), p. 147.

15 Althusser plays, in this passage, on the similarity between the French phrases meaning 'to go round in circles' and 'to run smoothly'.

16 Aristotle, *Politics*, I, 2 (1252 a 2–3).

17 Ibid., I, 4 (1253 b 3); I, 5 ff. (1254 a 2 ff.).

18 Aristotle, *Metaphysics*, Λ, 9ff. (1074 b 15ff.).

19 Averroës, *Ibn Rushd's Metaphysics: A Translation with Introduction of Ibn Rushd's Commentary on Aristotle's Metaphysics*, ed. C. Genequand (Leiden: E.J. Brill, 1986); Thomas Aquinas, *Aquinas Against the Averroists*, trans. R. McInerny (West Lafayette, Indiana: Purdue University Press, 1993).

20 Centre national de la recherche scientifique, a central, state-funded research organization in France.

Chapter 16

1 See Diogenes Laertius, *Lives of Eminent Philosophers*, 10, paragraphs 41–84.

2 Letters of Epicurus to Herodotus, in Diogenes Laertius, *Lives of Eminent Philosophers*. See especially, on atomic motion, 10, §43–44 and 10, §60–62.

3 Lucretius, *On the Nature of Things/De rerum natura*, Book 2, lines 216–293; Book 5, lines 432–494.

4 Cf. Althusser's letter of 15 March 1969 to M.A. Macchiocchi, in Macchiocchi, *Letters from inside the Italian Communist Party to Louis Althusser*, trans. S.M. Hellman (London: New Left Books, 1973), p. 306: 'An encounter may occur or not occur. It can be a "brief encounter", *relatively* accidental, in which case it will not lead to any *fusion* . . . An encounter which is, or becomes, a long encounter must necessarily take the form of a *fusion*.'

5 Althusser introduces the concept of the 'take' in a posthumously published 1966 text, 'Three Notes on the Theory of Discourses', *The Humanist Controversy*, p. 59, translation modified: 'I am here using the term "take" in the sense in which one says that mayonnaise "takes."'

6 S. Freud 'Sexuality in the Aetiology of the Neuroses' (1898), in Freud, eds. J. Strachey and A. Freud, *The Standard Edition of the Complete Psychological Works of Sigmund Freud*, Volume 3 (London: Hogarth Press, 1957), p. 280: 'It seems that in man the sexual instinctual forces are meant to be stored up so that, on their release at puberty, they may serve great cultural ends. . . . But they produce their effect only to a very slight degree at the time at which they occur; what is far more important is their deferred effect, which can only take place at later periods of growth.'

Chapter 17

1 The present chapter develops ideas outlined in *On the Reproduction of Capitalism*, pp. 57ff.

2 I. Kant, *Groundwork for the Metaphysics of Morals*, ed. and trans. A.W. Wood (New Haven: Yale University Press, 2002), p. 10: 'The good will is good not through what it effects or accomplishes, not through its efficacy for attaining any intended end, but only through its willing, i.e., good in itself.'

Chapter 18

1 W. Leibniz, 'Über Spinozas Ethik', in *Sämtliche Schriften und Briefe* (Berlin: Akademie Verlag, 1980), pp. 384–385: 'Sir Tschirnhaus told me many things about Spinoza's book. . . . He claims to demonstrate things about God. . . . *Vulgus philosophiam incipere a creaturis, Cartesium incepisse a mente, se [Spinoza] incipere a Deo.'*

2   The English translation reflects Althusser's translation of Spinoza's Latin. A common English translation is 'the face of the whole universe'.

3   M. Gueroult, *Spinoza I: Dieu (Éthique, I)* (Paris: Aubier-Montaigne, 1968), p. 318; *Spinoza II: L'Âme (Éthique, II)* (Paris: Aubier, 1974), pp. 169ff.

4   Spinoza, *Theological-Political Treatise*, trans. M. Silverthrone and J. Israel (Cambridge: Cambridge University Press, 2007), p. 32: 'Revelations differed, moreover, not only in form but also in clarity. What was revealed to Zechariah was too obscure for him to be able to understand it himself without explanation, as is clear from his account of it, and what was revealed to Daniel could not be understood by the prophet himself even when it was explained to him.'

5   Spinoza, 'On the Improvement of the Understanding', p. 9; Spinoza, *Ethics*, pp. 112–113, Book 2, Proposition XL, Note 2.

6   Spinoza, *Ethics*, p. 41, Book 1, Definition 6. Althusser bases his conception of the 'general theories' of the sciences by means of which concrete knowledge is produced on the model of the Spinozist attributes: thus he declares that the 'General Theories . . . are our attributes' ('Three Notes on the Theory of Discourses', p. 65), and, in a debate with P. Ricœur, invokes Spinoza's thesis that God has an infinity of attributes to justify his own claim that there exist scientific 'continents' unconnected to one another ('Lénine et la philosophie', in *Solitude de Machiavel et autres textes*, ed. Y. Sintomer (Paris: Presses Universitaires de France, 1998), pp. 139–142, n. r).

7   First draft: 'saw it running off into the distance [*fuir loin de lui*]'.

8   Hegel, *The Philosophy of History*, pp. 15–16, 21: 'The ill will that is found in the world [should be] comprehended, and the thinking Spirit reconciled with the fact of the existence of evil. Indeed, nowhere is such a harmonizing view more pressingly demanded that in Universal History. . . . But even regarding History as the slaughter-bench at which the happiness of peoples, the wisdom of States, and the virtue of individuals have been victimized – the question involuntarily arises – to what principle, to what final aim these enormous sacrifices have been offered.'

9   A. Gramsci, *Selections from the Prison Notebooks*, ed. and trans. Q. Hoare and N. Smith (London: Lawrence & Wishart, 1971), pp. 533ff.

10 The more cynical version of the French proverb that Althusser has in mind runs: 'The prettiest girl in the world can only give what she has. But she can take a lot more.'

Chapter 19

1 K. Marx, *A Contribution to the Critique of Political Economy*, in *Marx and Engels Collected Works*, Volume 29 (London: Lawrence & Wishart, 2010), pp. 365–381. See also Marx, *Grundrisse*, pp. 81–111.

2 Beginning in 1967, with 'The Humanist Controversy' (pp. 269–270), Althusser replaces his original, 'much too abrupt' formulation of the thesis that there was 'a true break ... between Marx and Hegel ... that it was possible to locate in 1845' ('Preface to *Capital* Volume One', p. 93) with the thesis that what was involved was, albeit 'irreversible', a 'continuing break'. Cf. 'Elements of Self-Criticism', pp. 107ff.

3 Lenin, *Materialism and Empirio-Criticism*, pp. 185–189, 194–195; Lenin, *Philosophical Notebooks*, 'Abel Rey: Modern Philosophy, Paris, 1918', p. 433: 'Agnosticism = shamefaced materialism'. Cf. Engels, *Ludwig Feuerbach*, p. 368: 'a shamefaced way of surreptitiously accepting materialism, while denying it before the world.'

4 Lenin, *Materialism and Empirio-criticism*, Chapter 6, Part 4: 'Parties in Philosophy and Philosophical Blockheads'. Cf. 'Lenin and Philosophy', pp. 64–65, and Engels, *Ludwig Feuerbach*, p. 398.

5 'Wer den Feind will verstehen/Muss in Feindes Lande gehen.' Adaptation by Ivan Turgenev, cited by Lenin in *Materialism and Empirio-criticism*, p. 306, of a couplet by Goethe: 'Wer den Dichter [the poet] will verstehen/ Muss in Dichters Lande gehen.'

6 E. Husserl, 'Foundational Investigations of the Phenomenological Origin of the Spatiality of Nature: The Originary Ark, the Earth, Does Not Move', in Maurice Merleau-Ponty, *Husserl at the Limits of Phenomenology*, eds. L. Lawlor and B. Bergo (Evanston, Illinois: Northwestern University Press, 2002), pp. 117–132.

Chapter 20

1 Lenin, *Materialism and Empirio-criticism*, p. 123. Cf. 'Is it Simple to be a Marxist in Philosophy?', pp. 228–229.

2 Engels, *Ludwig Feuerbach*, p. 363: 'Whoever placed the emphasis on the Hegelian system could be fairly conservative in both spheres; whoever regarded the dialectical method as the main thing could belong to the most extreme opposition, both in religion and politics.' See also Engels, *Dialectics of Nature*, in *Marx and Engels Collected Works*, Volume 25 (London: Lawrence & Wishart, 2010), p. 361.

3 Engels, *Dialectics of Nature*, pp. 364–365; cf. Engels, *Ludwig Feuerbach*, p. 383: 'Thus dialectics reduced itself to the science of the general laws of motion.'

4 Cf. L. Althusser, *The Future Lasts Forever*, trans. R. Veasey (New York: The New Press, 1993), p. 222.

5 Lenin, *Philosophical Notebooks*, pp. 251–252: 'Dialectics in the proper sense is the study of contradiction in the very essence of objects.'

6 D. Lecourt, *Proletarian Science? The Case of Lyssenko*, trans. B. Brewster (London: New Left Books, 1977), pp. 14–15.

Chapter 21

1 Compare Marx's *critique* of Max Stirner in *The German Ideology* (New York: Prometheus Books, 1998), pp. 84–85: 'The statement which frequently occurs with Saint Sancho that each man is all that he is through the state is fundamentally the same as the statement that the bourgeois is only a specimen of the bourgeois species; a statement which presupposes that the bourgeois class existed before the individuals constituting it.'

2 P. Valery, 'The Crisis of the Mind', in *The Collected Works of Paul Valery: History and Politics*, trans. D. Folliot and J. Mathews (Princeton, New Jersey: Princeton University Press, 1971), p. 23: 'We later civilizations . . . we too know that we are mortal.'

3 Crossed out: 'besides the Third-World countries, let us cite Italy, the USSR and so on.'

4 In 'Ideology and Ideological State Apparatuses (Notes towards an Investigation)', trans. B. Brewster. First published in *La Pensée* in 1970, this text brings together, in lightly revised form, several extracts from a 1969 manuscript, 'On the Reproduction of the Relations of Production'. It has been published together with the original manuscript and the 1976 'Note on the ISAs' in *On the Reproduction of Capitalism*, pp. 232–272.

5 In the mid–1970s, Althusser waged a campaign against the abandonment of the dictatorship of the proletariat by the French Communist Party, devoting a polemical book to the subject that he left unpublished in 1976: *Les Vaches noires: Interview imaginaire*, ed. G.M. Goshgarian (Paris: Presses Universitaires de France, 2016, English translation forthcoming from Bloomsbury). In the 1970s, Gramsci was often mobilized against Althusserian 'orthodoxy' by communist theorists such as L. Sève, C. Buci-Glucksmann, N. Poulantzas, and B. De Giovanni.

Chapter 22

1 R. Descartes, 'Fifth Set of Replies', in *The Philosophical Writings of Descartes*, Volume 2, trans. J. Cottingham, R. Stoothoff and D. Murdoch

(Cambridge: Cambridge University Press, 1995), pp. 246–247: 'But why should it not always think, since it is a thinking substance? It is no surprise that we do not remember the thoughts that the soul had when in the womb or in a deep sleep.'

2   K. Marx and F. Engels, *The Communist Manifesto* (London: Pluto Press, 2008), p. 51.

Chapter 23

1   According to a late tradition, the first witness to which seems to be John Philoponus (sixth century of the Christian era). John Philoponus, Commentary on Aristotle's *De Anima*, in *Commentaria in Aristotelem graeca*, Volume 15, ed. M. Haydruck (Berlin: Reimer, 1897), p. 117, line 29.

Chapter 24

1   The rest of the present book develops ideas put forward in two lectures that Althusser delivered in Spain in March–April and July 1976: 'The Transformation of Philosophy', trans. T.E. Lewis, in *Philosophy and the Spontaneous Philosophy of the Scientists*, pp. 241–265, and 'Sur la dictature du prolétariat' and 'Les formes politiques de la dictature du prolétariat', the central chapters in *Les Vaches noires: Interview imaginaire*, ed. G.M. Goshgarian (Paris: Presses Universitaires de France, 2016 [1976], English translation forthcoming from Bloomsbury), pp. 193–248.

Chapter 25

1   Engels, *Ludwig Feuerbach*, p. 362.

2   Lecourt, *Proletarian Science?*, pp. 156ff.

3   Althusser, 'Philosophy and the Spontaneous Philosophy of the Scientists', pp. 147, 149–165 (Appendix: 'On Jacques Monod').

4   See Chapter 5, n. 13. Althusser pursued his warning in private correspondence with Monod, in vain.

5   Althusser, 'Lenin and Philosophy', p. 68: 'Marxism in not a (new) philosophy of practice, but a (new) practice of philosophy.'

6   See, for example, 'Matérialisme historique et matérialisme dialectique', *Cahiers marxistes-léninistes*, no. 11 (April 1966), p. 97, p. 113: 'In founding this new science [the science of history], Marx founded, *by the same stroke*, another theoretical discipline, *dialectical materialism,* or Marxist philosophy ... The object of dialectical materialism is ... *the history of the production of knowledge as knowledge* ... Marx's philosophical revolution ... brought philosophy from the state of an ideology to that of a *science.'* Cf. *Reply to John Lewis,* p. 68.

Chapter 26

1   G. Lukács, *History and Class Consciousness: Studies in Marxist Dialectics,* trans. R. Livingstone (Massachusetts: MIT Press, 1971), pp. 21ff., 148– 149ff.

2   K. Marx, 'Theses on Feuerbach', p. 571, Thesis 11: 'The philosophers have only *interpreted* the world in various ways; the point is to *change* it.'

Appendix

1   *Cercle ouvert,* no. 9: 'Chacun peut-il philosopher?' (January 1958), pp. 13–16.

2   J.-F. Revel, *Mémoires: Le voleur dans la maison vide* (Paris: Plon, 1977), p. 356; M. Merleau-Ponty, 'Merleau-Ponty in Person' (interview with Madeleine Chapsal), trans. J. Barry, Jr., in *Texts and Dialogues: On Philosophy, Politics, and Culture,* ed. B. and H. Silvermann (Amherst, New York: Humanity Books, 1992), p. 7; C. Lévi-Strauss, *Structural Anthropology,* p. 337; J.-P. Sartre, 'Pourquoi les philosophes?', *Le Débat,* no. 29, March 1984, pp. 29–42 (first publication of the text of this lecture); Revel, *Pourquoi des philosophes?* (Paris: Julliard, 1957).

3   The French transcription reads: 'the mode of existing social relations'.

INDEX

Saint-Simon, C. 62
salvation 22, 32, 53, 104
Sartre, J-P. xiv, 37, 52, 80, 89
Schelling, F. W. J. von 6
science
  and the development of social
    classes 69
  Forms 89
  history of 60
  human sciences 26, 33, 70, 138
  labour of science 67
  objects of 24–5, 31, 73
  origins of 128
  and philosophy 22–30, 31, 48–9,
    70–1, 74, 89–90, 98, 119, 129,
    130–3, 135–6, 142
  scientific knowledge 56–7, 68
  spontaneous philosophy of
    scientists 136
  theory of science 69–71
  and truth 45
science of history xv, xvi, xxiii, xxvii,
    43
science of philosophy xvi–xviii, xx,
    xxi–xxiii
scientific philosophy xv, 20, 23, 24, 60,
    119, 131, 141
Selbst 92
self-criticism xv–xvi, xix, xxiii, xxviii
sensory perceptions 19, 56, 69
Sève, L. 116, 117
sexual relations 56, 67
signification 80
singular essences 108
singularity 92–3, 106, 107, 109
slaves 5, 39
socialism xxvi, 82, 142
social practices, philosophy addresses
    all xxiii–xxiv, xxvii
society and language 55–6, 124
sociology 26
Socrates 3, 4–5, 8
Soviet philosophers 76, 81–2, 116,
    142

speculation 73–4
Spinoza, B.
  abstraction of difference 67
  encounter 101
  eternal truths 75
  Ethics 10
  experimentation 30
  God 107–11
  Grusha's Donkey 5, 6, 7
  and idealist philosophy 113
  marginality 88
  and Marx xiii, xv, xxviii
  materialist philosophy 58
  mathematics 56
  objects 72, 73
  parallelism 46, 65–6
  and politics 40
  religion 77
  truth 45, 49, 50, 68
  truths 13
spiritualism versus materialism 64
spiritualist psychology 26
spiritual power 62
spontaneous philosophy of scientists
    136
Stalin, J. 26, 43, 117, 142
Stalinist deviation 60, 142
state, the xxvii, 121–2, 131–2,
    138–9
state ideology xxii, xxiii, xxvi, 82, 110,
    131–2
state of the whole people 83
Stoics 99
structuralism 33–4, 62
subject 74–5, 89, 91–6, 101–2, 103–6,
    107, 108
subjectivity xxi, 11, 46, 71, 140
subject/object 46–54, 64–75, 76–90,
    91, 107–8
subsistence 121
substance 94, 98
Summa theologica 10
superstructures 120, 121
supplement of order 85